THE

LAST ENEMY;

CONQUERING AND CONQUERED.

BY

GEORGE BURGESS, D.D,

Bishop of the Protestant Episcopal Church in Maine,

"THE LAST ENEMY THAT SHALL BE DESTROYED IS DEATH."

PHILADELPHIA:
PUBLISHED BY H. HOOKER,
SOUTH-WEST CORNER OF EIGHTH AND CHESTNUT STREETS.
1850.

CONTENTS.

PROEM.

Tired with the sultry noonday toil,
I laid me on the grassy soil,
Where stately o'er my head,
An oak's broad branches, with the sound
Of winds on distant errand bound,
Their fanning coolness spread,
And, glistening through them, far on high,
The summer sun went down the sky.
The strange, low notes that nature blends,
Like soothing words of ancient friends,
Came gently on my soul:
A child once more, I heard the bee,
The bird, the wind, the whispering tree,
And that unearthly harmony
O'er all my senses stole;
Till, stretched along the hillock's side,
I dreamed, and in my dream I died.

With one short moment's bursting strife,
My spirit upward sprung;
But on the verge of either life
Yet one short moment hung:
Above the dead I seemed to bow,
I seemed to touch the clay-cold brow,
And close the fading eye,
And still the murmuring branches stirred,
And, soaring still, the forest bird
Sent out its joyous cry.

But these were like the scenes of night,
While I awoke, and bathed in light
That round me far unveiled to sight
A world all dim before:
And life, as if an inward fount,
O'erflowed me and upbore,
As on light plumes of love to mount,
And journey and adore.
I was as one who on the main,
Has caught and lost a landward strain,
That came, and broke, and came again,
Mid the hoarse billows' roar,
But near as now his vessel floats,
Sound matched with sound, the choral notes
Pour warbling from the shore:
So all which e'er to joy or prayer
Had moved my grateful heart,
Seemed in one glorious hymn to bear
Its own melodious part.
The solemn voice of woods and streams;
The song of evening's fading beams;
The ocean's swell and fall;
And this fair chain of living things,
From glittering clouds of insect wings,
To nations rallying round their kings;
As from ten thousand thousand strings,
One music spread from all:
A strain of glory, heard above;
And heard on earth, a strain of love.

But oh, with what a bounding thrill
I felt the airs that never chill,
The strength that knows not years!
No cloud in all the heaven's sweet blue;
No more of doubt, where all was true;
No death, to close the longing view;
No dream of future tears!
The way was passed; and I could stand,

As if on Jordan's farther strand;
As if, the palm-branch in my hand,
    The chaplet on my brow,
A wanderer resting at his home,
A pilgrim at the holy dome,
To Zion's mountain I were come
    Eternity was now!
Oh joy, beneath the gathered sail,
To hear from far the howling gale,
    And feel the haven won!
Oh joy, along the well-fought field,
To see the conqueror's spear and shield
    Give back the setting sun!
All, all was mine, and battle's din,
And the wild sea of grief and sin,
No more with morn should yet begin;
    For all their work was done.

I took no note of earthly hours;
    Alike if months or moments sped:
I stretched the wing of inward powers,
    And far or near might tread:
And now it seemed as I had bowed,
Where rides in heaven some sabbath cloud,
And still a lingering gaze had cast
On those green vales whose woes were past.
Then forth the fire of gladness broke,
And all my new-born memory spoke,
And all its raptures rushed to meet
    In yon best psalm of happiest days,
"My thought on God shall still be sweet,
    And all my being shall be praise."
I praised the Maker's breath that gave
A life that bloomed not for the grave
I praised the Saviour, that to save
    From more than mortal loss,
He was the brother of the slave,
And drank the deep and bitter wave,
    And triumphed by the cross:

I praised the Spirit's sevenfold flame,
That now from all my spirit's frame,
With might that last in death o'ercame,
    Had melted all its dross.
"And now, O Lord of life," I cried,
"Around me spread, unknown and wide
    Thy ways, a pathless sea;
But thy dear love till now is tried,
And I will go where Thou wilt guide,
And where Thou art I dare abide,
    For ever safe in Thee!"

THE LAST ENEMY.

PART THE FIRST.

I.

Life.

"O thou great Arbiter of life and death!
Nature's immortal, immaterial Sun!
Whose all-prolific beam late called me forth
From darkness, teeming darkness, where I lay
The worm's inferior, and, in rank, beneath
The dust I tread on; high to bear my brow,
To drink the spirit of the golden day,
And triumph in existence; and couldst know
No motive but my bliss, and hast ordain'd
A rise in blessing; with the patriarch's joy
Thy call I follow to the land unknown!"

YOUNG.

THE earliest record in the history of man could come only from his Maker. It is, that the Lord God determined to make man in His own image, "formed him of the dust of the ground, and breathed into his nostrils the breath of life; and man became a living soul." His existence was to be a type and symbol of Deity; but he had the same body, and the same animal life, with the beasts, the birds, the fishes, and the insects over whom he had dominion. The dust from which he was formed was not more precious than theirs; and the breath of life was their possession before he was created.

In fact, the skeleton of the animal frame is composed of the same limestone which is scattered over the earth, from the depths of ocean to the ridges of the mountains. It is the beginning of animal structures in the coral and the shell; and it is the last remnant that is discovered in graves and catacombs. The great gaseous elements, oxygen, hydrogen, nitrogen, and carbonic acid, gather around it, with a little iron, sulphur, and quartz, and form in such proportions the fibrin of the muscles, the albumen of the brain and nerves, the gelatinous substances, and the fat, that of the whole weight of the body, when its parts are separated, three-fourths are water. Fearful and wonderful is the mechanism in which these chemical constituents meet; a mechanism so compact, so delicate, and so mighty; capable of being deranged by a touch, yet equal to the mightiest tasks of action and endurance.

But the body of man was not formed to excel the other animal systems in their peculiar glories. It lacks the massy strength of the elephant and the whale: it cannot rival the muscles of the lion: the antelope and the greyhound are far more graceful: man has no pinions to mount on high: he cannot live in the deep: the falcon has a keener eye, the grouse a quicker ear, the dog a more discerning smell, the bat a more susceptible touch; and of all the beasts the most hideous is that which most resembles him in form, gestures, and visage. His body, notwithstanding, has been fitted to be the house of a guest that could dwell in none beside. It is to stand erect, as becomes the ruler over all other earthly creatures; the eye can look to heaven; the mouth is made for speech, the hands for works of skill, the smooth, uncovered skin for expression and beauty of a higher kind than that of fleeces or plumes: man most easily weeps, and man alone can smile.

Into this body, Omnipotence breathed the breath of life; that unseen, incomprehensible principle, through which motion, action, and sensibility began, never to cease. Like the tree yielding fruit, whose seed was in itself, the life of the first man contained in itself the lives of all future generations. At once the lungs inhaled the vital air; the blood ran through the arteries and veins; the nerves bore every sensation to and fro; the muscles moved the whole frame; the heart throbbed within; the eye had its flash, the cheek its crimson, the mouth its smile: man had become a living soul, the chief of the animal creation. In most languages, the name of the soul is derived from a word which signifies wind or breath, as in the Hebrew, the Greek, and the Latin. For, independent motion is the first and last token of the presence of animal life, and the breath is the beginning of independent motion; and there is indeed a mysterious connexion between life and the air, a connexion perhaps deeper than that of mere physical adaptations. The creature that breathes has life, and, in the lower sense, has a soul: but the soul of man, which, on the side where it meets the body, is allied, but far, far superior to the life of all other animals, has also another side, where it meets the Spirit of God, and becomes itself a spirit. Body, and soul, and spirit form indeed a threefold division of our nature, which has been sanctioned by some of the profoundest thinkers of antiquity, by early Christian writers like Justin and Irenæus, and by the phraseology of St. Paul, who prays that all the three may be preserved blameless. In this division the second term is employed for that animal life which uses the organs of sense, and receives their impressions; and the third for that higher and more active part or operation of the inward man which is chiefly the divine image. But in the Hebrew, the Greek, and the Latin, the name of the spirit is also derived from words that express a wind or breath; and therefore the original signification of soul and spirit is essentially the same.

It is the spirit, or it is the soul in those higher properties and acts which give it the name of the spirit, that knows, that imagines, that wills; that employs the tongue in speech, and the whole body in free and moral action. When man became a living soul, these powers were given to him; and they were given to no other earthly creature. These are the strength of his arm, the grace of his figure, the beauty of his countenance; for, if the imagination could quite dismiss these, the noblest or the loveliest form would but produce the impression of the tiger or the swan, or, were it possible, of a majestic or a blooming idiot. But when the divine breath gave life to the body of man, a spirit shone in his glance, spoke from his features, and acted through his free movements. He alone could know himself, the visible world and its invisible Maker, and ripen for ever in this knowledge. The moral image of God was in man alone; and before him was that path in which he might go on from perfection to perfection. Male and female were they made, that strength and sweetness might every where be united in exquisite joy; and that the broad earth might be replenished and subdued by a vast family, whose ancestral home should be Paradise.

II.

The Tree of Life.

> "In this pleasant soil
> His far more pleasant garden God ordained;
> Out of the fertile ground He caused to grow
> All trees of noblest kind for sight, smell, taste,
> And all amid them stood the Tree of Life,
> High eminent, blooming ambrosial fruit,
> Of vegetable gold; and next to Life
> Our death, the Tree of Knowledge, grew fast by."
>
> MILTON.

THE first state of man was one, of which no later generation could form a just picture or conception. It was like infancy, which leaves no trace in recollection. The parents of the human race lived amidst a world of speaking symbols. They saw the properties of animals at a glance; the fit names came at once to their lips; and the foundation of all language was laid in the analogies of nature. The voice of God breathed to them as distinctly in the garden, in the cool of the day, as the murmurs of the wind. In the subtlest of all beasts lurked the presence of their spiritual tempter, with his hissing whisper, and his envenomed sting. The trial of their obedience, with all its vast issues, was a symbolical transaction. Amidst all the trees, the fruit of one was forbidden; and all their happy domain was held under the tenure of this compliance. One other tree was made the pledge and means of their perpetual preservation. The Tree of Life was planted in Paradise, that, eating of its fruit, mankind might live for ever.

2

All the material creation tends to decay, and requires incessant renewal: such is the law of its existence. The life of man was always sustained, as at this day, by continual supplies from a Providence, which has scattered over the earth, and gathers to his feet, those substances whose elementary composition is adapted to that of his body. But these supplies could only prevent, from day to day, that incidental decay which would ensue were the human body separated from any of the surrounding elements which are necessary to the coninual renovation of its vital energies. The great, constant, essential tendency to decay, under which all bodies, however nourished, grow old, and at last sink without disease, and notwithstanding all surrounding elements, could not be thus removed. For this, the bounteous Creator had provided another antidote, in the fruit of that blessed tree which stood distinct and pre-eminent amongst all the growth of the garden. It was ordained to be the sacramental symbol of immortality; perhaps, to be even the physical agency through which the decay of nature should perpetually be counteracted. The pulse, which grew cold and languid after the flight of years, was thus, perhaps, to be quickened and warmed into more than youthful strength. Or, it may be that he, who, at an appointed season, should approach and eat its fruit, was to pass through some gentle transformation, as if from glory to glory. Without dying, the insect lies down to its chrysalis slumber, and then spreads its light wings, a beautiful inhabitant of the air. The bud expands into the blossom, the blossom into the fruit, and yet there is no interval or violence. Two of the family of men have entered a brighter state of being without corporeal dissolution. It may be that the Tree of Life was not only the pledge but the means of such a transition, when the time should come to exchange Eden for some bliss yet nearer to the angels. These have been the opinions of wise and holy interpreters. "In the other trees," says Augustin, "there was nourishment; but in this a sacrament." Irenæus and Chrysostom suppose that it had a virtue to preserve the organs in their original state, without disturbance, till the period of translation. The words of Gregory Nazianzen make either the translation, or the perpetuity of a blissful existence here, the direct consequence of the taste. "If we had continued what we were, and kept the commandments, we should have been what we were not, by coming to the Tree of Life, being made immortal, and approaching nigh to God."

We can imagine that, had men multiplied in innocence, they might have come from the ends of the earth, on pilgrimage to Eden. In that pleasant land, the aged, the ripe, might say, "come and let us go up to

> "that sovereign Plant, whose scions shoot
> With healing virtue, and immortal fruit,
> The Tree of Life, beside the stream that laves
> The fields of Paradise with gladdening waves!"

There they might pluck from its branches, unforbidden and in safety. If they returned to their own regions, it would be with strength renewed like that of the eagle, for another career; as in the summer of countries that approach the pole, the sun just reaches the horizon, and, without setting, ascends anew, so that no night intervenes between the evening and the morning. If they passed into another and a higher being, it would be as angels have disappeared from the sight of men, and entered within the glorious veil. No thought of suffering would have attended their departure; and, perhaps, with the powers of their higher nature, they would no more have been always absent from such as they left behind, than the angel visiters, who disappeared, indeed, but "walked the air unseen," and at times came visibly again, on messages of love.

III.

The Sentence of Death.

> " One arrow more,
> The sharpest of the Almighty's store,
> Trembles upon the string—a sinner's death."
>
> KEBLE.

"IT is one thing," says St. Augustin, " not to be able to die, as God has formed some creatures; another thing to be able not to die, as the first man was created. Separated from the tree of life, he could die; but if he had not sinned, he could have been exempt from death. He was mortal by the constitution of his animal body; immortal by the gift of his Maker."

Placed, for his trial, under a single prohibition, he saw before him the two symbolical trees; and it was announced to him that, by tasting the one, he must forfeit the right and power to taste the other; that if he would know evil as well as good by his experience, he must surrender the peace, the joy, and the very life which would else have been perpetual. "In the day that thou eatest thereof," was the divine word, " thou shalt surely die." The name of death was spoken: it was heard in Paradise: the thought was written on the mind of man, in characters of fear, and it has never been effaced. In the present languages of the world, it is a simple, primitive word: there is no more elementary idea from which this could have its derivation. Man needed not to see death, that he might feel its horror; no more than he needs to see annihilation, that he may shrink from the conception, and rejoice in his existence. He understood that death was the opposite and the destruction of life; and life was all which, within him, or around him, moved, acted, or enjoyed. The sentence which awaited his transgression was, that he should be deprived of his present blissful being. As his body was dust by its original composition, it would be but dust when its life should have departed: the elements would claim their portion in its substance. His spirit, the gift of God, would return to the Giver, subject to His sovereign disposal, tainted by its own guilt, and burdened with His displeasure; a vessel that, having disappointed the use for which it was designed, might now be cast aside, and, if it could not lose its individual existence, could exist only in darkness and woe.

The penalty was vast and terrible; the more terrible, were it possible, even for its obscurity. The temptation was slight, the resistance yet slighter: the simple lie of the evil one was believed, against the dread word of the Almighty Father: evil was known as well as good: sin entered into the world, and death by sin. In that day man died in effect; for the decree went forth from Him with whom to command is to execute The seeds of sickness and decay were at once planted in the human frame; of sickness which would else have been an unknown thought, and of decay, which the fruit of the unforbidden Tree of Life would for ever have averted. Shame and fear accompanied the consciousness of guilt and the conviction that death was now a reality. In the very act of sin, our progenitors died to their peace as well as to their innocence. They now stood before their Judge, awaiting the fulfilment of the residue of His sentence. The manner was still with Him; they only knew that they were already dying creatures, and that the life for which they had been formed was already departed. They now heard the yet unknown process by which their death should be made complete; the mighty load of woes which was bound inseparably to death; the tremendous conflict of which the earth was to be the battle-ground, that death might not reach the spirit; and the final victory in which death, and he that had the power of death, should be trodden under foot, notwithstanding their present triumph.

The sentence which before had been only awful, now breathed compassion. Its thunders fell upon the head of the tempter. He, like his poor instrument, the brute serpent, was doomed to make his path in the dust, hated and hating, and at length to be crushed by the heel of a human conqueror. A mark of peculiar sorrow was fixed upon the hour which gives birth to a mortal; a mark, that should fitly betoken the gateway of a world of tears. But she who bore it should still be the mother of the living; her desire, submissive but affectionate and full of solace for her griefs, should be to her husband; and love and hope were still left to her who had forfeited Eden. A curse was laid upon the earth, that it might produce spontaneously the fruits of death, all noxious and useless herbs, and only yield to the hard toil of man his necessary food. While he should open its surface, he was ever to be reminded, too, that there his own limbs must find their final rest: but it should still give him abundant bread; and labour, with all its weariness, would be his relief and his protection. After a longer or a shorter space, thus crowded with anxiety and sorrow, the close must arrive: the dissolution of his original state, gradual as it was, should be completed; and he should return to his kindred dust. But if he had lost Paradise, and even life, through the fraud of the tempter; and if that tempter was yet to be no victor, but a foe trodden under foot by the seed of that woman whom he had deceived, this close itself could be no mere triumph of the author of evil. The soul, which would not die, might find a release in death, and the very body, which seemed through the sentence his inalienable prey, might yet be rescued through his defeat, and live again.

Hoping, therefore, in the midst of grief, the first man named the first woman, "Eve," the "living," as the mother of all living.

"Man is to live, and all things live for man."

But Paradise, however it might be changed, was no fit abode for those to whom the Tree of Life was now forbidden. To have tasted that fruit, if its original effect could now have followed the taste, would have been only to have made sorrow and sin immortal. Our parents were, therefore, in mercy as well as in justice, banished from Eden; and angels and a flaming sword forbade every presumptuous approach; till Paradise itself was no more. The flood left no tradition of the time when these bright guards were last seen by human eyes; and no mortal beheld when the trees of the garden, and with them that wondrous tree in their midst, withered away. Over the soil from which they grew, and into which, perhaps, they sank, the waters may have spread some plain of sand, where now above the wreck of Paradise, some Mesopotamian caravan, weary with the journey, and fearful of attack, halts for a night.

IV.

The Number of the Dead.

"Earth has hosts, but thou canst show
Many myriads for her one!"

CROLY.

THE mind sinks under the number, almost numberless, of those who have been successively the inhabitants of this world, and have bowed, in their turns, to the common sentence. Scarce one in many, many thousands, has left more than the briefest echo of his name; yet of each it is true that

"He was whatever thou hast been,
He is what thou shalt be."

The present population of the earth is estimated, with seeming probability, at a thousand millions. Almost six thousand years are numbered, since the creation. The first two thousand years embraced about eighteen generations, before the life of man had its present limits. During the later four thousand years, three generations have lived within each century. The succession of generations may therefore be computed at a hundred and forty. Of the population of the earth before the flood, not even the most conjectural calculation can be ventured; but probably the prevalence of violence and crime may have prevented that vast increase, which, in so long a space, and when the frame so defied disease, might else have overspread the globe. After the flood, the Eastern lands, Egypt, Assyria, India, China, were soon the seats of mighty empires; of which some were for a time, and others have been to this day, obeyed by the most compact and multitudinous populations. The remoter lands were more gradually and more thinly peopled, and the history of many generations is covered with impenetrable darkness; but except among the wildest barbarians, the population supposed before accurate knowledge could be obtained has commonly been less than that which actually appeared after better inquiry. It will not be an extravagant, although an uncertain computation, if the average number of each generation be reckoned at one fifth of the present; and then the entire number would be twenty-eight thousands of millions. To admit such a number into the imagination, we can conceive that twenty-eight of the chief empires of the earth contained each a hundred provinces, and that each of these provinces contained five cities of the magnitude of London. These fourteen thousand Londons could perhaps embrace the armies of the dead.

The city of Nineveh must have been inhabited, through several ages, by more than five hundred thousand persons; and probably its mounds look down upon what remains of six or seven millions. A still vaster multitude is covered by the desolate plain of Babylon. Not less than fifteen millions of bodies must, in the space of twenty-five centuries, have been mingled with the dust of Christian and Pagan Rome. At least half as many more must sleep under the new Rome of Constantine. Some of the great capitals of the remote East bury several millions in a century. But, in truth, the bones of hosts more numerous than ever stood living on one spot have been laid beneath many a fair town whose inhabitants may scarce ever have thought how the progress of ages had made their home so prodigious a sepulchre. Two millions of skulls are arranged in the catacombs of Paris. The ten thousand parishes of England contain ten thousand churchyards; and the clay of every churchyard contains a part of thousands of frames, once warm and buoyant. It is enough to make the simple comparison between the present population of any old district or town, and its collective population in all the past; and the mind will grasp the superior number of the dead beyond the living.

> "All that tread
> The globe, are but a handful to the tribes
> That slumber in its bosom."

The surface of the earth, so far as it is dry land, is estimated at nearly forty millions of square miles. If twenty-eight thousands of millions of inhabitants have sojourned upon it, and could once more be distributed over it, every square mile would receive seven hundred persons. The average population of England is about two hundred and sixty for a square mile, that of the whole territory of the United States less than eight. Could the dead live again upon the earth, they would make every spot almost three times as populous as the British isles, and almost a hundred fold more than the American Republic.

On individuals so numberless the decree that sends man to his dust has already passed into execution. The dead exceed fivefold the minutes since the creation; and in the last hour more than three thousand bodies must have fallen. Every year, one individual amongst twenty-seven dies in Russia and in the city of New York: one amongst thirty in Greece: one amongst thirty-two in Sicily: one amongst thirty-six in Prussia: one amongst thirty-nine in France and Holland: one amongst forty-two in Philadelphia: one amongst forty-three in Belgium: one amongst fifty-three in England. Till the end of time this mighty train must be swelled by all who shall live: the extent of the procession can be known only when it has completely passed. So immeasurable has been the triumph of the last enemy of man, while but those two exceptions forbid us to name it universal. One was "translated that he should not see death;" the other "went up by a whirlwind into heaven," with "a chariot of fire, and horses of fire;" that what, in the last day, shall be seen in millions, might already have been recorded of more than one.

V.

The Period of Death.

> " As the long train
> Of ages glide away, the sons of men,
> The youth in life's green spring, and he who goes
> In the full strength of years, matron and maid,
> And the sweet babe, and the grayheaded man,
> Shall one by one be gathered to thy side,
> By those who in their turn, shall follow them."
>
> BRYANT.

THE period at which man should return to dust was left under a solemn uncertainty. Time would reveal the thousand methods in which it could be hastened by every possible agency in earth and air, around and within; and would fix the limits beyond which, when every hazard should be escaped, the issue could no longer be delayed. The utmost length and the average length of human life were then the secrets of the unfolding future, as now they are the results of the recorded past.

Amongst those eight antediluvian patriarchs who completed the natural term of their days. he who died youngest was seven hundred and seventy-seven years old, and he who lived longest was nine hundred and sixty-nine. It is as if one now alive could have seen the face of one who had witnessed the crucifixion. Although the years of Methuselah have surpassed those of every other mortal, yet as Adam began his existence in full maturity, and then lived through nine hundred and thirty years, the most protracted resistance to decay may thus have been allotted to the frame of our first father. So far as life, amongst the wicked of the antediluvian world, was not extinguished by violence, the general length of the days of man must have been ten times their present duration: a space sufficient, had intellectual vigour been widely developed, to have comprehended the most amazing works of toil and skill, the profoundest discoveries in science, and enterprises and achievements of magnificence since unparalleled. But that world left neither pyramids nor books; and if great exploits of intellect were not attempted, tremendous, no doubt, must have been the progress of brutality and crime, when the body had such might, and when death and judgment were so distant. There were giants in the earth in those days, men of renown; but the wickedness of man was great, all flesh corrupted his way, the earth was filled with violence, and that mighty race was doomed to death without posterity.

The descendants of Noah, the second father of mankind, were permitted to add to that nourishment from the fruits of the earth, which had been assigned to Adam, the flesh of all animals. But it was not in the design that new vigour should be given to their bodily system, which was rather destined to yield more and more rapidly, till their days should at length be fixed at threescore years and ten. The son of Noah died at six hundred; the grandson of that son, at four hundred and thirty-three; the grandson of that grandson at two hundred and thirty-nine; the patriarch of the third generation after, at a hundred and forty-eight; and then the ages of Terah, Abraham, Isaac, Jacob, and Joseph were two hundred and five, a hundred and seventy-five, a hundred and eighty, a hundred and forty-seven, and a hundred and ten. When the Israelites were in the wilderness, the common term of life was already as brief as now; and though

Moses lived, with an undimmed eye and with unabated strength, to a hundred and twenty years, and Joshua died at a hundred and ten, these were amongst those extraordinary prolongations of life, of which every age has witnessed some examples. That such longevity fell to the lot of the two great leaders of Israel, was a part of the wondrous scheme of Providence which guided the destinies of a chosen nation. Since the days of Jacob, no authenticated instance remains, of a life that has exceeded a hundred and seventy years. If, amongst African slaves, or Russian peasants, or Arabian hordes, a greater age has been ascribed to some venerable remnant of a past generation, the evidence of records was wanting, and the credulity of barbarism too easily supplies its absence. There were in the city of Cairo, in 1800, thirty-five persons amongst the less indigent inhabitants, whose years were stated to exceed a hundred. In Birmingham, on the contrary, amongst a population of a hundred and thirty thousand, only six persons died at that age or beyond it, within a period of ten years. In a census of the Emperor Vespasian, a hundred and twenty-four such persons were found in the region between the Po and the Apennines. The census of the United States, in 1840, gave of such persons a thousand five hundred and ten males and a thousand two hundred and fifty-nine females, amongst a total population of rather more than seventeen millions. But of these numbers a thousand and thirty-four males and nine hundred and forty-three females were of African descent, amongst a black population of less than three millions, and may be excluded as generally ignorant of their own age or of computation. Seven hundred and ninety-two white persons are then left, from more than fourteen millions; or, about fifty in a million, or one in twenty thousand. In London one infant amongst three thousand lives to complete his hundredth year; in the Belgic states a careful table gave less than one-third of that proportion.

St. Polycarp seems to have been one of these exceptions to the common lot; Simeon, the second bishop of Jerusalem, is said to have reached a hundred and twenty years; and both died by martyrdom. Many of the saints and anchorets of the earlier ages are famed for their length of days: Paul the Hermit, it is said, lived to be a hundred and thirteen; his follower, Antony, to be a hundred and five, and John the Silent, to be a hundred and four; the cenobites of Mount Sinai attain not unfrequently an extreme age; and instances, more wonderful but more doubtful, occur in legendary biographies and in the tales of travellers. The actor Macklin appeared on the stage, as Shylock, after he had passed his hundredth year; and a Baptist minister, in our day, has, at a hundred and eight, addressed a congregation from the pulpit. Remembering the person of King Richard the Third, who fell in 1485, the Countess of Desmond lived till the reign of James the First, and died at a hundred and forty-five. In poverty and not without vice, "old Parr" survived till a hundred and fifty-two. But the oldest man of whom we have sure record, since the patriarchs, was Henry Jenkins, who died in Yorkshire, in 1670, at a hundred and sixty-nine.

This is the utmost limit at which one lonely traveller arrived; while, at less than half the distance, lies the common term of vigour and of healthful enjoyment. Our universal history has followed the saying of the mournful prophet, "The days of our years are threescore years and ten; and if by reason of strength they be fourscore years, yet is their strength labour and sorrow." Of all who are born into the world, scarce five in a hundred, it is probable, attain this natural term of their present being. Amongst all those Jewish kings whose age is recorded, not one survived so long; of the English sovereigns since the Norman Conquest, only three amongst thirty-four, and these three all of the robust house of Brunswick; in France, since Charlemagne, only Louis the Fourteenth, Charles the Tenth, and Louis Philippe. Under every advantage, the hereditary peerage of the British realm numbered, in 1840, amongst some five hundred and sixty members, one hundred and two who were beyond the seventieth year; but amongst the fourteen millions who composed the white population of the United States, there were, of that age, fewer than two hundred and thirteen thousand.

At less than half of this distance of threescore years and ten, itself less than half the utmost period of longevity, a majority of the pilgrims have already sunk by the wayside. Such are the various effects of climate, of the state of society, and of many accidental causes, on the duration of life in different lands, nations, and ages, that its average length for the whole human family cannot with much accuracy be determined. Buffon placed it just below thirty-five, and supposed that one third died before the age of ten; Hufeland has reckoned that only half attain even that outer gate of early childhood. In a town parish of New England, the average, in a computation of some three hundred deaths, was thirty-three; but two thirds of those who died before that point died within the first ten years of life; and such a result, when compared with the great destruction of infancy in regions less favoured, would tend to justify the calculation of Hufeland

It is not without interest to note the age at which human beings of different kinds of eminence have closed their earthly developement. Amongst the poets, whose fame is not seldom acquired early, Kirke White died at 21, Drake at 25, Novalis at 28, Brainard at 32, Otway and Churchill at 34, Byron at 36, Parnell and Burns at 37, Rowe and Gay at 44, Spenser at 45, Schiller at 46, Addison and Thomson at 47, Cowley at 48, Akenside at 49, Tasso at 51, Shakspeare and Lessing at 52, Gray at 53, Camoens and Alfieri at 55, Dante and Pope at 56, Prior at 57, Ariosto at 58, Racine at 59, Coleridge and Scott at 61, Laharpe at 63, Milton at 66, Cowper at 68, Dryden and Petrarch at 70, Mason at 72, Lope de Vega, Corneille, Klopstock, Claudius, and Crabbe at 78, Wieland at 79, Anacreon, Sophocles, and Pindar about 80, Goethe at 82, Voltaire and Young at 84, Southern at 86, and the Persian poet, Sadi, it is said, at 120. Amongst other literary persons, Olympia Morata died at 29, Pico de Mirandula at 31, Mrs. Godwin at 39, Politiano at 40, Glanvil at 44, Sir William Jones at 48, Ascham at 53, Herder at 59, Grotius and Richter at 62, Gibbon at 63, Cervantes and Stolberg at 69, Selden and Lamb at 70, Locke, Richardson, Thomas Paine, and Lady Mary Wortley Montague at 72, Cobbett at 73, Johnson at 75, Swift at 77, Lord Bolingbroke and Lord Orford at 79, Godwin at 80, while Mrs. Barbauld reached to 81, Mrs. Carter to 89, Hobbes to 91, and Hannah More to 92. Amongst artists, Bewick died at 35, Vandyck at 42, Vanbrugh at 54, Bacon at 59, Gainsborough at 61, Hogarth at 67, Romney at 68, Reynolds at 79, Northcote at 85, Nollekens and Beechey at 86, and Michael Angelo at 90. Amongst actors, Kean died at 45, Booth at 52, Garrick at 63,

Matthews at 65. Philologists, in their tranquil pursuits, have often survived to a very ripe old age; for, while Ockley died at 42, Wakefield at 45, and Porson at 49, Valpy lived till 62, Joseph Scaliger and Parkhurst till 69, D'Herbelot till 70, Ainsworth till 73, Walker till 75, Cyril Jackson till 77, Castel and Bryant till 74, Bentley till 80, Morell till 81, Heyne till 82, Markland till 83, and Pocock and Rennell till 87. Amongst antiquaries, too, Ritson was 51, Anthony Wood 63, Prynne 69, Ashmole 75, Cave 76, Baker 77, Willis 78, Stowe 79, Dugdale and Coxe 81, Rushworth and Whitaker 83, and Pegge 92. Amongst naturalists and philosophers, Cotes died at 34, Pascal at 39, Davy at 50, Tycho Brahe at 54, Saunderson at 57, Bacon and Boyle at 65, Smeaton at 68, Sir James Edward Smith at 69, Bradley at 70, Flamstead and Gilbert White at 73, Maskelyne at 79, Plato at 81, Theophrastus, Newton, Evelyn, Halley, and Hutton, all at 85, Long at 90, Sir William Herschel at more than 80, and his sister at 97. Amongst physicians, Beddoes died at 48, Freind at 53, Radcliffe, Cheselden and Percival at 64, Sydenham at 65, Fothergill at 68, Jenner at 74, Harvey at 79, Mead at 81. Amongst eminent lawyers, Dunning, Lord Ashburton died at 51, Lord Nottingham at 61, the first Lord Shaftesbury at 62, Lord Somers at 64, Lord King at 65, Hale and Holt at 67, Lord Ellenborough at 68, Lord Tenterden at 70, Lord Thurlow at 74, Lord Camden at 80, Coke at 84, Lord Eldon at 87, Lord Mansfield at 88, and Lord Stowell at 91. Amongst divines and religious writers, President Davies died at 36, Hugh James Rose at 44, Hervey at 45, Hooker at 46, Toplady at 48, Oecolampadius, Jewel, and Doddridge at 49, Mede and Sacheverell at 52, Thomas Fuller, Burkitt,

Joseph Milner, and Bishop Middleton at 53, Samuel Clarke at 54, Hammond, Poole, Bingham and Legh Richmond at 55, Jeremy Taylor, John Scott, Smalridge and Whitefield at 56, Junius and Waterland at 57, Cardinal Pole, Donne, and Wilkins at 58, Bunyan and Butler at 60, Luther, Heylin, Horne, and Paley at 62, Melancthon, Gastrell, and Kennicott at 63, Tillotson, Stillingfleet, and Dwight at 64, Bernard Gilpin at 65, Musculus, George Fox, and Herring at 66, Owen and Seabury at 67, Cardinal Baronius, Claude, Stanhope, and Drew at 68, Atterbury and Isaac Milner at 69, Beveridge, Sharp, and Kippis at 70, Bullinger, Paolo Sarpi, Cudworth, and Priestley at 71, Lightfoot, Pearson, and Potter at 73, Gill, Watts, Jones of Nayland, Thomas Scott, and Tomline at 74, Sanderson, Howe, Bull, William Law, and Secker at 75, Baxter at 76, Lowth, Porteus and Simeon at 77, Derham at 78, Bellarmine, Tenison, and Bishop Newton at 79, Wake and Emlyn at 80, Patrick, Warburton, Romaine, and Lawrence at 81, John Newton at 82, Bishop Law and Lardner at 84, Hoadley at 85, Beza at 86, Whitby, Hurd, and Wesley at 88, Nowell and Bishop Lloyd at 90, and Bishop Wilson at 92. Of the Fathers of the Church, Basil lived to be about 53, Ambrose about 58, Tertullian about 60, Chrysostom 63, Gregory of Nyssa 65, Origen 69, Eusebius and Augustin 76, Athanasius 77, Jerome 89, and Epiphanius almost 100. Amongst statesmen, Mirabeau died at 42, Pitt at 47, Halifax at 54, Fox at 58, Canning at 59, Lyttelton at 64, Clarendon at 66, Walpole at 69, Chatham and Carnot at 70, Hardenberg at 72, Wilberforce at 74, Talleyrand at 84, and Warren Hastings at 86. Of illustrious warriors who have died the death of nature, Hoche was removed at 33, the Marquis of Granby at 49, Davoust at 53, Massena and Augereau at 59, Collingwood at 61, Cortez at 62, Anson at 65, Washington at 67, Suwarrow at 71, Marlborough at 72, Howe at 73, Rodney at 74, Amherst at 80, Hood at 82, Townshend and Dumourier at 84. Amongst sovereigns, Alexander died at 32, Titus at 40, Canute at 41, Napoleon at 51, Henry the Seventh at 52, Charles the Fifth at 58, Marcus Aurelius at 60, Adrian at 62, Ferdinand and Isabella at 63, Severus and Henry the First at 65, Edward the Third at 66, Elizabeth at 68, Vespasian at 69, Tamerlane at 71, Antoninus Pius at 74, Augustus, and Cosmo de Medici at 75, Richard Cromwell at 86, and Artaxerxes Mnemon at 94.

The progress of society in cultivation and in the arts of peace and the science of health, have doubtless postponed a little the average limit of life. Its utmost term is probably unchangeable; and those examples of longevity which have approached that term were due to no influence of social improvement. Ten thousand human beings set forth together on their journey. After ten years, one third at least has disappeared. At the middle point of the common measure of life, but half are still upon the road. Fast and faster, as the ranks grow thinner, they that remained till now, become weary, and lie down, and rise no more. At threescore and ten a band of some four hundred yet struggles on. At ninety, these have been reduced to a handful of thirty trembling patriarchs. Year after year, they fall in diminishing numbers. One lingers, perhaps, a lonely marvel, till the century is over. We look again, and the work of death is finished.

VI.

The First Death.

> "Javan !" said Enoch, " on this spot began
> The fatal curse;—man perish'd here by man
> The earliest death a son of Adam died
> Was murder, and that murder fratricide !"
>
> MONTGOMERY.

FROM the author of death came the temptation, and man was already so much in the bondage of that mysterious corruption which had followed the great transgression, that the temptation was heard, and actual death was first introduced in demoniac hatred. The impulse of hatred, which is only just when it is turned against some entirely and irrecoverably evil being, is, to work a partial or a total destruction. Life is the utmost which it is in the power of man to destroy. Beasts had been struck down, and had ceased to exist, before the eyes of Cain: his hatred moved him to wish that Abel might thus be destroyed: his arm dealt the blow; and his brother, like one of the lambs of his own flock, sank in his blood, and breathed his life away. The murderer was smitten with desperate horror: he knew, by an inward instinct, that all men would hold it just to slay him: but the death by violence, the murder, the fratricide which he had wrought, could never be retraced, but was to be the dreadful type of many future horrors.

For wealth and rule, Abimelech, the son of Gideon, poured out on one stone the lives of his seventy brothers, and gained the horrible distinction of the most enormous murder in human history. In revenge for a most unnatural wrong, Absalom commanded his servants to slay his brother Amnon, when his heart was merry with wine. Many a sovereign, especially in the East, has not shrunk from securing his throne by the sacrifice of fraternal blood, and this has passed into a proverb, amongst the Ottomans. Cambyses, king of Persia, ordered the execution of his brother Smerdis, and with his own brutal foot inflicted a fatal blow on his sister Meroe. Seven fratricides occurred in the line of Darius Hystaspes; and three at least amongst the Ptolemies. Mithridates began his reign with the slaughter of his mother and brother. Tryphena, the wife of Antiochus Grypus, caused her sister Cleopatra to be slain in a temple, clasping the image to which she had fled for refuge. Onias, the Jewish high-priest, after being supplanted by one brother, was slain by command of another. In the house of Hyrcanus, the Asmonean prince of Judea, Aristobulus slew Antigonus his brother, by the hands of his guards; and Alexander Janneus, a third brother, caused a fourth to be put to death. Geta was butchered in the arms of his mother, in the presence, and by the order of his brother Caracalla. The ambition of Richard the Third prepared his way to the throne by the death of his brother, George, Duke of Clarence, and of his royal nephews. In humbler spheres, brothers have been waylaid by brothers for their estates, or struck down in wrath or revenge. It has been dreadful, too, even though the guilt of murder were not incurred, when one of princely rank, dying for treason, has been put to death with the direct consent of one who had been cradled in the same arms. Thus, Adonijah died by the sentence of Solomon; and the name of the

Protector Somerset was the first signature to the warrant for the execution of his brother, Thomas, Lord Seymour.

Less often, perhaps, has a parent thus inflicted death upon a child; except when some Brutus, or Torquatus, or Manlius, has nerved himself with the old Roman ferocity of justice. A Spartan woman is related to have killed her son for returning safe from a battle, where his companions fell. It is said that one of the Medici slew, with his own arm, one of his two sons, who had slain the other on a hunting excursion. Herod the Great put to death the uncle of his much-beloved wife Mariamne; then, her grandfather Hyrcanus; then, in a fury of jealousy, Mariamne herself; then, his own sons by her; and at last, his son Antipater.

But children have imbrued their hands in the blood of parents, even though the conscience of Pagans once clothed the punishment of parricide with peculiar horrors. The proud Sennacherib was murdered by his sons, Adrammelech and Sharezer, while he worshipped in the temple of his god Nisroch. Cleopatra, the mother of Antiochus Grypus, prepared poison for him, which he compelled her to drink. Bajazet the Second was poisoned by his son Selim. Through a signal triumph of the tempter, aged parents have been left by their children, in savage nations, to die by hunger or by wild beasts; and little children have been exposed to death by their parents; and the act has been followed by no remorse, and perhaps has been deemed religious. The king of Moab, in the contest with Israel, offered up his son for a burnt-offering; and if the daughter of Jephthah was really sacrificed, her father had borrowed the dreadful thought from the heathen. Manasseh and the idolatrous Jews caused their own sons to pass through the fire to

Moloch; which, if not a direct immolation, must often, no doubt, have been fatal. The ancient Arabs buried female children alive. An African tribe buried all their infants, and adopted the children of their captives. The Panches of Bogota destroyed all girls who were the first-born of their parents. In China, such multitudes of female infants perish, that the annual number exposed in the streets of Pekin by night is estimated at four thousand, all of whom, with the morning light, are thrown, living or dead, into the grave. Along the Ganges, till the British rule forbade, the mother very often, cast her offspring, to the goddess of the river. In New Holland and the Polynesian islands, a large proportion of each generation; in the Society Islands, before the introduction of Christianity, so large a proportion as three-fourths, have perished by the parental hand or direction. The child of the American Indian was not murdered, unless in some moment of impatience.

Ties of remoter kindred have been severed by the sword with still less of remorse. Joab, with ferocious vengeance or envious treachery, slew his two kinsmen, Absalom and Amasa, as well as Abner, with his own hand. Athaliah destroyed all the seed royal of Judah. The death of Prince Arthur of Brittany was ascribed to his uncle, King John; that of Richard the Second to his cousin who dethroned him; and that of Henry the Sixth to his victorious kinsmen and supplanters. The Italian chronicles, as well as the histories of the East, are red with these tales of unnatural murder.

As with Herod and with Henry the Eighth, the appetite for blood has found peculiar and horrid satisfaction in the slaughter of defenceless women. A brutal jealousy consigned the wretched sultana to the Bosphorus, and lifts the club of the coarse village drunkard against the wife who has borne with his enormities. Nero killed his wife Octavia, as well as his mother Agrippina. Amalasuntha, queen of the Ostrogoths, was strangled in the bath by the order of a husband whom she had elevated. Gonzaga, prince of Mantua, ordered the execution of the princess, his spouse; and a prince of the house of Caraffa slew his wife from jealousy. The infuriated demon often strikes in his frenzy at the nearest object; and thus it is that, of all murders, that of a wife or of one who has been admitted to the place of a wife, is probably the most frequent, as well as the most shocking.

Less often has the guilt of the murderess been found in the bosom of the wife. But Alboin, king of the Lombards, was a victim to the revenge of Rosamond, his queen, for the death of her father; Edward the Second was murdered through the instigation of his "she-wolf" wife; Catharine the Second mounted the throne over the corpse of her husband; and Mary of Scotland at least wedded the murderer of Henry Darnley. In common life, the assassin of the husband has sometimes been the paramour of the wife; and there have been instances in our times when a strange thirst for destruction has been infused by the devil, and women have administered poison to one after another whom they had first allured to the nuptial bed.

But as murder is the terrible exception from common death, so these are the terrible exceptions from common murder. They have been the utmost advances of sin and death and of their infernal author. Except where infanticide or human sacrifice has been a custom, and except the unlawful offspring destroyed as soon as born, very few in a million have died by the stroke or device of brother, or parent, or child, or kinsman, or consort. Still, almost every spot has its tale, of some half maniac father who has butchered his whole family as they lay asleep, or some frantic mother who has flung child after child into the rushing stream. Insanity, with which the powers of evil seem often to sport, as with a fortress forsaken by its garrison, very often inspires a deadly purpose towards the nearest objects of love: dark, dreadful thoughts shoot over the bewildered mind; and, though the guilt be wanting, the death is sometimes accomplished. It is as if it was designed that the first death which befell a human creature, with all its train of later fratricides and kindred crimes, should tell from how terrible a depth the victory of the seed of the woman must deliver the victims of sin.

VII.

Death by Murder.

> "Seest thou that lifeless corpse, those bloody wounds?
> See how he lies, who but so shortly since
> A living creature was, with all the powers
> Of sense, and motion, and humanity!
> Oh, what a heart had he who did this deed!"
>
> BAILLIE.

APART from the more horrible atrocities of parricide, fratricide, and the murder of consorts or kindred, a multitude of men have been slain by the secret assassin, or the open, infuriated assailant. Monarchs in their palaces; chiefs at the head of armies; rich men lying in their chambers; travellers on the highway; husbands waylaid by the adulterer; adulterers in the arms of their paramours; men whose own crimes have been followed by the swift foot of the avenger; men who have been hated for the strict execution of their duty; men who have been involved in national, political, or family feuds; each in the moment when he was most unguarded, have felt the sudden knife, or club, or axe, or ball, and fallen by the malice, the fury, the lust of gold, or the revenge, of a fellow-man.

The fifth in descent from Cain was Lamech, who was remembered for those verses in which he owned that he had "slain a man to his wounding, and a young man to his hurt." It was no murder, when Eglon died by the dagger of Ehud, and Sisera by the nail and hammer of Jael. Whether the arm of the slayer was moved by a divine impulse or only by a patriotic determination, whether the act could be justified or only excused, the tyrant who had violated every right was the enemy of all the oppressed people, and had nothing to expect but from his own strength and vigilance. Such deeds can never be imitated under the Gospel; but they are not to be read as if we were reading of crimes. It was otherwise when Ishbosheth, as he lay on his bed at noon, was slain by the two sons of Rimmon, who hurried with his head across the plain. Four kings of Israel, and three of Judah, died through conspiracy. Gedaliah, the governor of the conquered Jews, was murdered by those who had just eaten his bread; and Hazael, who had just before recoiled at the prediction of his deed, smothered his sick and confiding sovereign.

The brother and the son of Alexander the Great were successively placed on the throne, to fall after a little while by murder. His father, Philip, was struck by Pausanias, as, in great pomp, celebrating the marriage of his daughter, he entered the theatre. The magnificent Xerxes was murdered in his bed by one of his courtiers; three of his successors were also assassinated; and in the lines of Syrian, Egyptian, and Parthian princes, domestic slaughters were so frequent that the reader is scarcely shocked by the occurence, in their history, of less unnatural homicides. Scipio the younger was found, apparently strangled, in his bed: Pompey was murdered in a boat by three Egyptians, in sight of his wife from whom he had just parted; and Julius Cæsar fell down at the foot of the statue of Pompey, stabbed by the daggers of several senators. The Emperor Caligula was pierced in the neck by the poniard of one of his officers, as he passed through a gallery between the theatre and the palace:

Claudius died by poison: the gross Vitellius, dragged through the streets of Rome, was murdered with many blows: Domitian was overpowered as he went to dinner: Commodus, after being poisoned by his concubine, was strangled by a strong wrestler: Caracalla was assassinated by a hired soldier, as he paused on a journey: the firm Galba, the rich Didius Julian, Macrinus, already deposed, the upright Pertinax, the wretched Heliogabalus in the arms of his mother, Alexander Severus in his tent, the gigantic Maximin, the associates Pupienus and Balbinus, Philip with his young son, Gallus and Gallienus, Aurelian and Probus, all were slain by their own soldiers; Carinus by a wronged husband; Numerian by his father-in-law, in his litter: thus died the Pagan lords of the world. Of the Christian emperors, Constans was put to death in his bed by a rebellious officer: the second Valentinian was strangled, the third was murdered in the midst of his capital: Maurice was cruelly destroyed with his children: and so died by the sword of the assassin, or by poison, Phocas, the murderer of Maurice, the second Constantine, the second Justinian, Constantine the Sixth, Leo the Armenian, Michael the Third, Romanus the Second and the Third, Nicephorus and Alexius the Fourth. Omar, Othman, and Ali, the second, third, and fourth, successors of Mahomet, all perished by the poniard; and so died, or by the bowstring, many a later caliph and sultan. In the earlier history of the modern nations of Europe, murder was as commonly the end of royalty. King Edmund the elder fell by the hand of a robber who had boldly sat down at his board, and then, having provoked him to seize him by the hair, stabbed him to the heart. Edward the Martyr was murdered at the instigation of his stepmother, Elfrida; Edmund Ironside by two of his chamberlains. The murder of Duncan by Macbeth is no tragic fiction. The Emperor Albert was stabbed by his nephew, in the presence of his court, on the bank of the Reuss. Henry the Third of France was pierced in his palace by the dagger of Jacques Clement; Henry the Fourth in his carriage by Ravaillac. William, the great, Prince of Orange, fell by the hand of an enthusiast. In the civil wars of France, the heads of the royal houses of Orleans, Burgundy, and afterwards of Guise, were successively destroyed by mutual treachery. Humphrey, Duke of Gloucester, was found dead in his bed by violence. Galeazzo Maria, Duke of Milan, was assassinated as he entered a church in solemn procession; Giuliano de Medici just as the host was lifted: Becket was hewn down at the foot of the altar. Cardinal Beatoun was murdered by several conspirators in his chamber. The Regent Murray was shot from a window, as he rode through Linlithgow. From the feet of Queen Mary, Rizzio was dragged into a neighbouring room, and despatched with many wounds. Wallenstein was assassinated, with the approbation of his emperor. Pizarro, too, was murdered. A stab in the breast from a man of maddened mind destroyed the great Duke of Buckingham, the favourite of two kings. Monaldeschi, the supposed paramour of Christina, was slain by her order in the gallery of Fontainbleau, and almost in her presence. Cardinal Bambridge, Sir Thomas Overbury, and Ainsworth, the Puritan divine, were poisoned. Archbishop Sharp was surprised on a moor, dragged from his carriage, and butchered before the eyes of his daughter. Gustavus the Third was shot in the groin, at a masquerade, with a pistol loaded with slugs or nails. The Czar Paul was assaulted and strangled. The Duke of Berri, son of

Charles the Tenth, was killed in the heart of Paris. An infernal machine, discharged from a window as Louis Philippe rode by with his train, destroyed instantly the Duke of Treviso, and other officers. Of all assassinations, that one which the mind recalls with least pain, was when the monster Marat, in his bath, was struck to the heart, by the knife of Charlotte Corday; and one of the saddest was when a frenzied wretch, on the steps of Westminster Hall, shot down the excellent minister Perceval.

The name assassin is derived from a tribe who inhabited Mount Lebanon and some other regions of the East, in the days of the Crusades, and obeyed a chief who sent his emissaries wherever he would, against his enemies, without the possibility of defence. By the stroke of one of them died Louis of Bavaria; and Conrad, Marquis of Montferrat, was murdered by one, in the very street of Sidon. But the most amazing and horrid of all systems of murder, exceeding the combined operations of all the bandits of all ages, has been the long concealed union of the Thugs of Hindostan; whose life, whose delight, whose glory, and whose worship consisted in the secret, remorseless destruction of defenceless travellers by strangling. Their antiquity was unknown; their cruelty was uniform; and many thousands must have been their victims. The glimpses of savage history which can be won, disclose innumerable murders in wild lands; the proofs of an almost inconceivable amount of bloodshed which has cried from the ground, in spots whose history has never been told. Amongst nations not simply barbarous, the avenger of blood has, from the beginning, assumed the task of executing the doom ordained for the murderer; and bloody feuds have passed from fathers to sons, and from families to tribes. Spain, Italy, and the East, have been the chief scenes of those private assassinations, which, in a more advanced condition of society, have been prompted by revenge, pride, or the love of gold. In Spain, in the year 1826, twelve hundred and thirty-three persons were convicted of murders. Death by murder is, in Northern and Christian lands, the rare work of a peculiar atrocity of mind. Still, our own age has seen the ruffian, plunging his blade into the breasts of a whole family; the youth stabbing the old man in his midnight sleep; the mistress, torturing her servant till death was the release; the poisoner, gaining a kind of fiendish delight in her trade, till her victims were a numerous company; and the loathsome monsters, who, for the price of a dead body in the schools of anatomy, smothered their unhappy associates. If, in the most favoured regions of the earth, all those be numbered who die by wilful, private violence, they are probably more than one in a hundred thousand; a proportion which would yield from the present population of the globe the number of ten thousand. But when the condition of all the earth is weighed, we shall deem a tenfold estimate small; and the murdered of all times may be millions.

VIII.

Death by Massacre.

"Tumultuous murder shook the midnight air."

CAMPBELL

THE terrible sight of a multitude of human beings slain without armed resistance has been sometimes witnessed by indignant angels. This is not the indiscriminate slaughter of ancient war, when the whole population that could not flee was often destroyed; nor the relentless bloodshed, which in later times may have followed a hard victory; but it is that deliberate extirpation, that vast execution, which, if it cannot be justified as punishment, is massacre.

When all the Canaanites who withdrew not from the armies of Israel, were slain, it was by the express command of the Creator of all; and it was for their dreadful and unnatural iniquities. When Elijah slew hundreds of prophets of Baal, it was an execution of the national and the divine law, and was sanctioned by stupendous miracles. Seventy sons of Ahab were put to death by Jehu; but he had a commission from heaven. When, however, he gathered a company of the worshippers of Baal within a temple at Samaria, and slaughtered them there, his commission from above certainly comprehended not his bloody treachery. The Spartans perfidiously massacred two thousand Helots, who had served bravely in the wars of Sparta, and were therefore feared as slaves. Fourteen hundred Athenians were butchered on one spot by the Thirty Tyrants. On a tumult amongst the Jews at the passover, Archelaus sent out his troops, and slew three thousand around the temple. Before the last Jewish war began, the Syrians in different cities arose and massacred of the doomed nation, in Cæsarea twenty thousand, in Scythopolis thirteen thousand, in Askelon two thousand and five hundred, in Ptolemais two thousand, while, if indeed the large numbers of Josephus be not habitual exaggerations, fifty thousand of the slain were heaped up at Alexandria. The slaughter of the Jews by Vespasian and Titus was the result of an obstinate war and an indomitable resistance. Five days and nights the soldiers of Marius murdered at pleasure throughout the streets of Rome; but the speedy retribution of his rival Sylla was yet more terrific. Sylla assembled seven thousand of the opposite faction, and caused them to be put to the sword, in the circus; while, within the sound of their cries, he completed his stern harangue to the senators. Then, he prepared his list of proscription; and five thousand more fell by the stroke of any blade that would strike an outlaw. From a secure place at Alexandria, Caracalla directed the massacre of many thousands of strangers and citizens. Offended by the mutinous fury of the populace of Thessalonica, the Emperor Theodosius the Great, admirable as he was, adopted a fatal resolve. The message sped; the retraction was too late; and without discrimination of age, sex, or character, seven thousand persons, assembled in the circus, were slain with promiscuous butchery. Well might Ambrose repulse the bloodstained sovereign from the altar of the Prince of Peace, till he had proved his bitter penitence, and enacted a law which made such haste to shed blood impossible. The Caliph Abdallah, after the treaty with the Ommiades princes, assembled them, to the number of eighty, slew them with clubs, spread a carpet over their bodies, and made a banquet on the spot. The Sicilian Vespers, on the eve of Easter-day, in 1282, were a tumultuous onset of the maddened natives of the island upon the French under Charles of Anjou; and the Italian rage was not appeased till the seven thousand Frenchmen who were in Sicily lay in their blood. The Burgundian faction in Paris, under the reign of Charles the Sixth, surrounded the Chatelet, called forth the two thousand Armagnac prisoners, one by one, and beheaded them as they issued from the door. After more than three centuries, the same scene was repeated in the same city, when the murderers stood at the door of each prison; eight thousand men and women were struck down with pikes and swords; hundreds of priests perished; and the head of the beautiful Princess de Lamballe, its tresses draggled in gore, was lifted on a pike to the window of the imprisoned Louis. In the massacre of St. Bartholomew, and the subsequent slaughter throughout many cities of France, fifty thousand Protestants are said to have been slain in cold blood; the foremost of all, the good Coligny. England has scarcely witnessed a massacre: the slaughter of Glencoe extended to less than forty. But in France, during the Revolution, an almost undistinguishing cruelty was often let loose: seven hundred priests were butchered at Nantes: hundreds of victims were placed in rows at Lyons, and cannonaded: hundreds were drowned in the Loire; and many thousands were shot after the suppression of the Vendean insurrection. Slavers have thrown overboard whole scores of sickly negroes; but in the Haytian revolt a nation of untaught slaves took dreadful vengeance for the oppression of their race; and thirty thousand whites were slaughtered, many in their own halls and gardens. On the sandhills near Jaffa, Buonaparte shot a small army of Turkish prisoners, whom he could not feed, and dared not release. When Mohammed Ali of Egypt wished to shake off the troublesome Mamelukes, who had been so terrible, he looked on while five or six hundred, pent within a large court, were laid in their blood, one only leaping his horse over the barrier. The slaughter at Scio aroused the sympathies of all Christendom. But no bloodshed related in history was like that where the Sultan Mahmoud destroyed the whole army of his janizaries, whose strength threatened his throne. Thirty thousand were inclosed within walls, in one dense mass, through which his cannon ploughed, till all was over. Yet Timour built pyramids, of seventy thousand skulls at Ispahan, and ninety thousand at Bagdad.

Asia and Africa could furnish many of these awful tales of cruelty. So have hundreds of thousands died; and each death had all from which man shrinks in agony. When a single person like Hypatia, or Vitale Michieli, doge of Venice, or James Van Artevelde, or Delaunay, or Dewitt, or Marshal Brune, or Basseville, or like so many in the earlier days of the French Revolution, has been torn in pieces by the crowd, or hurried to the lantern, we seem to feel all which is possible. The mind is stupified by the horrors of those scenes, in which one such death has been many thousand times multiplied.

IX.

Death in Single Combat.

"For double murder armed, his own, and his
That as himself he was ordained to love."

POLLOK.

MEN have fallen in single combat with their fellow-men, in a manner which has partaken of the several characteristics of war, murder, and suicide. It has been like war, because there was mutual hostility; it has been like murder, so often at least as it was in private quarrels, and in violation of the laws; and it has been like suicide, because the exposure to death was voluntary and needless.

At first, all single fights could have been no more than parts of more general war, or else attempts to murder which were met by armed resistance. These were afterwards imitated in games; and then at length the imitation itself, for more intense excitement, grew into a bloody contest. Through six centuries, gladiatorial combats were held at Rome and other great cities of the Roman dominion. Julius Cæsar, when he was ædile, exhibited more than six hundred combatants; and on a single occasion, Trajan brought out ten thousand. All were compelled to fight to the last; and if one was borne to the ground, and quite overcome without a mortal wound, his life depended upon the caprice of the people or emperor, to whom the victor looked for the sign to spare or to slay. Christianity by degrees abolished a diversion worthy of demons; but an Asiatic monk, Telemachus, was first the martyr of humanity. He threw himself between the gladiators, and was overwhelmed beneath a shower of stones. The Emperor Honorius then decreed that these sports should exist no more; and as the decree was not always observed, they were finally suppressed by Theodoric.

The idea of combats for the decision of individual guilt or innocence, honour or dishonour, is of later origin. It sprang up in the dark ages, amongst nations trained to arms, addicted to superstition, standing between the ancient and the modern civilization, and too little able to appeal from violence to independent tribunals of justice; and it was connected, too, with the half sportive and half earnest exercises in the lists which were the amusement of such nations. The trial by combat was an appeal to the God of battles. Both the accuser and the accused, or his champion, were supposed to offer themselves, as if to the immediate realization of their oath;

> "And as I truly fight, defend me Heaven!"

But the test was unauthorized; and the slaughter may have been indiscriminating. Such trials and such deaths, however, were probably rather noticed for their interest than for their frequency.

Sometimes, in the less serious encounters of the tournament, one of the champions might receive a fatal fall or blow; as Henry the Second of France was mortally wounded by the lance of Montgomeri, which pierced his eye. Sometimes, in the rude struggle of boxers, an unfortunate man, fighting with blind desperation, has been beaten till life itself gave way. But these were accidents: the sports, however perilous or barbarous, were not designed to destroy.

The modern duel has been the offspring, on one side, of the trial by arms; on the other, of the brutal yet playful contests of chivalry. A revenge only satisfied with blood has often armed the challenger. In a public duel, the celebrated Chevalier Bayard slew a Spaniard, piercing his throat with his sword, and, when they were down, driving his dagger into his eye and brain. The most recent times, permitting duels, if at all, only to prove the honour by proving the courage of both antagonists, have made them a kind of infernal mockery, in which lives have been thrown away with reluctance on both sides, because neither could defy the contempt of the contemptible. Happily, such deaths have been confined to a limited sphere, composed chiefly of the more boisterous amongst military men, and of a particular class of political leaders and public characters. In the reign of James the First, the two sons of Lord Wharton and Lord Blantyre fell by the hands of each other at Islington; and the Earl of Dorset and Lord Bruce fought with swords under the walls of Antwerp, till Bruce fell down dead, and his opponent was borne wounded to a neighbouring monastery. In 1712, the Duke of Hamilton met Lord Mohun, whose hand was already red with other blood: they fought in Hyde Park, and both were fatally wounded. Forty years before, the profligate Duke of Buckingham slew the Earl of Shrewsbury, whose wife was his paramour, and was said to have held his bridle during the combat. One of the Lords Byron slew his neighbour in a quarrel rather than a duel; and the death of the duellist closed the dissolute lives, in 1804, of Lord Camelford, and in 1809, of Lord Falkland. So died, too, Sir Alexander Boswell, the son of the biographer of Johnson; John Scott, an ingenious writer; and Pushkin, a distinguished poet of Russia. Ireland has been fruitful in such crimes: one Fitzgerald, who was hanged at last, had the bad eminence of having destroyed more lives in duels than any of his contemporaries. Men fell by the pistols of future judges; and the blood of an adversary left a stain of remorse on the conscience of such a man as O'Connell. In America, it must have clung painfully to the memory of Jackson in the devotions of his old age. Many have been these scenes of useless death on the soil of the republic. So fell one of the signers of the Declaration of Independence; so, the gallant, unreflecting Decatur; and so, by the shot of the vilest man remembered by American history, died Alexander Hamilton; just as his son had died before.

The savage encounter which knows no rules, such as is seen in the south-western portions of the United States, is the mere warfare of murder and self-defence, but of a self-defence that is generally not unwilling to become murder. It is horrible enough that our age should have invented the Bowie knife and the revolving pistol. It is more horrible that in the streets, in houses, even in the seats of law and justice, they have been drawn and wielded with fatal ferocity, by the men of Virginia, Kentucky, and Arkansas. The whole number of the victims of single combat in all ages is not vast; but if only a hundred in a year should thus perish throughout the world, many thousands must have been added, and with a terrible guilt of their own, to the company of the murdered: besides, the many thousands, who fell under the test of a mistaken ordeal, and the hosts of wretched gladiators,

> "Butchered to make a Roman holiday."

X.

Death in Battle.

> "Last noon beheld them full of lusty life,
> Last eve in beauty's circle proudly gay:
> The midnight brought the signal-sound of strife;
> The morn, the marshalling in arms; the day,
> Battle's magnificently stern array:
> The thunder-clouds close o'er it, which when rent,
> The earth is covered thick with other clay
> Which its own clay shall cover; heaped and pent,
> Rider and horse, friend, foe, in one red burial blent."
>
> BYRON.

WHEN men became tribes and nations, the danger of national contest arose: the utmost height of contention would be war; the utmost point of war would be battle; the utmost point of battle, death. The superior authority of laws might restrain the strife of individuals; but for nations, commonly, there has been no higher tribunal on earth. They have taken up arms: every age has had its wars: and to the traveller along the road of history, tales of battles are like vast and frequent mounds, marking the distances, but at the same time covering the bones of armies.

Many of the more barbarous tribes have lived in such perpetual warfare, that a fourth or even half of their mature male population may have died by the weapons of their enemies. The islands of the Pacific, the forests of America, the almost unknown heart of Africa, have been the scenes of ten thousand unrecorded conflicts; and such must have filled many of the more favoured lands at periods of which no history is left. The little that we know of countries like Japan, Madagascar, Abyssinia, and many portions of the East, is but a story of revolutions and slaughter. Historic wars begin with those of Nimrod, "a mighty one on the earth" within two or three centuries after the flood, the founder of the great empire of Assyria. A century or two later, the combat of four kings against five in the vale of Siddim was doubtless but one amongst many struggles of inferior princes. Nine hundred years after the deluge, the Israelites conquered Canaan: every step was a battle. Perhaps it was in the next century that twenty-five thousand men of Benjamin, with their households, almost all the tribe, perished in a contest with the other tribes, in which the victors also lost forty thousand. In the next century, as is probable, ten thousand Moabites fell before Ehud; and in the next, the host of Sisera before Barak, and the vast array of the Midianites before "the sword of the Lord and of Gideon." The next century witnessed the wars of Jephthah, when forty-two thousand Ephraimites were cut off, and those between Israel and the Philistines, when thirty thousand Israelites fell in one disastrous day. Not far from the same period was the siege of Troy; and then, in the eleventh century before the Incarnation were the wars of Saul and of David. In the tenth century are placed the mighty expeditions of Sesostris, and the wars between Abijah and Jeroboam. The ninth beheld the battle of Ramoth-gilead, and the hostilities between Syria and the ten tribes of Israel. In the eighth, the Assyrians extended their conquests, and swept those tribes away; while the first Messenian war introduced the drama of authentic Grecian history. The seventh was the period of the second Messenian war, of the great contests between Media and Assyria, of the overthrow of Nineveh, and of the fall of Josiah at Megiddo, while he placed himself between the hostile Babylonians and Egyptians. In the sixth, lie the conquests of Nebuchadnezzar and of Cyrus. The fifth opened with the Persian war in Greece, and closed with the Peloponnesian. The fourth was the time of the expedition of the younger Cyrus, the whole career of Philip and Alexander, and the irruption of the Gauls into Italy. In the third were the wars of Pyrrhus, and the first two of the great struggles between Rome and Carthage; in the second the wars of the Greek kings in Syria, and of Perseus, the third Punic war, and the Cimbric; in the first, those of Marius and Sylla, of Mithridates, of Pompey, of Cæsar, and of Antony and Octavius. The first century after the Christian era embraced the German wars of Rome, the Jewish, and the civil strife between the soldiers of Otho, Vitellius, and Vespasian; the second, the wars of Rome against the Dacians, the Parthians, and the Marcomanni, and those of Severus for his crown; the third, a succession of revolutions, and a perpetual series of hostilities all along the frontiers of a tottering empire; the fourth, the successes of Constantine, and the wars of Julian against the Persians, and of Valens and Theodosius against the Goths; the fifth, the destructive march of Goths, Huns, Vandals, of Alaric, Attila, Genseric, Hengist, Clovis; the sixth, the campaigns of Belisarius, Totila, and Narses; the seventh, the contest of Chosroes and Heraclius, and the first, wide victories of the Saracens; the eighth, the subjugation of Spain by the Moors, their check by Charles Martel, and the wars of Charlemagne; the ninth, the inroads of Normans and Danes; the tenth, the ravages of the Hungarians, and the wars of Otho the Great; the eleventh, the Norman conquest, the victories of the Turks, and the first crusade; the twelfth, the Turkish conquest of Egypt, and the second and third crusades; the thirteenth, the conquests of Genghis Khan, and the fourth and fifth crusades; the fourteenth, the wars of the English in Scotland and France, and the career of Timour; the fifteenth, the wars of Henry the Fifth, those of York and Lancaster, the Bohemian struggle, and the capture of Constantinople by the Turks; the sixteenth, the wars of the French in Italy, of the Spaniards in America, and of the Roman Catholics and Protestants in France and Germany; the seventeenth, the civil wars under Charles the First, the Thirty Years' War, and many of those which issued from the ambition of Louis the Fourteenth; the eighteenth, the wars of the Spanish succession, of Charles the Twelfth, of Frederick of Prussia, and the French Revolution, as well as the loss of America to Britain, and the conquest of India; the nineteenth, the bloody empire of Napoleon, and now the Austrian campaigns of Radetzki and Jellachich. These wars very much compose the history of the civilized world; the uncivilized world has been one confused mass of perpetual slaughter. To reckon the proportion of mankind that have perished in consequence of the ravages of war would be, if it were possible, a work that might daunt the imagination. Even the number that includes only such as have fallen in actual and recorded battles, though it may be expressed in figures, leaves no distinct conception, from its prodigious magnitude.

When Absalom fought against the army of David, there was a slaughter of 20,000 men. When Jeroboam and

Abijah met on Mount Zemaraim, there fell down slain of Israel, unless an error has found its way into the copies of numbers in the sacred text, no less than half a million. In that battle in which the ark was taken, 30,000 fell with Hophni and Phinehas. At Marathon, the number of the dead scarcely reached 7000; at the pass of Thermopylæ it was more than 20,000; while of 300,000 Persians who fought at Platæa, it is said that only three thousand survived. On the plain of Issus 100,000 dead, and at Arbela 300,000, are enumerated as a part of the price with which Alexander won the dominion over Persia. In the great battle of Ipsus, where Antigonus sank under a shower of darts, 30,000 of his army must have been left with him upon the field. On the bank of Lake Thrasymene, 15,000 Romans were slaughtered, and 70,000 on the fatal day of Cannæ. In the battle of Munda the younger Pompey lost 30,000; Hannibal 20,000 at Zama; Antiochus 54,000 at Magnesia; Perseus 25,000 at Pydna; 100,000 subjects of Tigranes fell in one battle against Lucullus; 15,000 Romans died at Pharsalia. The two legions of Varus, that were utterly cut to pieces in Germany, must have contained more than thirteen thousand men. Of the 1100,000 Jews who perished in their struggle against Rome, a vast proportion were slain in the siege of their sacred city. At the victory of the second Claudius at Naissus, 50,000 men perished: in the unfortunate battle of Adrianople, 60,000 died with Valens. When Aetius delivered the world from the terror of Attila, 162,000 are said to have covered the field of Chalons. How terrific must have been the bloodshed of that battle of seven days, in which Spain was lost by the Goths, and won by the Mussulmen! How terrific that resistance of Charles Martel at Poictiers, from which, after a century of victories, the Saracen hosts at length withdrew! At the battle of Fontenai, fought between the four sons of Louis the Debonnair, 40,000 were slain; at the victory of the Emperor Henry the Fowler over the Hungarians near Merseburg, 36,000; at Simancas, Ramiro the Second destroyed 80,000 Moors: probably 30,000 men fell when Jerusalem was taken by the Crusaders; and Richard Cœur de Lion slew 40,000 Saracens under Saladin, on the shore by Ascalon. The battle of Hastings strewed the English coast with 40,000 bodies; at Crecy 40,000 Frenchmen fell, and 15,000 at Agincourt; at Halidon Hill, 30,000 Scots; at Durham, 15,000; at Flodden, a host even of knights and nobles. Marignano was the field of death to 40,000; Towton, to 36,000; Ravenna, to 18,000; 20,000 perished at Neerwinden; at least 15,000 at Blenheim; 15,000 at Ramillies; 5000 at Almanza; 30,000 at Malplaquet; 9000 Swedes at Pultowa; 17,000 on both sides at Fontenoy; 20,000 at Colin; 30,000 at Cunnersdorf; 15,000 at Austerlitz; 8000 at Friedland; 8000 at Jena; 50,000 at Eylau; 13.000 at Aspern; 60,000 at Borodino; 15,000 at Talavera; 10,000 at Lutzen; probably 30,000 at Leipsic; probably 30,000 at Waterloo; and as many as 30,000 in the British battles on the Sutledge. When the Saracens first took Jerusalem, 90,000 Christians are said to have perished; 65,000 Mussulmen in the contests between Ali and the Caliph of Damascus; 150,000 natives at the siege of Mexico by Cortes. In rather more than sixty chief battles, almost three millions of men are numbered as the victims. But the whole carnage of the wars of Cæsar has been commonly estimated at two millions; and as many lives must have been shortened through the selfishness of Napoleon. The forces engaged in sea-fights have been smaller than those in actions on the shore, and the loss far inferior; but death in such strife has a form peculiarly appalling to the imagination; and sometimes the slaughter has been awful, in comparison with the theatre of the conflict. In the celebrated battle of Lepanto, 40,000 perished; 5000 Pisans fell, in 1284, in a sea-fight with the Genoese; 5000 died at Actium; 5000 at Navarino; and full 15,000 at Aboukir. The Earl of Sandwich, in the time of Charles the Second, fought his ship till out of its thousand defenders six hundred lay dead upon the deck; and at Aboukir the ship of the French admiral blew up with all who were aboard.

So many millions, and millions more, have fallen by the several weapons which human skill has devised for mutual destruction. The club or mace of knotty wood was first, like that which felled Magellan or Williams, on the Polynesian islands. Then came the bow and the arrow, sometimes dipped in poisonous juices. Saul, Ahab, Jehoram, and Julian were mortally wounded by the arrows of the East; and the Duke of Norfolk fell at Bosworth Field, and the greatest princes of France at Crecy and Agincourt, the Dukes of Brabant, Bar, Alencon, and the Constable d'Albret, by the bows of the English archers. A stone, hurled even by the hand of a woman, broke the skull of Abimelech; but the small stone in the sling, like that which entered the forehead of Goliath, was one of the most fatal weapons of ancient war. The dart, like those with which Joab pierced Absalom through and through; the short javelin, like that which remained in the wound of Epaminondas, till he heard that his victory was secure, and with which his life then issued forth; the longer spear or lance, like those which Arnold de Winkelried gathered into his own body, when he made a way for his followers through the hostile spearmen; the battle-axe, with which Clovis hewed down the second Alaric in battle, and two captive princes; the Saxon hammer; the pike, with which the Irish insurgents pierced Lord Kilwarden in his carriage; the bayonet, commonly destined for the humbler breasts of the common ranks on the field; the universal sword, struck by which, in fourteen or fifteen places, Gaston de Foix fell at Ravenna; and the dagger of closer warfare, and for the final blow: all these are one formidable class of instruments of death, "the murderous steel." A shot from an engine gave the death-blow to Richard the First of England; a stone from the machines of the besiegers of Jerusalem struck down that awful person who went about its streets for months, crying, "Woe! woe!" The introduction of gunpowder brought in more distant, and, to the inflicter, less horrid means of death—but to the sufferer, more sudden, and often more ghastly. Some, like Nelson, or Marceau, or Joubert, fall by the steady bullet of the rifleman—or like Benyowsky, or like Abercrombie, by that of the musketeer; others, like Moore, or Bessieres, or Duroc, or Brueys, or Sale, by the shattering grape which lays open their vitals. The great Duke of Berwick and Prince Francis of Brunswick were killed by balls which struck off their heads; a smaller ball struck Charles the Twelfth in the temple; Dampierre died after losing a leg by a cannon-ball; Turenne was killed by such a ball; and both Moreau and Lannes lost both their legs, and survived a few hours. Mounting the wall of Rome, the Constable Bourbon was struck by a ball from an arquebuss, and fell back dead into the ditch. The explosion of shells in the vicinity of magazines has sometimes thrown a multitude of blackened or bleeding corpses far and wide. Men have died without being even grazed by the ball, when it has passed through the air close to their bodies. A whole rank has been mowed down by a single shot. The Greek fire is now lost; but from the seventh to the fourteenth century, it defended Constantinople, pouring its liquid flame into the Turkish fleets and armies, and penetrating within the mail of the soldier.

But, wild as are these horrors of slaughter, and mighty as is this destruction, and uncounted as are the victims of all times, still it cannot be a very large proportion of mankind that has fallen in battle. The other victims of war are more numerous, and still more numerous its disastrous fruits; but three millions or ten millions, the bloody trophies of so many fields, are but a small body in comparison with even a single generation. Amongst these, however, are numbered a mighty company of renowned names: Pelopidas, Chabrias, Nicias, and the elder Demosthenes, Junius Brutus, Flaminius, Paulus Emilius, Asdrubal, Catiline, Crassus, Pompey the younger, Judas Maccabeus, Leonidas, Darius, the elder and the younger Cyrus, the Emperor Decius, Roderick of Spain, Harold of England, Malcolm Canmore, Simon de Montfort, Edward Bruce; the Dukes of York and Suffolk at Agincourt, the great Earls of Salisbury and Shrewsbury and Thomas, the royal Duke of Clarence, all in France; a host of nobles in the civil wars of England under the Roses; Richard the Third, Philip Van Artevelde, the Scottish Regent Lennox, Sebastian of Portugal, the last Constantine, James the Fourth of Scotland with a squadron of his peers around him, Charles the Bold of Burgundy, the Duke of Nemours, Garcilasso de la Vega,

Gustavus Adolphus; the Duke of Hamilton, the Earls of Lindsey, Dundonald, Northampton, Denbigh, Sunderland, Lichfield, and the Lords Brooke, Falkland, Aubigny, in the later civil wars of England; John Hampden; the Earls of Falmouth and Portland, at sea; the Dukes of Grafton and Schomberg, in Ireland; Lord Downe, Lord Howe, Mackay, Graham of Claverhouse, Wolfe, Braddock, Montgomery, Warren, Kleist, Korner, Scharnhorst, Moore, Desaix, Bagration, Picton, Bozzaris, the Dukes of Brunswick, sire and son; and, to close the catalogue with a name of Christian eminence, the gallant and pious Gardiner.

XI.

Death by Punishment.

"Now, men of death, work forth your will,
For I can suffer and be still;
And, come it slow, or come it fast,
It is but death that comes at last."

SCOTT.

It was a divine ordinance or prediction, that the blood of the murderer should be shed for retribution, for warning, and for the common safety. As soon as families became states, this power of punishment was reserved to the sovereign jurisdiction. Necessity, fear, revenge, and cruelty, extended the same doom to other crimes; and under some form and process of law, the lives of the guilty, and too often of the innocent, have been exacted amongst every people.

The first instance recorded in history is that of the chief butler of Pharaoh, who was hanged; a mode of death to which disgrace has been attached, and which may have been adopted, from the ease of making the dying culprit a spectacle to a multitude. So, by divine command, those heads of Israel were punished who had led the people into guilt; and thus seven of the posterity of Saul were claimed by the Gibeonites, and put to death while Rizpah, the mother of two of them, watched below, and drove the vultures and dogs away. The murderers, the robbers, and even the forgers and thieves of Britain have thus died; and thus the ignobler persons who were charged with treason; and the sufferer was often taken down from the gallows that his body might be quartered, while his heart was yet throbbing. Amongst this unhappy throng, the half frantic Earl Ferrers, the ingenious Aram, the fallen Dodd, the once elegant Fauntleroy, the atrocious Thistlewood, were conspicuous malefactors. Thus died, too, David, the last Welsh sovereign, Hugh Despenser, Roger Mortimer, the favourites of a king and queen; the patriot Wallace; two successive primates of Scotland, Beatoun and Hamilton, the gallant Kircaldy of Grange, the Jesuit Campian, the unfortunate Sir Everard Digby, the fanatic Hacket, the noble Marquess of Montrose, the enthusiast, Hugh Peters, and such of the judges of Charles the First, as had neither sought clemency nor escape; thus the captive Guatimozin; and thus, bewailed by countrymen and foes alike, the victims of military rigor, Andre and Hale. The immediate cause of death in hanging is strangulation, or the fracture of the neck; and the Spaniards have therefore strangled criminals by an iron band or ring at a stake, sometimes before burning the body. Thus, not as criminals, died the last of the Incas, and Savonarola, and Tyndal.

Decapitation has been almost every where a punishment of common infliction. It was the mode by which John the Baptist, Justin, and Cyprian, suffered martyrdom. So died Cicero, the Constable de Luna, Biron, the young king Conradin, Egmont and Horn, Almagro, Balboa, Gonzalo Pizarro, the Doge Marino Faliero, Carmagnola, Barneveldt, and Lally. Charlemagne beheaded in one day forty-five hundred Saxon rebels. Christian the Second put thus to death ninety-four distinguished persons at Stockholm. In Britain, this kind of execution was appropriated to crimes of state, charged upon persons of birth; and thus the axe fell upon the necks of the illustrious Waltheof, of Piers Gaveston, of one Percy, Earl of Northumberland, and another, Earl of Worcester, of a Plantagenet, Earl of Lancaster, another, Earl of Kent, another, Earl of Cambridge, another, Earl of Warwick, and the last, the aged Countess of Salisbury; of several Howards, Nevilles, Staffords, Poles, Fitzalans, Grays, Scroops, Tuchets, Bohuns, Beauforts; of the aspiring Essex, the brother Seymours, the kingly Dudley, of Fisher, More, Laud, Strafford, Raleigh, Hamilton, Capel, Derby, Holland, the two Argyles, two Huntleys, Vane, Monmouth, Stafford, Russell, Sidney, of Thomas Cromwell, of several Douglasses and Homes, and Ruthvens, of Derwentwater, Kenmure, Lovat, Kilmarnock, Balmerino, of Anne Boleyn, and Catherine Howard, and Mary Stuart, and her royal grandson, Charles the First. The Swiss culprit sat in a chair, while a blade loaded with lead was swung by the arm of the executioner. In France, when the Revolution demanded a speedier process than the single stroke of a headsman, the guillotine was invented: the victim was but laid upon a board, the blade hung in a groove, the board was thrust in, the blade dropped, and all was over. Louis the Sixteenth, Marie Antoinette, the Princess Elizabeth, the Duke of Orleans, Barnave, Bailly, Malesherbes, Lavoisier, Madame du Barri, Charlotte Corday, Vergniaud, Brissot, Madame Roland, Manuel, Guadet, Barbaroux, Kersaint, Danton, Camille Desmoulins, Robespierre, Hebert, Westermann, Chabot, St. Just, Custine, Houchard, Clootz, Dillon, Beauharnois, Fouquier Tinville, were but the foremost of a company of thousands whose heads fell under this dreadful machine, by which the peculiar terror of a death instantaneous and unfelt, and yet fixed to a known moment, was substituted for all other fear or solemnity.

The horrible punishment of burning appears even in patriarchal times; for Judah commanded Tamar to be burned for adultery, though the command was not executed. Two false prophets of the Jews were burned by the King of Babylon; and the fiery furnace was there for all who, like Shadrach and his companions, refused to worship the golden idol. Fire was made by our Saviour a frequent figure of the future misery of the lost; and this seems the great cause for which it was chosen in the darker of modern ages as the doom of unbelief and heresy at the hands of human vengeance. Jews and blasphemers, Paulicians and Albigenses, Lollards and Hussites, and Socinians, and all who denied the spiritual sovereignty and infallibility of Rome, have been exposed to the stake. There, in one day, fifty-four Knights Templars suffered at Paris, in 1310, after thirty-six others had died upon the rack. There was the end of the days of the aged Polycarp; of Huss, and Jerome of Prague; of Joan of Arc; of Cranmer, and Latimer, and Ridley, and Ferrar, and Hooper; of Bilney, Frith, Barnes, Lambert, Anne Ayscue, Patrick Hamilton, Rogers, Bradford, Rowland Taylor, Saunders, Philpot, Palmer; of Algerius, of Giordano Bruno, of the bewildered Servetus, and the unhappy Vanini. The Spanish Inquisition presided over the most terrible and comprehensive of such inflictions; and what was called an Act of Faith included the agonizing death of such victims in the presence of a shuddering, shocked, and yet satisfied people. Sometimes, in England, gunpowder was allowed that the torment might be shortened; sometimes a barrel of pitch was suspended above. Cortez burned a Mexican chief with his son, and seventeen others; and in our own age and land, negro criminals have been executed by fire with a brutality which told that the soul of man could still find a pleasure in vindictive tortures.

The East has been inventive in forms of punishment by death. Besides the ancient custom of hewing down with the sword, as Joab and Adonijah appear to have been slain; and the modern practice of strangling with the bowstring, as so many Turkish viziers have died; besides the common Jewish mode of stoning, as Stephen suffered martyrdom; and the occasional practice of drowning, which was transferred to Venice; besides the poisoned draught, like those which were drunk by Phocion, Socrates, and Philopœmen; besides the opened veins of Seneca and Lucan; tyranny or revenge has multiplied deaths of a far more appalling aspect. At Bochara, and often elsewhere, criminals have been hurled from a tower to the ground, as at Rome from the Tarpeian rock. Murzuphlus, a fallen usurper of the Byzantine throne, was doomed to lose his eyes, and then to be dashed from a lofty column. The Persians sometimes filled a tower with ashes, into which the victim, like their prince Sogdianus, was thrown, when a wheel stirred the ashes, and he was suffocated. Parysatis caused Roxana to be sawn asunder, a doom which is said to have befallen the prophet Isaiah. But most horrible was the torture, when a person was laid between two boats, and fed, his head only being exposed, till after ten or twenty days, his body was consumed by the worms which were engendered within its loathsome prison. The Oriental and African nations, too, have buried alive, as the Romans buried the Vestal virgins when their purity was lost; they have empaled the wretched sufferer, by thrusting a stake through his body, and leaving him to writhe and die; and they devised that awful torture of crucifixion, by which Titus put hundreds to death, around the walls of Jerusalem, by which died Bomilcar the Carthaginian, and Regulus, and in Christian times, Arnold of Brescia, and which has been consecrated for the Christian believer. They have trodden under the feet of elephants: they have cut men piecemeal: they have flayed off the skin, as befell the heretic Mani in Persia; and they exposed human beings to the desperate conflict with lions, which Rome learned from the East. So died Ignatius, Attalus, Blandina, Perpetua, Felicitas, and many martyrs.

Soldiers, since the introduction of fire-arms, have been shot to death for military offences; and the punishment has been extended to others in times of war or revolution. Byng suffered thus his unjust doom upon the deck; the Duke d'Enghien, Ney, Murat, Iturbide, Charette, D'Elbee, were thus slain. A whole company of soldiers, with their officers, were shot by Custine, for some excesses at the capture of Spires.

Queen Brunechild was fastened by one hand and one foot to a wild horse, who tore her in pieces. Chatel, Ravaillac, and Damian, the last after being tormented with pincers, were drawn asunder by horses, limb from limb. This punishment had been known at Venice, where also criminals were sometimes suspended by one foot, and left to perish. The cook of Cardinal Fisher, for poisoning, was destroyed in a caldron of boiling water. Many an unhappy man has perished in Russia under the inhuman strokes of the knout. Criminals, on the continent of Europe, were long broken upon the wheel, the executioner successively crushing the parts of the body with a bar; so died Calas and Struensee. Under the English law, a criminal who refused to plead to a capital charge, was pressed to death by weights placed upon his body; and one firm man was thus killed at Salem, under the charge of witchcraft. Men have been starved in dungeons: so, many noble persons died by the order of King John of England. Monks and nuns, who were untrue to their vows, have been walled up with stone and mortar, and left to expire. So late as the last century, a negro in St. Eustatia was hung in irons, and survived three days.

The annual number of capital executions in Christian countries is now exceedingly small, not more than a few hundreds. There have been times when the proportion to the whole population was an hundred fold greater; and at other periods it has passed computation. The Paris guillotine, in thirteen months, struck off the heads of twenty-five hundred persons. Two thousand were guillotined at Arras. It was the boast of the Duke of Alva that, in a short space, he caused thirty thousand executions in Flanders. Queen Mary sent several hundreds to the stake for their religion. The capital executions under Henry the Eighth have been reckoned as far more numerous in every year than all which are now witnessed in the civilized world. Thousands on ten thousands were the victims of the Inquisition; no less, it is said, than eight thousand eight hundred in the eighteen years during which Torquemada presided. It is probable that the number of those who, justly or unjustly, have been put to death by some sentence of law or authority, has equalled or exceeded that of those who have died by private violence. At the utmost, a dreadful necessity, and through the bad passions of men, a varied and horrid cruelty, death in punishment has been surrounded by terrors of its own, which only the innocent heart, trusting in the only Disposer of life and death, could look in the face without dismay.

XII.

Death in Sacrifice.

> God, whose almighty will created thee,
> And me, and all that hath the breath of life,
> He is our strength; for in His name I speak,
> And when I tell thee that thou shalt not shed,
> The life of man in bloody sacrifice,
> It is His holy bidding which I speak."
>
> SOUTHEY.

THE custom of sacrifices, at first a divine institution, preserved itself in almost every region, under almost every perversion of the primeval truth. When, for successive generations, the corruption of man had so suppressed the light, that it became deep darkness, and the knowledge of the true God had been gradually supplanted by dreams of deities who were but personifications of human vices, it was at last suggested that such deities might hold in highest acceptance the altar on which the blood of man was the offering. Once indeed, one, and he the father of the faithful, was commanded from heaven to slay his son in sacrifice. But he knew that his son, in whom was the promise of such future blessings for all men, must be preserved, even though it were by a resurrection; and that the act, if it had not been commanded, would have been the most tremendous presumption and enormity. When some of his descendants caused their children to pass through the fire, the Most High denounced such cruelty as a thing which, emphatically, He "had not commanded, neither came it into his heart." But if the thought was not from the Creator, it was from the tempter; for, to take life, when it is not a duty, is the chief of crimes.

These sacrifices were practised amongst the Canaanites and the neighbouring nations of Syria. Princes and magistrates, amongst the Phœnicians, in times of public calamity, offered the dearest of their offspring to those whom they feared as avenging deities. The Ethiopians sacrificed boys to the sun, and girls to the moon. Those gloomy oaks, which overshadowed the rites of Scythian superstition, were sprinkled with the blood of every hundreth prisoner. Red-haired men were sacrificed by the Egyptians at the tomb of Osiris; and they were accustomed, it is said, to fling a young and beautiful virgin into the Nile. The Chinese histories record the self-oblation of the monarch Chingtang, to avert great calamities from his subjects. Human victims were immolated in Persia by the sword, or buried alive. The dread rite was known to the ancient people of Hindostan; and in various forms, has been practised even till our day, with the consent or by the act of the victim. In the heart of a wood, the Druids slew their captives in sacrifice; and in Gaul, they set up an immense wicker figure of a man, in which a hundred victims were enclosed, to be consumed by fire. The Greek states, in their early history, offered human sacrifices before their troops went on an expedition. A man was sacrificed every year by the Athenians. The custom existed amongst the Romans, even after it was forbidden by law, and scarcely ceased before the overthrow of Paganism. It existed amongst the Goths, amongst the Arabians, and with peculiar atrocity, amongst the Carthaginians. In the north of Europe, it prevailed till Christianity came in; and the grove of Upsal and the island of Rugen were made memorable by such horrors. Amongst certain tribes of the Mahrattas, victims distinguished by their bloom and beauty are fattened for the altars. The African kings slaughter many prisoners in sacrifice to some fetish: sometimes infants are exposed to the sharks; and in the funeral rites of Congo and Ashantee at the burial of princes, hundreds of their wives and attendants have been destroyed. Such sacrifices, too, were found in the Pacific islands.

It was in America, however, that the number of victims, elsewhere not very large, swelled to an annual sum of many thousands. The Peruvians, when they offered solemn prayers for their princes, slew children in great companies. But in Mexico, human sacrifice most outraged the eye of Heaven, till it drew down the retribution of

"Th' heroic Spaniard's unrelenting sword."

The yearly victims in the capital were estimated at twenty thousand; and the accursed high places of slaughter arose in the other cities of the empire. Seventy thousand human beings are said to have perished at the dedication of one great temple. The skulls of such sufferers were preserved in certain edifices, in one of which a hundred and thirty-six thousand were counted by the companions of Cortez. Stretched on a block of stone, the victim was held fast by several priests; while one, in a scarlet mantle, opened his breast with a sharp knife, and, tearing from it the palpitating heart, held it towards the sun, and then threw it at the feet of the idol. He who was intended for this, in some instances, had been splendidly arrayed and attended, and every luxury had been heaped around him, for a certain period before the fatal day; in other instances, the most exquisite tortures had first been inflicted. In Mexico, as often elsewhere, the sacrifice was associated with the cannibal repast.

As few, perhaps, since tradition said that these bloody rites had been introduced into Mexico but two centuries; as few, perhaps, as a single million may have been the whole multitude of human sacrifices in America; and, although the nations in which such customs have had sway must have been without cultivation or history, yet, in the absence of estimates, should we reckon those of the elder continent at another million, it would seem a large conjecture. But if the sacrifice of Iphigenia, told in poetry or on the canvass, has drawn such tender tears; if the supposed fate of the daughter of Jephthah has aroused the indignant sympathy of all ages; if no eye ever read unmoved the story of Isaac on the mountain of Moriah; how must thought recoil from that mass of anguish which has thus been heaped upon the altars of the spirits of evil.

XIII.

Death by Suicide.

" 'The term of life is limited,
Nor may a man prolong nor shorten it:
The soldier may not move from watchful sted,
Nor leave his stand until his captain bid.'
'Who life did limit by almighty doom,'
Quoth he, 'knows best the terms established;
And he that points the centinel his room,
Doth license him depart at sound of morning drum.'

SPENSER.

BY the same physical power which can destroy the life of another, man can fix a sudden period to his own. If at any time he become so weary of his present state, and so hopeless for the future, that he prefers the uncertainties, or imagines that he prefers the certainties of death, the temptation to suicide may be at hand, unless repelled by higher sentiments of duty. These sentiments may be overpowered by frenzy, supplanted by selfishness, silenced by pride, or extinguished by atheism; and then the man may be his own destroyer.

Both Abimelech and Saul were already wounded to death, when they besought their attendants to give the finishing blow. Ahithophel, rejected as a counsellor, and despairing of a wicked cause, went and hanged himself; a mode of death, which, possibly because the horror of bloodshed was wanting, has always been a ready suggestion. Such was the death of the traitor Iscariot, when the full anguish of his guilt burst upon him, and drove him to despair; and Pontius Pilate, long years after, died too by his own hand.

The chief senators of Saguntum, when their city was about to be taken, threw themselves into the same flames in which they consumed their treasures. Josephus relates how, when Jotapata was captured, he, with forty others, was hidden in a pit, where suicide was preferred by all the rest to a surrender; and lots being cast at his suggestion, he who had the first lot was slain by him who had the second, till Josephus and another were alone left. In the days of Richard the First, more than five hundred Jews are said to have destroyed themselves at York, to escape their persecutors. Eight hundred mothers and children, when Missolonghi was conquered by the Turks, fled from their cruelty, and cast themselves into the sea to perish there. It was made a question in the age when Rome was sacked by Alaric, whether those Christian virgins who preserved their purity only by casting themselves into the Tiber, had violated the divine law; and their act was excused rather than justified by St. Augustin.

Sardanapalus, the last Assyrian emperor, died with his eunuchs, wives, and concubines, on one vast pile, amidst his treasures, while his enemies burst in upon his capital. Imilcon, the Carthaginian general, slew himself after ill success; and Annibal, who always carried poison in a ring upon his finger, used it when he saw before him only his enemies and ignominy. It is said that Bajazet, confined in a cage by the victorious Timour, perished by dashing himself desperately against the bars. Men in Japan, under very common mortifications or losses, plunge a knife into their bowels. For ages, till British rule dissolved the murderous spell, the

Hindoo widow had mounted the pyre with the corpse of her husband; and the Hindoo devotee had lain down before the wheels of the car of Juggernaut. Within thirty miles around Calcutta, two hundred widows sacrificed themselves in a year; and female slaves sometimes threw themselves also into the flames.

When all hope of safety was at an end, Demosthenes swallowed some fatal substance, and fell dead in the temple of Neptune. But suicide never became to the enjoying Greeks, what it was amongst the iron Romans, the almost usual resource of great men under misfortune. From the treatise of Plato on the immortality of the soul, Cato arose to plunge the dagger into his own body. Brutus fell upon his sword; and Cassius ordered his freedman to run him through. Portia, the wife of Brutus and daughter of Cato, swallowed burning coals. Mark Antony stabbed himself; and Cleopatra died by the bite of an asp, which she placed on her arm or bosom. Piso opened veins in both his arms. Nero was compelled to destroy himself or be destroyed, and tremblingly inflicted a fatal wound. Otho, after an unfortunate battle, calmly slew himself with a dagger. The elder Gordian, Julia Domna, widow of the emperor Severus, Pœtus, and, giving him the example, his wife Arria, died this "Roman death." In Christian lands, it has been left, with few exceptions, to the maniac and the unbeliever. The Venetian admiral, Dandolo, taken prisoner by the Genoese, was insultingly exposed, and in a frenzy dashed his head against the side of the galley and was taken up dead. England was said to have the unhappy distinction of an undue proportion of suicides, from melancholy and discouragement. The Earl of Northumberland, committed to the Tower in the reign of

Queen Elizabeth, was found dead with three bullets in his body; and the Earl of Essex, under Charles the Second, in circumstances exactly the same, appeared to have cut his throat in the same gloomy prison. Creech, the translator of several classics, Budgell, one of the writers of the Spectator, who threw himself into the Thames, and young Chatterton, who took arsenic, are the only English authors, whom distress and sadness have driven to so desperate an end. Maitland of Lethington, a sagacious man of intrigue, poisoned himself, to shun the block. Sir Robert Calder and Colonel Brereton were goaded by the loss of professional reputation. But most often perhaps the suicidal blow has been struck under sudden delirium, or the gloom of derangement; for this is one of the most frequent and the most frightful perils of insanity. Three conspicuous statesmen in one age, Whitbread, Romilly, and the Marquess of Londonderry, died thus by their own hands; and thus died Lord Clive the conqueror of Bengal. When the French nation caught the spirit of unbelief, in a period of immense political revolutions, the heathen practice of suicide revived with the heathen uncertainty of life hereafter. Many of the democratic leaders, in their downfall, attempted thus to escape, and many succeeded in thus escaping, the guillotine; like Petion, who was found dead in a field; Roland, who ran himself through with a stiletto by the road-side; Condorcet, who carried poison, and used it in prison; Rebecqui, who threw himself into the sea; Valaze, who stabbed himself when his sentence was pronounced; and those five, with Romme the mathematician at their head, who plunged the dagger successively into their breasts, before the judges could interpose, each passing it to the next as he fell wounded, and three of them dying on the spot. Berthier, a favourite of Napoleon, threw himself from a window, in delirium; and Junot, too, with an alienated intellect, accomplished his own destruction. Christophe, deposed and deserted, shot himself with a pistol. Admiral Villeneuve took an anatomical plate of the heart, marked the exact spot, and then, at that spot, drove a pin into his own heart, and expired.

Every week, indeed, bears its tale of suicide. Men, like the painter Haydon, made desperate by misfortunes or mistakes; men overwhelmed with sudden disgrace, by the detection of crime; men and women, under the pangs of blighted affection; women for whose fair fame there is no refuge; men weary of the world, and anticipating only an old age without enjoyment; even children under an exasperated bitterness, which has made them willing to revenge themselves by the pain which their death might inflict; all have dared to tear asunder the soul and the body which their Maker had united. They have been found hanging in garrets, barns, or lonely rooms, by ropes or handkerchiefs, even with their knees resting on the floor: they have cast themselves from wharves, and the decks of vessels, and high edifices: they have swallowed arsenic, laudanum, prussic acid, every variety of poison; they have drawn the razor across the throat; they have placed the muzzle of the pistol in the mouth or ear, and thrown the shattered bone and brains upon the wall. After a desperate sea-fight, the conquered commander has set fire to the magazine. Murderers in their cells have often been their own executioners. A shipwrecked man has even been known to shoot himself rather than die by drowning. Romantic and godless lovers, in France, have chosen to die together, and have preferred the easy mode of stifling themselves with the fumes of charcoal.

One annual suicide amongst ten thousand people is probably no extravagant estimate; one death, perhaps, amongst three hundred. In France, there were, in the year 1846, three thousand one hundred and two; about one third by strangulation, one third by drowning, and one eighth by firearms. Even this estimate would yield an aggregate of a hundred thousand needless and guilty deaths in every year; needless, as anticipating the appointed mode and time; and guilty, because most unnatural, presumptuous, and desperately impious, except when they are the work of frenzy.

XIV.

Death through Eruptions in Nature.

> "The hills move lightly, and the mountains smoke;
> The rocks fall headlong, and the valleys rise;
> What solid was, by transformation strange
> Grows fluid; and the fixed and rooted earth,
> Tormented into billows, heaves and swells,
> Or with vertiginous and hideous whirl
> Sucks down its prey insatiable. * * * *
> Ocean has caught the frenzy, and upwrought
> To an enormous and o'erbearing height,
> Not by a mighty wind, but by that voice
> Which winds and waves obey, invades the shore.
> * * * * They are gone,
> Gone with the refluent wave into the deep,
> A prince with half his people."
>
> COWPER.

A PORTION of mankind have been exposed to death through the direct and extraordinary operation of the more stupendous agencies in nature. When the world was destroyed by the deluge; when fire from heaven fell on the cities of the plain, or on the captains and their troops who were sent against Elijah; when Korah and his associates were either burned or engulphed, these agencies were employed to attest miraculously the divine displeasure. But inundations, lightning, the volcano, the earthquake, the avalanche, without any special token of that displeasure, and without a miracle, have put an end to many lives in a single hour.

On those lowlands which sometimes lie along the

margin of the seas, vast floods have rolled in, and swept multitudes away. The Zuyder Zee and the Harlaem Lake were formed by such inundations, when the dykes of Holland yielded, and many lives were lost; and thus, in the winter of 1808, four hundred bodies floated on the flood, near Arnheim. An inundation of the Neva, in 1824, destroyed three thousand; and six thousand were overwhelmed, in 1802, in the vale of Lorca in Spain, by the waters of a reservoir. Earthquakes have often hurled a mass of mountainous billows upon the shore: thus the sea at Lisbon came in like a wall, and in a moment bore back a crowd of dead into its bosom; and thus, at Alexandria, in 365, fifty thousand lost their lives, when an earthquake was followed by a similar inundation. In 1780, a single wave drowned the whole town of Savannah-la-Mar, with all its inhabitants.

Even more terrific to the uninstructed mind might be that sharp interposition of a sudden, irresistible shaft, directed from the heavens, seeming to single out an individual, and blasting him in an instant. Deaths by lightning are few; yet so one Roman emperor, Carus, was reported to have died in the night; and so a distinguished orator of the American Revolution, James Otis, was struck down as he looked from his door on an approaching storm.

Scattered over the earth are those peaks from which the internal flame finds issue; and around their bases lie the habitations of men. Torrents of lava and showers of ashes, poured from the craters, have surprised and overwhelmed individuals, or even the population of villages or cities. In that eruption of Vesuvius, which destroyed Herculaneum and Pompeii, there was, notwithstanding the general flight of the inhabitants, a wide loss of lives: the skeleton of the mother with her infant, has been found, and that of the householder, or steward, with his keys; the elder Pliny was fatally overtaken by the ashes, when he had drawn too near; and an Agrippa perished with Drusilla his mother. When Catania, in 1669, was almost buried by the earthquake and the attendant eruption of Etna, the flood of lava was stopped by the city walls, sixty feet in height, till it rose above them, and fell over like a cataract of fire, while about twenty-seven thousand perished, more by the earthquake than the lava.

At Antioch, in 526, two hundred and fifty thousand are said to have been destroyed by an earthquake; at Port Royal, in 1692, two thousand persons perished; at Lisbon, in 1755, sixty thousand in six minutes; at Damascus, in 1759, six thousand; at Caraccas, in 1812, nine thousand; at Safed, in 1837, five thousand. Bagdad, Aleppo, and Lima; Jamaica, Guadaloupe, and the islands of the West Indies, have been visited with a like tremendous destruction. The sufferers have been crushed by the falling walls, or engulphed in the waters or the fissures. At Callao, in 1747, a great multitude were gathered upon a quay or pier, which so sank with them all, that none of the bodies ever were seen upon the surface: one man alone escaped. A vast number were swallowed up in the earthquakes in Italy, under the Emperor Gallienus. In the earthquakes of Calabria, between 1783 and 1786, twenty-nine thousand died under the ruins.

Avalanches of ice have occasionally swept the hunter or the traveller down some precipice or ravine, burying him as he fell. The village of Leuk, with its baths, was overwhelmed in 1719, and many of the people perished. Avalanches of earth, which have been gradually undermined and separated from the hill-sides, have covered houses and hamlets; as the inhabitants of the village of Goldau, in Switzerland, died, almost to the number of five hundred, under a mass of rocks and sand from the neighbouring mountain.

But these events, although they so startle all men, and impress themselves on history, or on memory, are yet rare; and all the thousands to whom death has come through these great and extraordinary agencies of nature, might scarcely be considered in an enumeration of the modes of death, if numbers alone claimed regard or yielded instruction from the grave. There is, however, a peculiar power in deaths like these, the greater because they are unusual. It was thus that Omnipotence interposed to destroy, when it was designed that the terror of death as His immediate judgment on a multitude, a city, or a world, should be manifest. The heathen, in all ages, felt the divinity of such visitations with a special awe, either the awe of remaining truth, or that of blind superstition. No long chain of causes and effects here joins the event to the hand of its supreme Author, and distracts the attention of man: he sees himself brought into direct contact with those tremendous powers which no human skill or strength could ever attempt to baffle. He seems left with his Maker, who wields the earth to entomb him, or bids it pour forth its flames or its waters to sweep him from its bosom, or sends to his frame an arrow from the heavens. It is no special judgment, no preternatural instrument: the Almighty decree is just as truly and as directly fulfilled at the calmest and easiest deathbed: but to man the letters are here more burn ingly visible.

XV.

Death by Water.

> "Peril and dismay
> Wave their black ensigns o'er the watery way."
>
> FALCONER.

THE greater part of the solid globe is covered by an element at once too dense to allow our organs to act within its embrace, and not dense enough to sustain our weight upon its surface. Man cannot long survive in the waters; and yet he cannot venture far without standing on their brink, or crossing their brooks, rivers, bays, lakes or seas. Then, the slightest accident, a step beyond the edge, a breath of wind, a wave higher than the rest, a leak, a loss of his footing for a moment, is death.

A mighty company, therefore, are they who have sunk beneath the waters. Attempting to ford the rapid stream, the savage is borne downward, and perhaps hurried over the cataract. Launching forth in his frail boat, another, by a single heedless movement, is plunged below, and disappears. As ages and arts advance, the bolder barks of commerce and piracy are dashed on rocks and shoals: the danger is first noted when the mariner has been overwhelmed, and the safer paths are gradually discovered, after the more perilous have been the graves of many. No triumph of science or skill has ever quite removed these perils of the ocean. It is computed that of those whose business is upon the deep, a proportion almost too large to be named come, earlier or later, to their end, by shipwreck. In a single disastrous winter, twenty-five hundred were drowned on the shores of New England. The hurricane sweeps down many a foundering vessel; many are shattered on the breakers; many are drifted hopelessly on the sands; some are broken by the shock of the ice-island; many in the darkness are driven together in fatal encounter.

When Xerxes assembled his immense fleet at Artemisium, a storm arose which engulphed far more than the Grecian arms could destroy. Prince William, the only son of Henry the First of England, with his sister and a gay train of nobles and courtiers, was drowned in crossing the channel from Normandy: a butcher alone clung to the mast, and was rescued. Returning from the scene of their unworthy attempts to supplant better men, Bobadilla and Roldan, the adversaries of Columbus, were lost with all their gold. A succession of tempests scattered the great Armada of Spain, and strewed the seas of Britain with foreign dead. The good Sir Humphrey Gilbert sat reading at the stern of his ship, when it was last seen by its companion, as a night of dreadful peril was closing in: "the way to heaven," cried he, "is as short by sea as by land:" and in the morning his vessel was seen no more. Hudson was turned adrift in a boat, by his mutinous sailors, and so perished. Sir Cloudesly Shovel, with three gallant ships of the line, and their crews, sank by the Scilly Islands. Many lamented Englishmen went down, when James the Second, with Marlborough and a few beside, escaped from his sinking ship. The Prince George, in 1758, took fire at sea, and five hundred perished by the flames or by the waters. Off Portsmouth, the Royal George, some twenty years after, while she was careened for repairs, and crowded with seamen and people from the shore, admitted too much water into her portholes, and thus in a few moments,

> "Kempenfelt went down,
> With twice four hundred men."

After the victory of Lord Rodney, in 1782, all the prizes, except one, were lost in a terrible storm, in which, also, two British ships of the line and many merchantmen foundered, with more than three thousand persons. The circumnavigator La Perouse perished, without a trace, till some relics of his vessel were found on an island, to which they had drifted. Falconer, after he had described his own fate in his beautiful poem, "The Shipwreck," embarked for India, and sank in the Eastern seas, where the same fate, covered with the same mystery and silence, awaited afterwards the brave Sir Thomas Trowbridge.

The safer voyages of travellers have yet been fatal to many honoured lives, even since all the advantages of modern discovery. In crossing the Atlantic, one of the signers of the Declaration of Independence was drowned; and at a later period the accomplished Professor Fisher and the veteran General Lefebvre Desnouettes; and still later, in one of the noblest steam vessels, the comedian Power and a son of the ducal house of Richmond. Lord Royston was lost off Lubeck. The Earl of Drogheda and his son were drowned in the short passage between England and Ireland. In little excursions of pleasure, a gust of wind has overturned the boat which was laden with many hopes and treasures; so sank an eminent admiral, Sir Joseph Yorke, near Portsmouth; so the shining, unhappy Shelley in the Gulf of Spezzia.

There is no river that has not swallowed up its dead. The first Sforza plunged in to rescue a drowning page, was shaken from his affrighted horse, and sank under the weight of his armour. A Duke of Brunswick was overwhelmed by the waters of the Oder, while he endeavoured to save the unfortunate peasantry during an inundation. Mungo Park, attacked by the Africans, leaped into the Niger, and was either drowned, or destroyed by their missiles. The young, gifted, and pious Spencer, was drowned while bathing in the Mersey; it has been the end of many parental anticipations. Wounded and exhausted, Poniatowski was unable to cross the marshy Elster, in the heat of the battle of Leipsic. Many were the columns that, at Blenheim, were driven into the Danube; many the fugitives who sank freezing from the bridge of the Berezina; many the Seiks whom the British cannon impelled into the broad Indus. A thousand Mamelukes sank in the Nile, at the battle of the Pyramids.

Each day and hour, perhaps, brings to some mortal its fatal peril by water. The inexperienced ship-boy, hurled from the yard into the deep, and struggling vainly for a while; the rowers, overset in attempting to pass the surf upon some dangerous bar; the seamen, washed from the deck; the crew, deserting their sinking bark, to be swamped in their frailer boat; the wrecked survivors, clinging to the side of the ship, till, one by one, they are swept away; the fishermen, surprised by the sudden gale, and striving, without success, to reach the shore; the heedless passer along the sands, where the returning tide hems him in; the boy, falling through the ice; the rider, drawn beyond his depth by his horse; these are a portion of the great throng whom the ocean, with its tributaries, numbers amongst the dead. When it shall give up those whom it buried alive and never restored, they must be an host as numerous, perhaps, as all who, at anv one time, float upon its bosom.

XVI.

Death by Poisons.

"The leperous distilment, whose effect
Holds such an enmity with blood of man,
That, swift as quicksilver, it courses through
The natural gates and alleys of the body;
And, with a sudden vigour, it doth posset
And curd, like eager droppings into milk,
The thin and wholesome blood."

SHAKSPEARE.

A CHEMICAL process incorporates the fruits of the earth, or the flesh of other animals, with our own, through digestion and assimilation. Another chemical process, when other vegetable or animal substances are introduced, dissolves and destroys the whole system. Like the electric fire, the very touch of prussic acid darts through the human frame one withering flash; and life has departed for ever. The slower and more painful operation of arsenic disturbs and distresses the vital functions, till they cease. Strong narcotics, like laudanum, oppress the brain; and the soul passes away under the thick cloud which envelops the senses and all the intellectual faculties. Conveyed to the blood, also, from without, many substances diffuse a blasting energy, which is mightier than all the resistance of physical life.

These poisons have been employed by the murderer, by the savage warrior, by the public executioner, and by the suicide. But they may also, through various accidents, find entrance within the body, and accomplish there their terrible work of dissolution. The Emperor John Comnenus was mortally wounded while he was hunting, by a poisoned arrow. A fatal quantity of some powerful drug, of which a little might preserve life, but much must destroy it, has sometimes been administered through the error of a nurse or attendant; and sometimes, that of the apothecary, the friend or the patient himself has substituted a poison for a remedy. Archbishop Stuart, son of the celebrated Earl of Bute, died from swallowing an embrocation which had been given him by mistake for a medicine. The beautiful poetess best known under her maiden name of Landon, appears to have heedlessly used a greater quantity of prussic acid than was her perilous custom, and was found dead, alone, in her chamber, at Cape Coast Castle. An apothecary in one of the Southern States, on the representation that he had perhaps sent a draught which he did not intend, was so confident of his correctness that he offered to swallow the draught, and actually destroyed himself by his rashness.

It is common to hear of those who, having mistaken the poisonous toadstool for the rich mushroom, have brought death into a family at a repast. Children and domestics have lighted upon arsenic which had been carelessly deposited within their reach, and have tasted it fatally, or, perhaps, mingled it accidentally with the food of a household. Diseases in the flesh of animals have been known to cause qualities so poisonous, that those who partook of the flesh, after the animal was slain, have sickened and died.

It has sometimes happened, that very slight wounds have spread, in an inexplicable manner, some strange effect, like that of venom, throughout the system.

There is a special peril in the dissection of dead bodies, around which floats so destructive an atmosphere. Some valuable lives of professional men have been lost, through the injury inflicted by a mere puncture with some instrument which had just been used in such anatomical investigations. In the bite of a mad dog, the mischief proceeds not from any natural fury of the animal, but only from an accidental malady, and is not in proportion to the severity of the wound, but only to the malignity of the substance infused. It may properly be placed, therefore, not with other fatal injuries from beasts, but with fortuitous deaths from the communication of poisonous matter. Amongst the victims of hydrophobia the most distinguished, perhaps, was Charles, Duke of Richmond, who died in 1819, while he was Governor of Canada, having been bitten by a favourite dog which was often near his person.

The blood, the nerves, the digestive organs, thus take up the seeds of death from a variety of substances; and man, with all his skill, cannot deliver his inmost frame from such enemies. They enter deeper into the secrets of nature than all his remedies or his knowledge. How amazing is that agency, and how far beyond all human discernment, through which one single drop received into the throat, a few grains deposited in the stomach, or a touch, and no more, reaching the blood-vessels, can prostrate the strongest form, defy all power of science, derange and absolutely dissolve the whole organization, drive the soul from its citadel, and rapidly convert the lifeless body into a mass of corruption! Nothing more clearly tells how fearfully and wonderfully we are made, and how manifold as well as mighty, are the means which obey the divine decrees, of judgment or of mercy. The men who die by these poisons, except when they are administered by the hand of suicide or of murder, are very few; only enough to remind the rest that all nature can become the armoury of death.

XVII.

Death from Atmospheric Extremes.

"On every nerve
The deadly winter seizes; shuts up sense;
And, o'er his inmost vitals creeping cold,
Lays him along the snows, a stiffened corse,
Stretched out, and bleaching in the northern blast."

THOMSON.

Two dreadful extremes, the heat that consumes, and the cold that congeals, threaten on either side the life of man, which commonly vibrates between them, at a secure distance. From the violence of the burning sun he shelters himself beneath the shade of roofs, trees, or rocks; and against the biting blasts he protects himself with the aid of fire, thick raiment, and continual exercise. But sometimes he is found unprepared, or is drawn forth from his refuge, and falls under the might of a natural force, which he was not framed to encounter. The air, too, which he breathes, may, through the accumulation of noxious vapours in close pits and depths, be so deprived of the just proportion of its vital elements, that to inhale it is to be suffocated.

Exposed without defence to the vehement heat of the sun, especially in the warmer latitudes, men have often dropped down, and survived but a few moments. A regiment of Prussians, in 1848, suffered as great a loss in this manner as would have been caused by a sharp skirmish. At the battle of Monmouth, several soldiers died merely from the heat; and General Greene, outliving the war, was afterwards smitten with a fatal sun-stroke on his plantation. Labourers in the fields have thus fallen in the season of harvest; and workmen on the roofs of houses have felt their life melting away beneath the blazing noon. But this is an uncommon fate; and the destructive power of extreme heat is more often exercised through exhalations and consequent pestilences, through drought and through the fiery blasts, that send the sands of the desert in whirlwinds against the caravan. The bones of men lie strewed along the plains where such whirlwinds have passed.

More directly destructive is the violence of cold. Every severe storm of the Northern winters surprises some wanderers, who may easily perish amidst the bewildering snows and the benumbing frost. The shipwrecked sailor sometimes escapes the rocks and waves, only to die frozen upon the shore. The squadrons of Charles the Twelfth and the legions of Napoleon sank in long files before the sharp winds of Russia. One of the earlier English navigators, Sir Hugh Willoughby, in the time of Elizabeth, was frozen to death with all his crew in the Arctic sea of Europe; and it is said that a Greenland whaler was found, about 1780, wedged in the ice, where she had been fastened some fifteen years before, with all on board in the very attitude in which they had died, stiff and undecayed.

An accident, not unfrequent and very distressing, is the destruction of the lives of sleepers through the change in the air which they breathe, produced by the fumes of charcoal, where there is no chimney or other outlet. The effect of the respiration of a numerous company, crowded for a long time into a very close room, would be almost as fatal: and thus the hundred and twenty-three British sufferers in the Black Hole at Calcutta were suffocated by the change in an air in which a few of them could have easily borne their imprisonment. In the same manner, seventy or eighty Irish passengers in a steamer died dreadfully under the hatches, where they had been crowded during a storm.

In pits and wells a noxious gas is sometimes formed, which becomes almost instantaneously fatal to the explorer; so that man after man has been lowered only to die in the attempt to rescue his predecessor. Such gases were found to be pent up in the earth so intensely, that often, when the miner has opened a passage, they have rushed forth, either stifling the unfortunate company, or taking fire at their torches, and wrapping all in destruction. Science has found preservatives; but in these more hidden places, nature will doubtless retain some stores of elemental ammunition, ready for mortal explosion. Many hundreds have thus perished in England within a single season.

The rapid dissolution of men in vast companies, when Providence visits them with fatal judgments, is usually through some agency which takes the form of an actual disease, however sudden and speedy. But when, in one night, a hundred and eighty-five thousand Assyrians were smitten by the destroying angel, this can hardly have been through any operation of the most violent and infectious malady, but probably through some such miraculous change in the surrounding atmosphere as made it death to breathe.

Thus the very means of life become the means of death. Man, since the sentence under which he dies, has been subject to natural influences, which in their appointed course, and within their just limits, nourish and preserve him, with all other creatures. But, when some irregularity disturbs that course, or when he invades those limits with a rash step, he only struggles against a power which is the basis of all corporeal existence. He has no strength to endure a temperature above or below that which is adapted to his feeble frame; and the air in which he lives must be blended from its constituent elements in exact proportions, or the vital machine is deprived at once of its moving power, and all the parts which compose the substance of his body hasten back to their sources in surrounding nature. These deaths are not very numerous; but more mightily, perhaps, than any other class, they speak the essential mortality of our present condition; for, though we could escape every disease and accident, we never could brave the might of extreme heat or cold, or of a decomposed and noxious atmosphere.

XVIII.

Death in Infancy.

"There thousands and ten thousands I beheld,
Of innocents like this, that died untimely,
By violence of their unnatural kin,
Or by the mercy of that gracious Power,
Who gave them being, taking what He gave,
Ere they could sin or suffer like their parents.
I saw them in white raiment, crowned with flowers,
By the fair banks of that resplendent river,
Whose streams make glad the city of our God."

MONTGOMERY.

IN an age of refinement and humanity, and in lands where a most watchful tenderness guards the cradle, one third of a generation die in early childhood. But the fragile life, which seemed to need but a gentler or a ruder breath to preserve or extinguish its flame, must often have ceased through the roughness or inattention of barbarians, ignorant even in their kindness. A multitude of infants have been born to die almost at once, with the consent or by the act of parents, brutalized through superstition, or extreme want, or habits of cruelty. All the calamities, too, by which whole communities and tribes have been visited, could not but act most fatally on the feeble beings whose lives were wrapped in the lives of fathers and mothers. From all these causes, the computation of Hufeland, if too large for the present age, may perhaps be admitted for the past history of the world; and it may be believed that half the human race have died within the first ten years of life.

It seems, at first sight, a mysterious ordinance, that death should hold such dominion, before the higher ends of life could be attained or attempted. The same principle seems to have presided over that arrangement by which one third of human existence is apparently lost in the inactivity of sleep, and that other by which almost all the waking hours of almost all mankind must be given to the mere labour of obtaining sustenance. It seems as if the greatest purposes were thus sacrificed or disappointed. But sadder views, compelled by human history, not only satisfy the mind of the wisdom of these ordinances, but result in adoration of the goodness which through them has turned aside so many perils. While labour employs the body, more than half the temptations which would else assail the soul are kept aloof. In sleep, the soul, as well as the body, is refreshed, and ripens passively; and if it makes little progress in good, advances as little in evil. Infancy, a kind of partial sleep of the moral nature, is unmolested by the worst of human temptations: and they who close their days within that region of but half waking thoughts, have never offended as men offend. They die without the burden of a guilt which has been contracted against reason, knowledge, admonition, deliberation and experience. If we knew no more, it would be but too certain a gain for a mighty proportion of mankind, to fall so early.

But more is known. For these, as for all who died in the first of men, there remains, through the seed of the woman, another life, in which the body that dies, and the spirit that never dies, shall alike participate. That the life to come should be to them a state of strict punishment for deeds done in this life, could neither be averred nor imagined; because, whatever be the tendency of the dispositions which they disclose, and whatever the abstract character and merit of those dispositions, it is impossible, with any knowledge which we possess, to impute any very high accountability to their persons. The future life, indeed, without being for such strictly a place of punishment, might still be the beginning of sorrows. To enter it with a mass of impious desires, all sure of their development, would be only to make it at the best a world like this, where evils, unchecked by any future redemption, must pass into evils still blacker and more unmitigated. Not, therefore, through their mere freedom from deliberate guilt can they who depart in childhood be secure of future felicity. But if the evil which they inherit, the downward tendency which has been the load of all men since sin came into the world, be once removed, there is then no bar to their free entrance on all the joy which the Sovereign Father has reserved for the creatures of His love. If they who, from the weakness of their years, cannot embrace a message that announces and offers redemption, may yet be embraced within that redemption, death may be to them the seal of their exemption from trial; of pureness once bestowed, and never again to be endangered; and of their free admission to a purchased possession. But it has always been believed that they could be and were embraced within the redemption which was promised before Paradise was forsaken. Its Author and Finisher gave to such as them an express inheritance in the kingdom of heaven.

The theological question between universal and particular redemption, seemed not necessarily to involve a question on the future peace of such as die in childhood. Should it be pronounced universal, as by the general voice of Christendom at this day, their peace would certainly be decided in that decision. But should redemption be pronounced particular, or limited to a chosen number, that number might still include all who were destined to die before conscious rebellion. Two theories, however, have alike, in their turn, darkened the hopes of the bereaved parent. Tertullian, at the end of the second century, intimates that innocent infants needed not, like older mortals, the sacrament of baptism for the remission of sins, and would die uninjured by its delay. But, fifty years after, Cyprian and the other African bishops were unanimous in urging that the youngest infant should not be debarred from the grace of that sacrament. Its absolute necessity was thenceforth declared with so little qualification, that after the time of Augustin, infants dying without baptism were generally believed to be excluded from the blissful abodes. But a state was imagined for them, which was little more than exclusion from heaven, without suffering, while the baptized were supposed to be in endless felicity. Even Melancthon speaks of those children only as admitted to grace, who are not Turkish, nor Jewish, nor Pagan, but in the church. It has been easy for some Protestant divines, in lands where scarcely, till of late, one unbaptized person in a hundred or a thousand could be encountered, to speak in a tone of uncertainty when they spoke of infants dying without baptism. But the fathers of the reformed church of England hesitated not to declare that, without doubt, unbaptized infants might be heirs of Heaven. Such, too, was the doctrine of Calvin and his followers; but their theory of an irrespective election inclined them to imagine a separation even amongst little ones; and they spoke of elect infants. While some, like Usher, seemed to allow the same difference of destiny in those who should pass into the world to come as in those who should survive in this; others, like some of the Synod of Dort, suggested that all who died in infancy might be of the elect. A part of the harsher doctrine was still that the condemnation of infants who might not be chosen would be the lightest of all future woes; but even from this the mild Watts took refuge in the strange conjecture that heathen infants might possibly cease to exist. The theory of election is now less agitated; the vastness of the redemption is seen in the word of truth; and Protestant Christians, almost with one sentiment, regard the infant world as safe in the hands of a faithful Creator and most merciful Saviour.

"Of such," said He, who knew the glory from which He came, and to which He returned, "of such is the kingdom of heaven;" of such as the little child before Him; not because it was a Jewish child, and circumcised; not because it was a child elected from the rest; but simply because it was a little child, like other little children. Not merely that, through His covenant, they may be heirs of glory, are they consecrated and regenerated in baptism; but because, in His design, they are already made heirs of glory. Therefore, the pious mind, surveying the manifold uncertainties and sorrows of protracted life, and understanding the dangers through which so large a proportion of mankind shipwreck their everlasting hopes, can contemplate, with grateful reverence, the decree under which half have been removed before the season of peril. How sweet must be the songs of that innumerable company, who die without knowing the sting of death, and exchange the vale of tears for a second birth into a world where their angels always behold the face of the Father!

XIX.

Death by Pestilence.

"Nature sickened, and each gale was death."
POPE.

THE air which we breathe is so affected by certain causes, and very mysterious causes, that from time to time it becomes loaded with disease. Some maladies, also, may be conveyed from man to man, by contact. These sources of death, thus distinguished by their origin in infection or contagion, are classed under the common name of pestilence; and they fill a very solemn place in the history of mortality.

Of one such visitation, at least, it is divinely recorded, that it was ordained in punishment for transgression; that an angel was the controlling minister; and that in three days 70,000 men died through the sin of their sovereign. At another time, almost 15,000 died in the camp of Israel; at another, 24,000; and of the people about Bethshemesh, when they dishonoured the ark, 50,000 fell. Men have always felt that these seasons of rapid, simultaneous death had a peculiar language, and demanded a special interpretation. All have bowed themselves before their Preserver, and have confessed that, as death is the fruit of sin, so extraordinary sin is justly visited with extraordinary triumphs of death.

The chief orders of pestilence, since medical science has been sufficient to distinguish their features and record their passage, have been the plague, the sweating sickness, the small-pox, the yellow-fever, and the cholera. In ancient and in modern times, the plague has haunted the cities of the East. During three years of the Peloponnesian war, it was in Athens, and furnished a terrible theme to the descriptive powers of Thucydides. Out of an expedition of 4000 men, 1050 died in forty days. It was fatal, perhaps, to Pericles; certainly to almost all his family. In the time of Justinian, 10,000 died of it daily in Constantinople; and, in a solemn procession at Rome for imploring deliverance, eighty dropped dead in one hour. When it passed over Europe, in 1345 and several succeeding years, Florence lost 100,000 of its population; Venice, 100,000; Naples, 60,000; Genoa, 40,000; and Trapani, in Sicily, all its inhabitants. It was computed, that in Asia and Africa, 23,000,000 had perished; and in Europe, sometimes a fifth, a third, and even three-fourths and nineteen-twentieths were supposed to have died from different cities and provinces. No visitation so dreadful has befallen the earth since the deluge. In the plague of 1406, 30,000 died in London; in that of 1603, 35,000; as many in that of 1625; and 68,000 in that of 1665, when, at times, about 1000 were buried daily. By the plague, Brussels, in 1489, lost 30,000, and in 1578 almost as many; in 1711, 30,000 died at Copenhagen; in 1720, 30,000, half of the whole population, at Marseilles, and a still larger proportion at Toulon; and in 1743, 20,000 at Messina. Its propagation, for a century past, has been prevented by the strict precautions of every Christian people; but in Egypt, where, in 1801, while the French army suffered little, 150,000 natives perished; at Constantinople, where, in the autumn and winter of 1836, 100,000 were swept away; and at Bagdad, where, amidst a tremendous destruction, the accomplished Rich was its victim; it is much more than an occasional visitant. Amongst those who have died by the plague, were Joanna, daughter of Edward the Third, who was seized at Bayonne, where she had just met her betrothed bridegroom; Holbein, the painter; Conrad Gesner, Jansenius, Simon Grynæus, Capito, and the dramatic poet Fletcher.

The small-pox is first mentioned in the seventh century, and amongst the Saracens. Its ravages seem to have become more and more terrible, till they were checked by the discovery of inoculation, and then of vaccination. At this day, the traveller in Europe is surprised at the number of faces which bear its marks, and can judge how great a host must have fallen before these preventives were suggested. The younger Queen Mary of England, Louis the Fifteenth, Joseph the First, and the great metaphysician and divine Jonathan Edwards, were thus removed from the world.

The sweating-sickness was an epidemic which visited England and the north of Europe about the beginning and middle of the sixteenth century. It swept away the learned Colet, and the two young Dukes of Suffolk, on whom many hopes reposed; and in a week eight hundred died in London. It was probably some fever, like those which are often infectious, but seldom spread themselves over so large a surface.

The yellow-fever has been terribly destructive in single ports within the warmer latitudes, especially in America; but disappears with particular seasons, and does not extend into the country. At Malaga, in 1803, almost 12,000 were its prey.

The cholera, originating in India, repeatedly passed over the Asiatic continent to Russia, Poland, Germany, the shores of the Atlantic, Great Britain, and the

United States. Its path was determined by no clear law, but was marked by the graves of thousands on thousands. In some Oriental towns; in Hungary, Bohemia, and Russia, the mortality far exceeded even that which was witnessed in the most crowded of the manufacturing communities of England. Amongst its dead, it has numbered Adam Clarke, Casimir Perier, and Marshal Bugeaud.

A disease was introduced into Naples, in 1792, by the Jews who were banished from Spain, of which 20,000 perished. Confinement in close prisons has produced fevers of fatal malignity; so that the number of persons who died in the British prison-ships at New York, during the Revolution, has been reckoned at more than eleven thousand. Once, in an English court, the judge, the sheriff, most of the jury, and a numerous company of persons present at a trial, were fatally infected with the disease brought from the jail by the prisoners. The scurvy may be reckoned amongst pestilential maladies: it destroyed more than half of the crew of Lord Anson's squadron. The dreadful leprosy, too, is contagious; and the influenza has assumed a very deadly aspect.

Whatever terrors belong to the death of individuals, by rapid, distressing and sharp disease, are accumulated in pestilence. It is always speedy, and not seldom loathsome; and, especially amongst Pagans, has been attended by scenes of revolting selfishness, or criminal desperation. Pestilences have abounded in armies, have haunted besieged cities, have been very fatal at sea, have followed in the track of famine. Whole tribes of savages, ignorant of all remedies, have been cut off, almost to a man. Families are thinned at a stroke, or entirely extirpated; cities are full of mourners; and death becomes a calamity of nations. It seems, and it is, a direct interposition of Omnipotence, hastening the doom of millions, and clothing it with peculiar dread; that all the world may start in its slumber, and feel itself dying.

XX.

Death by Casualties.

> "Each season has its own disease,
> Its peril every hour."
>
> HEBER.

THE universal necessity of death has made every scene a witness, and every object an instrument of its accomplishment. Man cannot live and move without subjection to the possibility of many accidents, of which any one may be fatal. The more he multiplies his weapons and aids, for self-defence, for labour, or for pleasure, the more he varies the armoury of death.

A fall from a tree or a precipice breaks the bones of the strong barbarian, for whom there is no remedy. Afterwards, when lofty edifices have been erected, workmen fall from scaffolds and ladders, heedless visitors from battlements, venturous persons from towers and steeples; men in their own houses, like Bruce the traveller, from the staircase; or like King Ahaziah, from a lattice or window. Seamen are tossed from the yard or mast upon the deck. Perhaps the whole frame is crushed; perhaps the neck is dislocated, and death is instant; perhaps the brain receives a mortal shock; perhaps the bruised sufferer lingers hopelessly under manifold injuries.

The wild beasts of the forest and the desert are often the foes of man, or at least sacrifice him to their hunger. Lions tear the poor Hottentot; wolves devour the Scythian shepherd; the tiger springs from the Indian jungle on his prey; the hyena steals to the unguarded tent, and seizes the sleeping infant; the crocodile fixes its teeth in the bathing Egyptian; the shark cuts off the limbs of the seaman; the envenomed snake plants its fang in the heel of the passer. Those animals whom man has subjected become sometimes the causes of his end: the dog, through his bite in the frenzy of disease; the horse, through his kick; the bull and elephant, by direct assault in moments of fury. Even bees and hornets in swarms; spiders and scorpions of a poisonous nature; and the loathsome and ferocious rat, have inflicted death.

When any of the quadrupeds have become beasts of burden, and men mount upon them, or upon the vehicles which they transport, the caprice of the animal, or any of a thousand accidental obstructions, may be the occasion of a destructive overthrow. The heir of the dynasty of Orleans was one of the many who have been fatally stunned by leaping from a carriage in a moment of danger. Theodosius the Second was killed by a fall from his horse; so perished Louis d'Outremer; so Isabella, wife of Philip the Hardy, of France; so Alexander the Third, of Scotland; so Casimir the Third, of Poland; so the laborious writer, Birch; so the ingenious Day, kicked by the animal that had thrown him; so Unwin, the friend of Cowper; while William the Conqueror received from his horse a blow which resulted in a fatal rupture; Louis the Third, a mortal injury from striking against the top of a doorway through which he was dashing in hot pursuit; and Bembo, from bruising his leg against a wall as he rode. The overturn of a stage-coach put an end to the life of Bishop Kemp, of Maryland. When steam became the agent of speed in travelling, the agent and the increased speed were alike perilous; and Huskisson, crushed under the tremendous wheels, was one of the first of a numerous company of sufferers. Scalded by the exploding boilers, or torn in the violent concussion, or hurled down the precipitous embankment; by water and by land alike, men have purchased greater triumphs over distance by exposure to deaths more sudden and shocking.

Fire is an enemy that can commonly be avoided, but never resisted. It sometimes seizes the sleeper, the infirm, the heedless, the child; breaks out beneath the chamber, darts from street to street, envelopes the vessel, and shuts up every avenue of escape. The wounded Emperor Valens was consumed in a cottage by his enemies; and Alcibiades perished between the flames and the darts of the pursuers. A sick prince, in the dark ages, wrapped up by empirics in clothes all covered with combustible ointments, was accidentally touched by the candle of a servant, and perished by flames which reached his very bones. Of six masquers, quaintly dressed, of whom Charles the Sixth of France was one, four were burned to death by a like accident. The Viscountess Molesworth and her two daughters; the Marchioness of Salisbury; Lord and Lady Walsingham; the brother of Archbishop Cranmer, were all burned in the accidental conflagration of splendid mansions. Three thousand were supposed to have died, between the water and the fire, when, about the beginning of the thirteenth century, London Bridge was in flames. In the midst of a bright festival, held in the palace and gardens of Prince Schwartzenberg, on the marriage of Napoleon, a fire broke out, and the sister of the Prince, with several other persons, perished. When the theatre at Richmond was burned, the Governor of Virginia, with many persons of eminence in society, was buried in its smoking ruins. With equally fatal rage, fire in the forests or on the prairies has surprised travellers, or enwrapped scattered habitations.

The weapons designed for labour or for war prove often the accidental instruments of destruction. With a careless stroke, the mower inflicts a fatal wound; the husbandman falls from the hay-loft on the points of his own pitchfork; the woodman gashes his foot with an axe; and death ensues, after mortification, lockjaw, or excessive bleeding. The shaft of a hunter slew William Rufus; Archbishop Abbot was so unhappy as to slay a man while he awkwardly aimed the crossbow at a deer; and many a time has the gun, held in a heedless hand, lodged its load in the bosom. Like Henry the Second of France, Geoffrey, son of Henry the Second of England, was accidentally killed at a tournament. Rocks, exploded by gunpowder; mills, for its manufacture, and magazines, flashing at a spark; heavy pieces of ordnance, bursting with terrific violence, have shattered and hurled afar off the frames of men: so, in an hour of gayety, several of the highest officers of the United States were destroyed before the face of the President, Tyler. In 1824, an explosion at Cairo was fatal to 4000 persons.

Machinery is an intensity of mechanical power; and such power cannot be closely approached without possible hazard to the human system and its feeble integuments. The immense wheel hurries round; and if the arm be caught by a band, drawn under a roller, or torn by sharp points, it is often the instantaneous assurance of a dreadful end, if it be not that end itself.

By the slightest and the strangest casualties; by the descent of a window upon the neck; by the entrance of a piece of glass, from a bottle held between the knees, in the act of drawing; by swallowing pins; by the pressure of a cat on the breast of an infant; by a sudden check in riding or running; by every variety of incident, the common doom has at one time or another been executed. Bishop Kidder was killed in his bed, and his wife with him, by the fall of a stack of chimneys, in a great tempest. Anacreon is said to have been choked by a grape-stone; Pope Adrian the Fourth, by a fly. The pressure of a crowd has crushed multitudes besides the nobleman in the gate of Samaria. It is probable, that at least one death in fifty may be the result of some fatal casualty.

XXI.

Death from Defective Organization.

> "Short was thy span; but Heaven, whose wise decrees
> Had made that shortened span one long disease,
> In chastening merciful, gave ample scope
> For mild, redeeming virtues, faith and hope,
> Meek resignation, pious charity;
> And, since this world was not the world for thee,
> Far from thy path removed, with watchful care,
> Fame, glory, gain, and pleasure's flowery snare;
> Bade earth's temptations pass thee harmless by,
> And fixed on heaven thine unaverted eye."
>
> CANNING.

SOME of the children of men are born with frames so deficient in some of the common requisites to the preservation of animal life, that they are necessarily doomed to an early dissolution. These die, often in the earliest months of their existence; sometimes, after lingering in much suffering through several years; sometimes, when the defect is less important, after they have been preserved with care to a much later period. In these, the general law of mortality has taken the form of a special provision, to be effectual in the defective part of the organization.

Not unfrequently the mind is, through the same cause, incapable of much development. In mountainous countries, like the Swiss Valais, are found those decrepit cretins, whose bodies are so painfully misshapen, while their intellect is more or less sunken in a state approaching idiocy. With such, it would be strange if life could reach its common limits. Where the organization of the brain is defective, all nervous action suffers; and the point at which the vital principle is in contact with matter becomes liable to destructive influences from every side. Where the heart is marked by some malformation, the circulation must always labour, till the organs give way, or become exhausted and stand still. Where the lungs or the digestive functions are originally imperfect, the life must be imperfectly indued with the power of self-preservation. When a defect or deformity is external, we perceive its injurious operation; but this is only the mightier when all is within.

Not dissimilar to these appear some instances in which the connection between the vital principle and the bodily organization seemed singularly easy of rupture. In July, 1846, a young lady died suddenly at Cincinnati, apparently from excessive heat. The next day, her sister died in the same manner, on her return from the burial; and a third sister, on the third day, returning from the second burial, died also in the carriage. It appeared, on an inquest in England, that sixteen persons of one family had, at different times, died of bleeding, without having received any serious injuries.

With malformation of the system must be closely associated that hereditary transmission of early and fatal disease, which makes of death, not a mere submission to the universal law, not an accidentally premature occurrence, but a necessary result of specific causes born in the individual. Scrofulous affections, and an inevitable tendency to consumption, are sometimes so planted from the birth, that children, and even families of children, descend, without any other than this original cause, and notwithstanding every preventive measure, to the grave of their kindred, before they can attain the strength of maturity. It would be indeed a melancholy sight, were the human destiny limited to this life, and were not the very scene of early death so often the scene of the purest triumphs of hope over sorrow and suffering.

Among those who are thus marked from the first, although often there may be no outward, at least, no decisive sign, names of celebrity cannot, of course, be recorded. But parents have thus outlived a large circle, amongst whom their hopes were once divided, till, while one after another fell like the blossoms in spring, they have felt it as a providential appointment that they themselves should die alone. At other times, the children have been early deprived of their parents, and reserved only for a short orphanhood, and the inheritance of that peculiar fragility that could not pass beyond a single generation. If the world has felt less of interest in such deaths, as such lives may have seemed to promise it less of vigorous operation, yet they have been the centres of an unspeakable mass of private and domestic feeling.

It is not always true, on the other hand, that the imperfections of the bodily organization, or its seeds of innate disease, have made the intellect feeble or languid. The very cause which has shortened the days has sometimes given them a wonderful brilliancy. That common class of proverbs, which, in all ages, have assigned a brief date to powers singularly developed, have their foundation. Some of the extraordinary instances of mental precocity which have delighted or amazed mankind, and ceased with an early death, have been, no doubt, connected with strong tendencies to disease of the brain, or to a development unequal, and therefore irregular and dangerous.

It would be very affecting, could we see the process

by which so many emphatically begin to die when they begin to live. As in a defective piece of mechanism, the absence or weakness of one part is the occasion of a continual strain upon others, or of an imperfect action of the whole. All is thus weakened by degrees, even while the natural accessions of force, as the system grows towards maturity, furnish some counteraction. The struggle between the powers of life and the deficiency of their instruments is vainly prolonged; for the deficiency is one which no possible addition to the strength of any other quarter could overcome. At length, the encroachments of disease are manifest: the enfeebled frame gives up its painful resistance; some accident, perhaps, however trivial, hastens the fatal progress; and the life which never knew health, is closed.

XXII.

Death from Diseases incidental to Youth or to Place.

> "The besprinkled nursling, unrequired
> Till he begins to smile upon the breast
> That feeds him; and the tottering little one
> Taken from air and sunshine, when the rose
> Of infancy first blooms upon his cheek;
> The thinking, thoughtless schoolboy; the bold youth
> Of soul impetuous, and the bashful maid
> Smitten while all the promises of life
> Are opening round her."
>
> WORDSWORTH.

A CLASS of diseases, often more or less infectious, befall so large a part of mankind, that they may be viewed as the common lot of a certain age and of certain localities. They are not seldom fatal to life, although, in their nature and under favourable circumstances, they do not necessarily inflict on the system any considerable shock.

The mere growth of the teeth causes, in many infants, a suffering which, especially when united with other inconveniences, is capable of becoming destructive to the frail receptacle of an immortal spirit. A general disease and commonly a slight one, the whooping-cough, yet sometimes exhausts the vital powers of little children. Still more dreaded, for its occasional severity, is the measles, an eruptive malady of every degree of violence, infectious and not unfrequently mortal. Less common and far more terrible, the scarlet fever assails the youthful family; and, when it takes its severer forms, sometimes sends several members at once to the grave. It deprived both France and England of heirs to the crown; France, of the Duke of Burgundy, grandson of Louis the Fourteenth and pupil of Fenelon; England, of the Duke of Gloucester, the son of Queen Anne. In certain regions, diseases are caused by the climate and atmosphere, such as are more fatal to strangers, but sometimes, though seldom, wear out the strength of the native inhabitant. Such are the agues and intermittent fevers of new countries, where the marshes fill the atmosphere with unwholesome vapours; and such, the indigenous complaints of tropical climates.

No human care can avoid these maladies. They are not, in the usual sense, accidental, but rather the necessary appendages of our earthly condition. They are severally allotted to different lands, but no land is exempt from them all. Some of them are but once the lot of an individual; others may break down the frame by successive encroachments. They argue no special infirmity of the constitution. They spring from no extraordinary circumstance. It is appointed that men should pass by the way of some such perils, and that many should fall by this necessity.

At certain seasons of the year, one-fourth of the deaths in the city of New York are ascribed to cholera infantum, to convulsions and to teething. At all seasons, convulsions furnish, to the classification of the fatal diseases, one of the largest numbers. The croup often dashes the cup of parental hope with an appalling suddenness. Another affection, extremely fatal to children, and into which other maladies easily pass, is dropsy of the brain; which, when it becomes seated, is necessarily though not painfully mortal. Complaints of the bowels also exhaust the feeble powers of a life so precarious. Scrofula, often transmitted by hereditary descent, exhibits itself in a variety of forms, and frequently makes a brief existence anxious and full of distress.

Perhaps the proportion of such deaths to all beside is greater rather than less, as society advances from barbarism to refinement. The savage wanders not far from the region of his birth; and local diseases fasten chiefly upon strangers. If the frame of the young barbarian has survived the first shock of exposure to the rudeness of the forest state, it will not be very liable to those imperceptible assaults which fix disease in the little children just escaped from their delicate cradles and warm nurseries. Light causes break upon the firm texture of a system hardened by early dangers. But, through such dangers, many must first have perished. The rough winds may sooner check the early blossom of life from without, although, if it be able to resist them, the inward strength of the plant may afterwards be greater for the trial. Fewer children, it is probable, grow up, amongst the same number that are born, in the wilderness than in the city. But fewer fall by absolute diseases of this class, and more without maladies, through simple exposure, harsh treatment and neglect. In civilized and savage society alike, the younger portion of the human race is thus thinned by causes which are quite unavoidable and resistless. An infant must, as it were, fight his way up to youth through enemies, by whom a large part of the army to which he belongs are cut off on the road. Even youth and manhood are not exempt from such a warfare; all are exposed, some sink, and many escape for other dangers.

XXIII.

Death in Childbirth.

"Visiting the bridal bower,
Death hath levelled root and flower."

SOUTHEY.

ONE form of death was the peculiar remembrancer of the original order in transgression. As woman had first yielded, so she was to bear her own special sorrow. The pains amidst which a child is born into the world are sometimes death; and they link themselves with diseases, their precursors and their consequences, through which the very season of highest joy is also a season of apprehension and anxiety, and sometimes of rapid transition into bitter mourning.

With such mourning Jacob wept at Bethlehem, over the beloved wife of his youth, Rachel, who gave him Benjamin at the price of her own life. The daughter-in-law of Eli, when she heard of the slaughter of her husband and his brother, the defeat of Israel, and the capture of the ark of God, bowed herself and travailed; and died, after she had given birth and a melancholy name to an infant son—"the glory departed." In secular history, similar scenes arrest our eyes as we look along that course of events, which, indeed, can scarcely be traced in its domestic influences, except where the palaces of the great and royal have fallen in its way. The young Princess Charlotte, daughter of George the Fourth, carried with her to such a grave the warmest hopes of a nation. Joanna, sister of Richard the First, and Blanche, sister of his Queen, died thus, both within a few days; and thus died Isabella, the second Queen of Richard the Second; Elizabeth, Queen of Henry the Seventh; Isabella, Queen of Portugal, and Jane Seymour, mother of Edward the Sixth. Whether it be that the young and lovely are pre-eminently exposed to such peril, or that the union of joyous expectations with forebodings too fatally realized gives a sad charm to such deaths, or that the approaching hour casts a peculiar, tender shadow over the spirit of the sufferer, or that there seems something like an involuntary generosity in dying that another may have life, whatever be the exact cause, such deaths are remembered with an interest all their own. A child dates his own existence, with a mysterious, affectionate gratitude, from the dying hour of a mother whom he never beheld. But very often the spirits of mother and child have departed almost together; and the solemn seal of death, placed on the volume of one life, has left that of another unopened for this world.

It is probable that this cause of death, also, is far more fatal in a refined state of society than amongst barbarians. But, even in our own cities, scarcely one birth in two hundred is mortal to the parent: scarcely one death, in as large a number, is in childbed. This cause, as almost the only stroke peculiar to the one sex, may be placed in the balance against the manifold accidents which attend on the more active pursuits of the other. It is not sufficient to equalize the scales; and the average age of the female sex is the greatest. Although foremost in that sin which brought death into the world, that sex has clasped with readiest affection the sovereign remedy; and even its greater length of days may be viewed as a pledge like that afforded by the birth of Him who was born of a virgin; a token of the completeness of redemption, since the restoration is most entire where the fall began.

XXIV.

Death from Sudden Derangement of Vital Parts.

> "His spirit, with a bound,
> Burst its encumbering clay:
> His tent, at sunrise, on the ground,
> A blackened ruin lay."
>
> MONTGOMERY.

LIFE often closes through a sudden and entire derangement of the vital organs. There may have been a morbid preparation for such a blow; there may have been an internal decay beyond the scope of accurate observation, or, perhaps, of possible knowledge; but an unforeseen touch forces the fatal instant on, and almost in that instant death begins and ends.

Thus, many fall by the effusion of blood upon the brain, or by the rupture of vessels near the heart, or in other vital regions; and apoplexy or paralysis closes the career of a very large proportion of those who survive beyond the first years of decline towards age. The accumulation of blood upon the brain, when it is mighty enough to be the occasion of fatal apoplexy, is often extremely sudden, often absolutely instantaneous. Men have died thus, in moments when any thing rather than death was expected by their companions. Several great American advocates, Pinkney, Harper, Winder, Emmet, and Wells, sank in the midst of forensic efforts. Bishop Heber, returning from the services of the sanctuary, exhausted with heat, went into a bath, and was found lifeless. The Empress Catharine the Second was smitten down in her private closet. Euler dropped to the ground while he was playing with his grandchildren; Bochart, while engaged in a discussion at the academy; Hermann and Sands while writing; and Clarke, a divine of Boston, and several other clergymen, in the midst of sermons. King David the First of Scotland, Sir Charles Bell, Bishop Jolly, and Dr. Chalmers, were found dead in their beds. Amongst those who have died of apoplexy are also enumerated the Popes Martin the Fifth and Innocent the Eighth, the Sultan Achmet the Third, Charles the Eighth of France, Charles the Second of England, John the Third of Portugal, Matthias Corvinus, two successive Dukes of Orleans, St. Francis de Sales, Sir Thomas Gresham, Lord Somers, Sir Peter Lely, Matthew Henry, Samuel Clarke, Vitringa, Spallanzani, Fracastorio, Mrs. Rowe, Garrick, Cheselden, the two Rousseaus, Marmontel, the grammarian Adam, the historian Belknap.

A stroke of paralysis surprised Archbishop Whitgift on his way to the council-chamber; and Archbishop Tillotson during divine service, which he would not interrupt: both lingered for two or three days, almost speechless. Those excellent prelates, Bramhall, Cumberland, and Horne, died also of paralysis; and so died the Emperor Henry the Fowler, Pope Pius the Sixth, Ben Jonson, Harrington, Hobbes, Lord King, Lord Heathfield, the painter Barry, William Hunter, Foote, Poussin, Richardson the novelist, Halley, Thomas Warton, Gilbert West, Smeaton, Cuvier, Sir Walter Scott, and John Quincy Adams. The original stroke, however, though sudden, has often been but the commencement of a weakness of years: thus, Bishop Jebb lived ten years, a patient invalid and a valuable author. Henry the Fourth of England died of epilepsy; the same disease snatched away the youthful Buckminster.

Diseases of the heart are often fatal at last, by an instantaneous blow, though less often than is popularly imagined. King George the Second died in a moment, through the rupture of the right ventricle. The celebrated John Hunter was seized with a spasm of the heart, at a meeting of surgeons, and died almost instantly. Bishop Berkeley was stretched on a couch, and listening while a sermon was read: his daughter approached to give him a dish of tea, and found him already stiff. Doctor Arnold, without previous disease, awoke with a sharp pain in his chest, and at the end of two or three hours breathed his last, as his father had died before him. Lord George Bentinck died while walking to a neighbouring mansion to dinner. Bishop Griswold sank at the door of his assistant and successor. Of disease of the heart, too, but not suddenly, died the pure Bishop Ryder.

Amongst those who have passed out of this mortal life by almost instantaneous prostration from different causes, was the renowned Earl Godwin, who died while at dinner with his sovereign. In later times, the Earl of Dorset, at the council-board, died of dropsy on the brain. Diderot arose from table, and fell dead. Prince Potemkin, the favourite of the Russian Empress, alighted from his carriage under a tree, and there expired. The great Prince Eugene suddenly breathed his last in his bed, after retiring for the night. Bishop Fletcher was sitting in his chair smoking the tobacco, then just introduced into England, when, with an exclamation to his servant, he fell back and died within fifteen minutes. Heyne died while washing his hands in the morning.

Petrarch was found sitting in his chair dead, with his book before him.

Every man has within his own recollection some deaths like these, from the circle of his acquaintance. In early life, they are heard with a peculiar dread; and to some minds the thought of such an end is always alarming. So often, too, is it attended with distress to affectionate survivors, surpassing that of the usual shock, and so large a portion of mankind are unprepared for immediate departure, that the Church may well include in its prayers, a petition for deliverance from sudden death. But, apart from this distress of survivors, he who strives to watch from day to day, and from hour to hour, may come to an entire acquiescence in that manner of death appointed him, secure that even the most instantaneous stroke has its peculiar and evident alleviations.

XXV

Death from Inflammatory Diseases.

> "You pitying saw
> To infant weakness sunk the warrior's arm;
> Saw the deep, racking pang, the ghastly form,
> The lip, pale quivering, and the beamless eye,
> No more with ardour bright."
>
> THOMSON.

THE fatal diseases which may be termed accidental in their occurrence are numerous and various, yet bear a resemblance. They do not befall the whole human race alike, or any one age, or any one people; but through special circumstances in the condition or constitution of individuals, seize them in the middle of their course, as with a grasp of iron. These deaths as much startle mankind as even those which are more abrupt; and, from their very nature, they are preceded by even less than the usual warnings, by which the probability of sudden dissolution is at some distance dimly intimated. Disease which, however instantaneous its issue, has its root deep in the system, may have given some token of its existence; disease which is the offspring of occasion, can utter no sign till the occasion has arrived and passed.

Such are the mortal attacks of fevers. A slight exposure, a cold, an occasion that often cannot be traced, is followed by one of these manifold fires within. They hold within their reach every part which is most needful to the continuance of life; and every organ may be their prey. They are either vehemently infectious; or, like the typhus, capable of communication rather than easily communicated; or not communicable, in any degree which can be appreciated, like the common bilious fevers, and most of the inflammatory maladies. They are often accompanied by delirium; always, sooner or later, by prostration. Under the extreme heat of the attack, life is sometimes, as it were, consumed; at other times it is unable to revive, when all has subsided. A few days, or a fortnight, must commonly decide the recovery or the dissolution.

Fever, the result of extreme intoxication, overpowered the strength of Alexander the Great. Henry the First of England died of a fever, caused by indigestion. A fever hurried away the fiery spirit of that martial Pope, Julius the Second. A fever was fatal to the great Emperor, Charles the Fifth. Lord Bacon took a cold through some experiments with snow, and died a week after, of a light fever, which was too much for an enfeebled constitution. A cold, caught on the Thames, caused, by a similar process, the death of Hooker. Bunyan, from exposure in the rain, was in the same manner overtaken by a fatal fever of ten days. Barrow died, rather suddenly, of a malignant fever which affected the brain. A burning fever dried up the energies of Mirabeau, in the midst of his power and renown. Hoche, seized with a cold, through his strenuous exertions, sank under a consequent fever. Putrid fever cut short the days of Akenside, and of Condillac. Kepler, Rapin, Jeremy Taylor, Owen, Thomas Fuller, Glanvil, John Gale, the physician Freind; and the poets Racine, Gay, Prior, Goldsmith, Thomson, Churchill, Burns, Byron, all died of fevers, and most of them in their prime.

That violent disease, the pleurisy, removed Corregio the painter, and Barthe the admiral. Mahomet the Second died of a vehement colic. Burckhardt, and Coryate, and many other travellers, have been the victims of dysentery, which closed the career of the royal Saint Louis, on the African coast. Cromwell sank under a tertian ague, and Cardinal Pole under a quartan. Pym, Archbishop Dawes, Hume, the sculptor Bacon, Adam Smith, all died of complaints of the bowels; Boccace, of a disease of the stomach; the Emperor Leopold the Second, of a diarrhœa; Margaret of Valois, of a catarrh; Dacier, of an ulcer in the throat; Limborch, of erisypelas; Dryden and Waterland, of inflammation of the foot, through the growth of the nail into the flesh; Bishops Babington and Senhouse, and Lord Kenyon, of jaundice. The deaths of Francis the First, of Shah Abbas, and of Raphael, are attributed to the disgraceful fruits of vicious indulgence.

In youth, or in middle age, and sometimes too in declining years, an accidental sickness thus withdraws men rapidly from their activity, and their usefulness or crimes. The cause seems rather to come from without than from within; or, at least, to be such as might have been avoided, could it have been anticipated, and could all circumstances have been arranged for prevention. Such care, however, and such foreknowledge are themselves impossibilities. Some accidents might be shunned; but no human prudence could anticipate and escape all. Some diseases of this order might be checked at their beginning, or quite prevented by special caution; but the seeds of many are beyond the most penetrating observation. They are a necessary part of the great system of mortality. As men are doomed to die, so a large proportion of their number are to be removed by these visitations, more accidental in their appearance, but appointed under the same law of dissolution. They have, like yet more sudden deaths, this happy effect, that they never permit a mortal to feel himself secure, at any age, in any health, after any precaution.

XXVI.

Death from Chronic Decay.

"Now spring returns; but not to me returns
  The vernal joy my better years have known;
Dim in my breast life's dying taper burns,
  And all the joys of life with health are flown.
Startling and shivering in the inconstant wind,
  Meagre and pale, the ghost of what I was,
Beneath some blasted tree I lie reclined,
  And count the silent moments as they pass;
The winged moments, whose unstaying speed
  No art can stop, or in their course arrest;
Whose flight shall shortly count me with the dead,
  And lay me down in peace with them that rest."

BRUCE.

THE gradual decay of some portions of the system, the growth of some obstruction, the undue preponderance of some elements, or the deficiency of others, through the slow operation of chronic disease, is to many of the children of men, both early and late, the manner of the close.

In dropsy, through the accumulation of one elementary part of our organization, the system becomes deranged, and in the end yields to the pressure. Its fatal effects are more common in advancing years. It caused the death of Robert Cecil, the famous Earl of Salisbury, of Joseph Scaliger, Monk, Duke of Albemarle, Waller, Maclaurin, Johnson, Gibbon, and Fox. Dropsy in the chest destroyed the lives of Bishop Cosin, of the pious Nelson, and of Pope; and Sir Matthew Hale and Addison sank under dropsy with asthma.

Gout, the painful, often hereditary malady, which, after many years of occasional suffering, at length brings down the edifice that has become thoroughly undermined, was destructive to Lord Shaftesbury, Condé, Lord Roscommon, Betterton, Congreve, Gray, Helvetius, and the learned Bishops Stillingfleet, Gastrell, and Conybeare.

The stone has been the torment of many men of learning, or of sedentary habits. By some such complaints died the Popes Pius the Fifth and Gregory the Fourteenth, the Czar Peter the Great, Tycho Brahe, Luther, Linacre, Julius Scaliger, Isaac Casaubon, Sir Kenelm Digby, Episcopius, Hammond, Bishop Wilkins, Anthony Wood, Horneck, Jeremy Collier, Buffon, and Sir Isaac Newton. An ulceration of the bladder was fatal to Linnæus.

The accomplished Marquess of Halifax, Sir William Petty, Sanderson the mathematician, and the learned Jacob Bryant, died of gangrene. So died the poet Mason, after a wound which he received in alighting from his carriage; and so Puffendorf, after a slight injury to one of his toes, in cutting the nail. Bishop Kenn and Robert Hall were worn out by protracted disease in the kidneys, and Christopher Smart by a complaint of the liver. The disease which Napoleon inherited from his father, as the source of his own death, was cancer in the stomach.

Chief, however, amongst all the causes of lingering decay and death, is the consumption of the lungs; a malady which sometimes has continued through one-third or one-half of the appointed years of man, and sometimes has done its work in a few short weeks. The hereditary tendency in many families; the originating occasions; the gradual developments; the struggle between apprehension and hope; the emaciation; the hæmorrhages; the peculiarly interesting traits which often irradiate the countenance; the ultimate difficulty of respiration; the final extinction of the breath; are but too well known, and too often witnessed. Of those who are thus removed, and who form by far the largest number of victims of any one disease, as reckoned in our statistical tables, many are in the bloom of youth or of early manhood. For this cause, they have less often attained celebrity than those whose path has been closed by other maladies. Still, the bright signs of precocious genius have frequently blazed up, only to be extinguished by consumption. So, at sixteen, died that young Josiah of England, Edward the Sixth; so, even earlier, the sweet songstresses, Lucretia and Maria Davidson; so, at twenty-one, Henry Kirke White; so Baratier, a prodigy of youthful learning. But the venerable Bede expired also under an asthmatic consumption; it exhausted the bodily endurance, but not the inward patience, of Donne and Scougal, of Bishop Davenant and Kettlewell, of Bishop Bagot and of Henry Thornton; it ended the days of Spinosa and of Bayle, and withered the laurels of Bürger, of the tender and profound Novalis, of the brilliant Keats in all his promise, and of our affectionate Brainard.

Those deep, internal maladies, which have their seat in the whole system of the circulation, or which plant decay in some particular organ, are met, it may be, for a time, and baffled by the resources of skill and experience. The body may partially, perhaps almost entirely, fulfil its work, even when its powers have become imperfect. With uneasiness and pain, however, in some of its functions, it bears up against the obstruction. The progress of the chronic disease is sometimes imperceptible, and sometimes interrupted; but the vital organization is ever like a besieged city. Barrier after barrier yields, till the citadel itself is assailed. The powers of life offer there their last resistance; but it has become feebler after so many losses; and at length the breath ceases, and the pulse throbs no more.

XXVII.

Death from Old Age.

"Like a shadow thrown
Softly and lightly from a passing cloud,
Death fell upon him."

WORDSWORTH.

IF no violence interrupt the life of man; if he escape the diseases incident to infancy, youth, and manhood; if his frame be complete, and be preserved from all occasional perils, or preserved through them all; if no particular portion of his system yield to a premature decay, he may live on to old age, the survivor of most of his contemporaries. Death finds him at last, through some lighter attack, which at an earlier period would hardly have seemed a sickness; or through a general cessation of all the wheels of life, as if they were merely brought to a stand by the exhaustion of the original force which had impelled their motion. This is the death of old age, when no other cause, or no other cause of importance, except old age itself, can be assigned for the general dissolution of physical nature.

A nervous fever cut off, with little violence, the life of the aged Kosciusko. Bishop Hurd, having lived to a great age, much beyond fourscore, and having passed his closing years in a dignified and devout seclusion, fell asleep one night and never awoke. The still more venerable Bishop Barrington, at ninety-two, read the

Sunday lessons to his household, told them it would be for the last time, and a few days after expired, almost imperceptibly to his attendants. In like manner, Archbishop Harcourt, who died at ninety, had worshipped at York minster on the Sunday before his death, and ceased to live as if through mere exhaustion. The death of the elder Adams and of Jefferson on the same day; and that day the anniversary, and the fiftieth anniversary, of the most memorable event of their lives, the Declaration of American Independence, is to be explained, no doubt, by their extremely weak hold on life—a hold so slight that it was relaxed by the excitement of the occasion and its recollections.

The ancient hermits and anchorets, after lingering through an austere and solitary life, often, in the extreme of old age, dropped gently into the grave. Even Simeon the Stylite became an old man upon his pillar, from which he descended only to die. Paul, the first monk, was found dead upon his knees. Anthony, his successor, surrounded by his disciples, stretched himself out and expired. In a milder retirement and later age, Thomas à Kempis passed beyond his ninetieth year. Huet, the learned Bishop of Avranches, survived as long. Bishop Leslie was much more than a hundred years old when he died, and Bishop Wilson at ninety-two, Sir Christopher Wren at ninety-one, and General Oglethorpe, the founder of Georgia, at ninety-seven, flickered and went out, like the last lights of their generation. Yet the gay and frivolous Ninon de l'Enclos faded away also at more than ninety.

So the mortal frame may remain till its very organization is dissolved by its own natural, unavoidable decay. The decline is very often attended by a loss of much of that intercourse with the external world which is carried on through the senses and the memory. Much of the beauty, as well as of the vigour of the form, has long since departed. The eye has lost its brightness, the skin its bloom, the hair has fallen from the hoary head, the teeth are seen no more, the step is weak and trembling; and every thing tells that man goeth to his long home. There is much of peace in this spectacle of death, when death arrives merely in the latest and easiest form of gentle, gradual, natural decline. But it is still a solemn fulfilment of that great sentence, which, in so many forms, is executed upon the race of men; thinning the ranks of a generation, and enfeebling more and more the few who linger behind, till at length they lie down and sleep, as if weary with watching.

PART THE SECOND.

XXVIII.

Essential Nature of Death.

> "Thou art the shadow of life; and as the tree
> Stands in the sun, and shadows all beneath,
> So in the light of great eternity,
> Life eminent, creates the shade of death;
> The shadow passeth when the tree shall fall."
>
> TENNYSON.

THE original doom was death; and it is death which, by all these various agencies, is sooner or later accomplished in every human creature. From the wide, general survey, as if from a mountain which overlooks all the vast family with their destinies, we now descend as into the valley of some individual lot, and consider what is that death itself, which was thus denounced and is thus executed.

Many may be the solemn precursors, many the sad appendages, from which it may not be quite easy to separate, even in thought, the event which gives them their significance and importance. But nothing is strictly a part of death, if it could have existed without death, or is found at any time where life is continued. However intense the suffering, however probable the sign, it is not death if men have met it and survived.

The arms and legs have all been amputated, and the heart and lungs have still played with vigour. Some parts of the body have been entirely mortified, and their removal has preserved the rest. The action of the brain, and with it life and sensibility, have existed for a little while, when, through injury to the spine, the whole body below the neck has been paralyzed. Even when the brain itself has been so fatally assailed that it could no more discharge its chief functions, and the intellect has thus been utterly deprived of its own organ, life may yet linger on, while the life of life is over. Death is something beyond all these changes. Suffering, in fact, belongs to life: all the pains of mortal distress are on this side of the boundary.

There is an expression by which those who watch a sick-bed, without scientific knowledge, often distinguish the state of actual dying from all previous suffering, however fatal in its issue. They speak of the sufferer as at length "struck with death;" meaning, that a certain change in his symptoms has occurred, which is never seen except when death is certainly at hand; that a point is passed which can never be repassed. He may still breathe, be conscious, speak and act, for hours; but a hand is upon him which cannot be mistaken, and will not be withdrawn. This popular mode of speech has its foundation. The actual dissolution of the bond between the body and the vital principle is begun, and is proceeding, and cannot be long delayed. It is not the same thing with any previous progress of decay in one organ, or in all. It is the lapse of the whole system from the state of organization into the state of dissolution. The beams may before have been weakened, or, one after another, removed; but now the building is falling to the ground.

Such, as to the body, is death; the absolute cessation of all which makes matter the instrument and dwelling, not only of the spirit, which is in man; but also of the soul or animating power which is in brutes; and of the vital operation which is in vegetables; and even of the cohesion which is in minerals. A dead body ceases to have an existence of its own: the merest stone has more: every moment carries off some of its atoms, till all have joined the surrounding elements, so far as the process can be traced by human eye or science. The particles of the stone adhere to one another, till they are forcibly driven asunder, or are separated by chemical action; the particles of the human body, after death, fall asunder of themselves, or through the chemistry of nature.

But the stone has no life; and there is life in the flower or shrub; life, from that great vital stream which pervades the universe; but a life simply passive. A similar life is that which carries on the involuntary operations of the human frame; and, in death, this life, too, is removed. Digestion, absorption, secretion, circulation, are, as it were, the vegetable parts of man; the power which gives them action returns at death into the general current of natural operations, from which it has been set apart in his person.

The brute has still a higher life: he is conscious of the vital stream: he feels, acts, resists, consents, dimly remembers, almost reasons. His is the same life which, in man, performs these various operations, so that, in certain states, when they are performed in the least measure, as in infancy, in idiocy, or when the brain has been grievously injured, little more is seen in man than in the inferior animals. In death, the senses go out, even before the corporeal machinery comes to an utter pause; and this animal life, too, passes from our sight and from its habitation.

That highest life of all; that which belongs, amongst all visible creatures, to man alone; that life of the spirit, which makes him capable of speech, and thus of distinct thought; which makes him a moral being, and therefore responsible to his Maker; that life returns not to the dust, nor to the current of vital powers which animates plants or brutes, for it came not from these sources. But it disappears like the rest; this moment it is here, perhaps as clear, as vigorous as ever; the next, we gaze on that which has neither power, nor sensibility, nor expression, and which is as far below the meanest living things as it was lately exalted above them.

The dissolution of the body, the withdrawal of the vital soul, the departure of the immortal spirit; this is death.

XXIX.

Immediate Cause of Death.

"Oft have I seen a timely-parted ghost,
Of ashy semblance, meagre, pale, and bloodless,
Being all descended to the labouring heart;
Who, in the conflict that it holds with death,
Attracts the same for aidance 'gainst the enemy;
Which, with the heart, there cools and ne'er returneth
To blush, and beautify the cheek again.
But see, his face is black and full of blood;
His eyeballs further out than when he lived;
His hair upreared, his nostrils stretched with struggling;
His hands abroad displayed, as one that grasped
And tugged for life, and was by strength subdued."

SHAKSPEARE.

THE life of the body may be destroyed by a shock which in an instant destroys the materials of the body itself. An explosion might tear limb from limb, and leave nowhere a sufficient portion of the frame to be recognised as human. However uncommon it be, such an instantaneous disruption of all which makes up the corporeal man is conceivable and possible.

In several kinds of violent death, the vital organs are directly rent asunder, or swept away. A cannon-ball may remove the head, the heart, or the bowels. The wheels of a railroad car may leave only a shapeless mass behind. When the axe falls, the twin seats of life are as utterly severed as if the whole world lay between them. These are forms of death which require no explanation; the machinery of life exists no more.

A violent shock from within may in a similar manner break some vital cord, and disconnect parts that are essential to the very existence of the system. Such is the death caused by the rupture of an aneurism, or of some important blood-vessel. More often, a portion of the frame may be so oppressed that the vital action must cease; as in effusions on the brain.

Decay of some of the organs, as of the lungs, may permit them to act till the instrument itself, more and more imperfect, becomes at last absolutely incapable of its office; and then obstructions intervene, and all is stopped. Through the inability of the lungs, an accumulation often takes place in the throat and upon the organs of respiration themselves, sufficient to suppress their already hesitating action.

The direct abstraction of large quantities of blood, from outward wounds or inward hæmorrhage, may produce such extreme weakness, and so deprive the body of its nutriment, that life shall be relinquished, as if for lack of fuel. Or, the substance of the frame, or of some of its parts, may become so changed and corrupted, as by gangrene, that the processes of circulation are checked, and the vital organs fail.

These are some of the immediate causes of dissolution. But often, the violence of an inflammatory attack seems so much to hurry the organic motions in one part, or to impede them in others, that the system becomes deranged and exhausted. Death may begin at the head, the heart, or the lungs; but, whatever be the process, the result, if all the organs remain, is, that the lungs pause in their play, the heart ceases to beat, the head is senseless, and every movement in every part is at an end for ever. Bacon still makes the distinction of supposing "that the immediate cause of death is the resolution or extinguishment of the spirits; and that the destruction or corruption of the organs is but the mediate cause;" a distinction founded perhaps on the nature of animal life, but which only pushes back the operating power into a more mysterious region.

XXX.

Phenomena of Death.

> "At length, no more his deafened ear
> The minstrel melody can hear;
> His face grows sharp, his hands are clenched,
> As if some pang his heartstrings wrenched;
> Set are his teeth, his fading eye
> Is sternly fixed on vacancy."
>
> SCOTT.

WHEN death is instantaneous, all the accompanying phenomena are, of course, unobservable. Either they do not occur, or they are crowded into a moment, and cannot fix a separate notice.

When the disease has oppressed and stupefied the brain, all those phenomena are wanting, which indicate the gradual decay of sensation. Then the breath becomes troubled and irregular, more painful, feebler, shorter. The pulse is trembling, and at length almost imperceptible. First the left ventricle, then the right, loses its motion. The hands and feet grow chilled. There is sometimes a labouring, groaning struggle, as if in a dream, while all is fainter and fainter at every successive moment. Perhaps a convulsive stretch precedes the instant in which, after successive ebbs, the breath expires.

But the phenomena of death, even such as are purely physical, are best seen where consciousness is still left, where the mind still acts on the body, as well as the body on the mind, and where every step is so slow that it may be measured by the observer. The first signs are like those of approaching sleep after deep weariness, but far stronger. At the same time, a cold sweat is often perceptible on the face and limbs; and the substance of the flesh is sunken and bloodless. There is, perhaps, an uneasy motion; the hands seem striving to pick small objects; the grasp is firm; the teeth fixed; the lower lip trembles; the body is stretched out; the extremities are cold. The senses, one by one, are enfeebled, perhaps extinguished. First, the sight fails: spots and flakes appear before the eye, and the finger strives sometimes to remove these from the covering of the bed; the countenances of friends are but imperfectly distinguished; the candle, held closely, shines as if through a thick mist; darkness comes on. Hearing endures longest; and often the voice of affection and the melody of a hymn are sweet to the last. Sometimes the ear fails not till long after the power of utterance has ceased; so that a pressure of the hand answers the affectionate question to which the tongue strives in vain to reply.

It is said, that the hair has suddenly become gray in the last struggle. This struggle, however, is generally past before the actual arrival of death. Very often there is no such struggle; but life, lingering faintly at its citadel, wanes till it imperceptibly goes out. At other times, the very departure of the spirit is in the midst of extreme agony. But, perhaps, more commonly, a season of considerable suffering attends the gradual disruption of the ties between the body and the spirit, but closes when the issue is decided, and leaves an interval of comparative rest for a few moments before the end. It is while the vital system still resists, that suffering is prolonged. When all has yielded, there is comparatively little appearance of deep distress;

but rather languor, faintness, the absence of sensation, and a mere tremulous lingering of the breath of life.

While consciousness remains, it often seems to the dying, that the outer and the lower parts are becoming lifeless before the inner and the upper. The fluids, driven to the surface, instead of becoming blood, and running inward, appear as cold sweat upon the skin. Warmth departs with motion and sensation. From some observations, however, it is said to appear, that life lingers in the gangliar nerves after it has forsaken the brain and the senses. But the draughts poured into the throat are no longer conveyed into the stomach, and the digestive organs, far from dissolving the food and medicines, are themselves dissolved by these. There are even instances in which the decay of the substance of the limbs has preceded the act of death.

Many persons, in their utmost weakness, have fallen asleep, and died without waking. The watching attendant has been unable to notice the moment of dissolution. John Newton says that he watched his dying wife some hours, with a candle in his hand, and when he was sure she had breathed her last, which could not at once be determined, she went away so easily, knelt down, and thanked the Lord for her dismission. So it was with the poet Werner. Many have fainted gently and gradually, and without the slightest token of suffering. But, very frequently, respiration, after the pulse has ceased to be felt, continues for a little while, becomes feebler and feebler, seems at an end, returns again, and perhaps again; and, when consciousness is past, still suggests the thought of distress. It is thus that the tenderest friends, standing by, become more than willing that the last breath should be over. When it is apparently over, they linger for a few moments, and are often surprised and pained by a convulsive movement of the features, as the muscles are for the last time involuntarily contracted; then to repose for ever.

The frequent remark is undoubtedly true, that the bodily suffering of the last hour, much as it appals, is not really to be compared with what has been endured again and again by many a sick man in the previous illness. Bacon observes, that "the most vital parts are not the quickest of sense." It is the ordinance of the Creator, that pain should attend the disorganization of the corporeal system. The more perfect the strength of the system, the more keenly alive must it be to this pain; and thus, the most painful deaths are probably those where, notwithstanding some mighty local disease, some of the vital organs have remained in vigorous operation. But the pain is by no means in the act of dying. A French soldier in Egypt, sinking under heat and thirst, said to Larrey in his last moments, "I feel myself in a state of inexpressible happiness." It is but accidental, that death and strong pain are sometimes associated; for, in most diseases, the chief disorganization has been previously accomplished; the sensibilities have been diminished, and a general languidness has come over the tired sufferer. Apart from those pains which may occur long before, death may be and often is absolutely without anguish. He who has ever fainted away, has probably felt all which is commonly felt in the mere act of sinking into the arms of death. Had he died when he fainted, it would have been no more. Those who have been recovered after drowning, have described the sensation, immediately before they became insensible, as far from being painful; and yet, had they never been restored, no other bodily suffering would have followed. Whatever throws us for the time into a state of complete unconsciousness, is equivalent to the mere process of death, apart from all previous decay. It is probably the same with that of the insensibility produced by chloroform; the same with that of severe epilepsy; the same with that of faintness; and essentially the same with that of sinking into profound slumber.

XXXI.

Apparent Death.

> "Why pause the mourners? who forbids their weeping?
> Who the dark pomp of sorrow has delayed?
> 'Set down the bier! he is not dead, but sleeping!
> Young man, arise!' He spake, and was obeyed."
>
> HEBER.

THE heart may have ceased to beat; the respiration may have entirely ceased; the frame may be stiff and cold; no sign of life may remain; and hours and days may pass; and still the body may not be dead. Men have recovered from such a state, and issued from the shroud, the coffin, and even the tomb. The instances are very few; and the tales by which fancy magnifies the terrors of the grave have very little support from actual evidence, or from probability. In some European cities, a room, adjacent to some cemetery, has been expressly provided for security, whenever any doubt of the reality of the decease remains; and a cord attached to a bell has been so placed that the least motion of the muscles would give the alarm; but these measures have resulted in no revival. Those who were believed to be dead have, however, in every age, been known to awake; and these are amongst the most remarkable facts within human knowledge. A French author has collected fifty-two cases of persons buried alive by mistake; four of premature dissection; three of recovery after seeming death; and seventy-two of death too soon reported; but the distinction between the third and fourth of these classes is not evident, or else the third might certainly be enlarged.

Persons who had been drowned have recovered, after remaining even for hours in the water. A man apparently dead from a grievous wound revived, though twenty-four hours were past. Recovery after suffocation has been particularly frequent. One Anne Green, who was hanged in 1650, at Oxford, on being cut down, was accidentally observed to be warm; and lived many years after. The appearance of death by apoplexy has sometimes proved deceptive, when almost every sign had long been manifest. Very seldom, if ever, has the state of seeming but unreal dissolution continued beyond the third day; still, it is said, that the seventh, and even the ninth, has witnessed restoration. During such periods, the substance of the body remains uninjured by the outward elements. The process of recovery, too, goes on; and they who have reposed upon the bier have arisen and walked.

To some who have thus revived, all which passed in the interval has seemed but as a deep sleep, or a state of fainting. Others, without the slightest power of motion, have yet retained some consciousness, and have even heard around them the preparations for burial. But often, the soul has been in a kind of entrancement. It preserves, after recovery, faint impressions of a sphere of existence distinct from those of its ordinary waking and of its ordinary dreams.

Several examples of seeming death are mentioned by Pliny; one, of a person who revived on the funeral pyre. Varro relates, amongst others, that of his own aunt. In modern times, they have been observed by men of the highest attainments in medical science, and narrated by very eminent writers. The case of Tennent is very familiar. It is also told, on the best authority, that an English gentleman had the power, and exercised it in the presence of the celebrated John Hunter, to throw himself into the state of apparent death, with almost every sign of an actual cessation of circulation, respiration, and the other processes of life. But after various trials, one was fatal; for, he awoke no more.

All such unusual phenomena may yet prove little more, as to the nature of death, than the common occurrences of fainting and temporary insensibility. If these continued, as under unfavourable circumstances they might continue, the result would soon be death. A warrior, fainting on the field of battle from loss of blood, would revive under the care of friends; but would perish, should he remain beneath a heap of slaughtered men and horses. Life, for a little season, hovers where it can be recalled: it has not forsaken its former sphere, but it is on the wing. Should death actually occur, the moment could not be fixed, except it were at the moment when the faintness came on; and this was obviously not the true moment. Minutes or hours may elapse before the anchor is quite cut loose. The utmost extension of this state is in the cases of apparent death, which sometimes end in revival, but perhaps more often in actual dissolution. There may be no greater mystery in this than in sleep, in common faintness, in catalepsy, in the magnetic slumber: all are mysterious, and all our nature is, like every work of God, a mystery to created intellects. The practical danger of premature burial is but the very slightest, and is easily made impossible. For there are signs enough of dissolution, which cannot be mistaken, and should be awaited.

It is said by Irenæus, that through fasting and prayer the dead were raised, even in his time; but in the same age, Autolycus, a heathen, challenged Theophilus of Antioch to point to a single instance. Certain it is, that such power was exercised by the apostles. From actual death came back the children for whom Elijah and Elisha prayed; the man who touched the bones of Elisha; the daughter of Jairus; the son of the widow of Nain; Dorcas, and Eutychus, and Lazarus. As, however, the interval was not longer than that which is stated to have been known between the moment of seeming death and the revival, we may well conclude that the spirit still remained in that intermediate condition from which it might yet return, without ever being consciously mingled with the departed in their own appropriate world. From that world, it would seem that none has come back to dwell in the body, except One, and perhaps a few who attended Him into His glory, as first-fruits of the general harvest.

XXXII.

Corruption of the Body after Death.

"I will not have the church-yard ground
 With bones all black and ugly grown,
To press my shivering body round,
 Or on my wasted limbs be thrown.
With ribs and skulls I will not sleep,
 In clammy beds of cold blue clay,
Through which the ringed earth-worms creep,
 And on the shrouded bosom prey."

CRABBE.

FROM real death the body hastens to corruption. The blood, which had been withdrawn from the extremities, now flows from veins which may have been opened, but which till now refused it a passage. It is not circulation, but dissolution, of the blood; but it sometimes gives a strange colour to the cheek. Gases engendered by the commencement of corruption soon swell the abdomen; the surface of the body becomes slightly darkened from its perfect paleness; and the outermost integument of the skin is dissolved.

It is now the time for interment; and the remainder of the process of decay is commonly to be hidden within the bosom of the earth. For seven or eight centuries, the interment of Christians was usually on the day of their death; as, indeed, Christianity most flourished then in the warmer climates. If, through the calamities of war, or through accidental desertion, the body was exposed, a natural provision, kindly though shocking,

> "Allured from far
> The wolf and raven, and to impious food
> Tempted the houseless dog."

In temperate climates, the stage at which nature forbids a longer view of the dead, is reached about the third day; but it is hastened by great heat, by dampness, by pestilential diseases, by poisons, and by lightning and tempests. Cold, on the other hand, a stream of air, salts, metallic oxides, and various other substances, retard decay. Through causes like these, human bodies have been found in a strange state of preservation, under glaciers, in mines, in vaults peculiarly exposed to a dry air, and even in the sandy deserts. Travellers in Europe visit many places where these natural mummies have been preserved for centuries.

One of the first productions of the grave is phosphorus, which has been seen in tombs, and on the walls of dissecting-rooms. Indeed, inflammable air has issued from cemeteries; and not only the dead body, but even the living, when the living has been corrupted by habits of excessive drinking, is known to have taken fire spontaneously. Such gases are of a very poisonous nature; and dissection has communicated a dangerous infection to the operator, when the dead matter has found its way into the blood through some slight wound.

After this stage of corruption, follows that in which alkalies and similar substances are formed, which consume like those that, for such a purpose, have been sometimes deposited in populous burial-places, or with the bodies of beasts. At a still later period, oily and fat substances are generated, and all unpleasant effluvia disappear. The bones remain still later, and, latest of

14

all parts, the teeth and hair; and at length these also are dissolved, and nothing distinguishes the dust of men from the surrounding soil, in which the worm has its habitation.

All this, in some soils, is accomplished with an amazing rapidity. In Yucatan, it is the custom to collect, after some months, the bones of the dead, and place them with those of their neighbours who have gone before, all in one heap, exposed to public view; and as they are buried without coffins, the decay is so speedy that only a few months need intervene. At the great burial-place in Naples, where the vaults are three hundred and sixty-five, and one is opened every day of the year, quick-lime is thrown in; and at the expiration of the year, scarcely the least relic of the human frame is apparent. But, in other circumstances, not only has the skull of Whitefield, seventy years from his death, been handled by a careless traveller; not only has that of Milton, at the end of a century, been dragged to the light of day; but the lineaments of kings who had been buried for centuries have been seen once more. The almost gigantic body of William the Conqueror, after it had been entombed four hundred and fifty years, was found almost entire. When the tombs of the French princes at St. Denys were rifled by the Revolutionary populace, the features of Henry the Fourth were perfect, while the body of his son, Louis the Thirteenth, was dry, like a mummy; for both had been embalmed. Of King Pepin, after a thousand years, there remained then but a handful of dust. It is very common to disinter human bones from spots where they have not been known to have been buried within the memory of man; but when ancient mounds have been opened, which had indisputably been raised over the dead in distant ages, nothing has remained, or nothing but what crumbled at a touch.

The most common and natural mode of disposing of a body which must so soon be reduced to earth, has been that of depositing it in the bosom of the earth itself. To dig a cave, or to use one which had been prepared by nature, was but an enlargement of the grave; and the costliest sepulchre is but a more spacious coffin. Mausoleums and pyramids could do no more. Some savage tribes, however, have exposed the bodies of the dead to the sun and the air, upon scaffolds or on the shore. Thus, the Parsees at Bombay even leave them to the vultures. The practice of burning the corpse prevailed, to some extent, amongst the classic nations of antiquity, and has found place in other regions, as amongst the Aztecs and the Brahmins. It is well known that the body of Shelley was burned by Lord Byron. The ashes were collected by the ancients into urns, which were deposited in sepulchres; and thus the earth enclosed them at last. Human bodies, too, have been devoured by wild beasts; and many have been swallowed up by the deep; but it is probable that very seldom can the substance have been so dissipated that the bones, at least, have not found a place in the earth, or upon its surface.

There, for the mortal eye and terrestrial history, closes the scene. Of the body, once so strong, so beautiful, so expressive, no trace is left, except it be such as superior intelligences alone can follow. But the skill of Egypt did succeed in preserving the very skin and integuments, shrivelled, blackened, but identical in feature. It is but a mere chemical resistance to the course of nature; and, since the very Pyramids are searched at the end of ages, it has only postponed the issue; that mummies might at last be scattered in museums, or burned for fuel. "Dust thou art, and unto dust shalt thou return," was the original decree; and on all the strong and the lovely forms of every generation, it has passed into its fulfilment, except on One, and two besides.

XXXIII.

The Mind in Death.

"E'en at the parting hour, the soul will wake,
Nor like a senseless brute its unknown journey take."
PERCIVAL.

WHILE the body yields to the sentence of decay and dissolution, the mind is not falling with it, but only loosens its own hold, and prepares for another destiny. It is only when disease impedes the functions of the brain, that we observe even an appearance of mental disturbance or inability. That appearance indicates no decay of the mind itself; for the same or similar appearances may be produced by sleep, by intoxication, by inhalation of gases, and by other causes, from the operation of which the mind arises as fresh as before. Through such causes, it only forbears, for a time, the use of its organs, whether of sense or of conscious recollective thought, and retires into a state in which its connection with the outward world is interrupted. There are not wanting, in those aged persons who take no note of passing occurrences, and do not recognise their nearest friends, some signs of an inward communion with a world of older recollections. When the chord is touched, the life of the soul reveals itself; that chord is the distant past; and we perceive that the inner man only lacks the power of fastening its own operations to the chain of external events. But commonly, not even this power is lacking, as the life of the body ebbs away. That kind of languor which is but to be compared with common drowsiness is indeed often witnessed; and often some lightness of head, or partial deliriousness. This is not decay; and very often, up to the last sigh, up to the very instant and act of departure, all perception, consciousness, recollection, and mental action is as clear, as strong, as vivid, as in the happiest moments of bodily vigour. Indeed, in many dying persons, the mind is unquestionably quickened by the partial release from many encumbrances of the flesh, and by the intensity of its own feelings. The senses themselves disclose more than their natural keenness; or else, there is an appearance as if of some new sense, or some state resembling clairvoyance, so that things otherwise imperceptible are known to be near. A dying person has perceived the arrival of a friend in the house, before it could be ascertained by any of the bystanders. Another has seemed, even when sight and hearing had failed, to be conscious of the presence or approach of an intimate associate. Delirium, and even long insanity, has yielded, as if before the light of a higher sphere. Unusual powers of utterance have appeared; a flow of thought and expression, such as characterizes other states, in which the mind is freest from the influences of the body. But, aside from any such extraordinary phenomena, it is certain that many die in the complete possession of every mental power at the very instant of the separation. The physician Haller, conversing calmly to the last, felt his own pulse: "The artery, my friend," said he, "ceases to beat;" and he expired.

So far as the consciousness of the dying can furnish proof, it is clear that they have no sensations which would forewarn them of any death of their inward faculties. They speak and think as if they were to pass on in one continuous being, and not at once to fall into nothingness. Even when the mind is most overclouded, it is but as when we sink every night in slumber. Whatever be the expectations of the dying man, he feels as yet no break of his existence. The very atheist who takes what, like Hobbes, he calls "the leap in the dark," would not call it such, had he not a secret recoil from a decision which that leap is to make, and of which he is to be conscious. When Hume, in his last hours, was jesting with his friends in allusion to the Pagan fable of Charon and his boat, the consciousness of continuous life was seen in the very choice of his jest. If Priestley expressed, almost as he died, his expectation of a sleep till the resurrection, such a sleep would be no extinction; but he looked to its close, as if to waking in the morning.

The mental sensations of the dying, apart from all spiritual diversities, must be very variously modified by the circumstances of their condition and character, until that point is reached at which all communication with the living is left behind. Many die without knowing that their end is so near, till they are actually insensible. Many actually die in sleep. Many fix all their thoughts on the world which they are leaving, on their affairs, their friends, their last requests; on their present sufferings, or the effect which their conduct may work at such a period. It is entirely possible thus to withdraw from the consciousness of the change which is actually passing, until the moment when the threshold of life is crossed, and the soul issues forth. But when it rather retires into itself, or turns its gaze from the things of this earth to the events which are each instant opening upon its knowledge, we can see, even upon this side of the threshold, an experience new and peculiar, and overwhelmingly interesting. Persons who were approaching their last hour have desired, after taking leave of their friends, to be left to themselves, and not to be interrupted; as if they felt that an untried scene was claiming all their souls. The hands have been clasped, as in rapt devotion; the eyes have been fixed as in intense contemplation; a smile of inexpressible peace, or a shade of deep sorrow, or yet deeper anguish, has lingered till the end; or even has left its trace upon the features of the dead. There is, indeed, much room for interpretations from the fancy or the affections of the spectators at such a season. But one who has watched many deathbeds will hardly be deceived; and the experience of the deathbed itself is not wanting.

Schiller, a little before his death, with a kind of reviving look, said, "Many things are becoming to me plainer and clearer." There seems to be, in the frequent declaration of the dying, that they now see the world and eternity as they had not seen them in life, something more than a merely religious significance. They probably feel that the intellect, when it is not oppressed by its remaining connection with the body, is indeed expanded through the looseness of that connection. The same fact may in part explain the ancient and common notion that the dying had prophetic knowledge.

Some conclusions may be derived from the experience of those who have been seemingly dead, and have recovered. For, notwithstanding that they recovered, they had been in the space between this living world and the world of real death. Those who have been drowned have declared, that in the moment of sinking the events of a lifetime came before their recollection, as if in one vast map of a superhuman memory. Then, with a gentle passage, rather pleasurable than painful, their breath went out, and they glided into unconsciousness. Men who have been hanged, and resuscitated, spoke of the first convulsive struggle, the flashing lights that seemed to swim around the brain, and the subsidence into repose, as all less painful than the revival. There has been a remarkable consent, amongst those who have seemingly died, as to the last images which hovered before the soul as it fell asleep. They have heard a rush of great waters, over which their way seemed to lie. "The world to come," says Schubert, "seems still to speak to the spirit of man in that same great language of figures, of which all visible nature is the work and expression." This assent has appeared amongst persons of different nations, different education, and even different religions, as in the instance of the Mexican princess, Papanzin, related by Clavigero, and beautifully versified by Sands. Others have seemed to themselves only to fall asleep and to awake in some wondrous scene, where they have remained till their resuscitation. Such was the remarkable experience of Tennent.

Doctor Nelson, the author of the excellent treatise on the Cause and Cure of Infidelity, was long a medical practitioner; and he speaks of a striking distinction which he had observed between those who seemed to be dying, and yet recovered, and those who actually died; a distinction in their experience, even when all things besides had equally appeared to foretoken the end. He compares it with the descent into a deep valley, before ascending a hill which commands a vast prospect. Those who approached death as near as could be without dying, had descended into the valley only; those who died had, even before they passed the summit of the hill, some prospect beyond. "It seems," says Newton, "as if the weakness of the bodily frame gave occasion to the awakening of some faculty, till then dormant in the soul, by which invisibles are not only believed but seen, and unutterables are heard and understood." However such evidence from such men be regarded in its highest bearings, it rests upon an accurate observation of mental phenomena in the sick and dying. A wonderful resemblance has been noticed in the dreadful objects which fill the fancy of those who die under delirium tremens, as well as of many whose departure is made terrible by great anguish of conscience. They see black figures, serpents, horrid forms, every wild, spectral appearance. A similar uniformity is observed in the softer and more pleasing pictures which float before the imagination of many, who wander in tranquil pastures, approach bright cities, obtain glimpses of celestial messengers, or catch the sound of unearthly music. The mind reverts with a peculiar readiness to the associations of childhood; and the recollection of early friends has the vividness of sight. "Touching was the scene," says a sketch of the death of the poet Hillhouse, "as the warm affections of that noble heart wandered forth in remembrance to the opening scenes of life, and the friends of childhood who had already gone." Shakspeare makes the dying Falstaff "babble of green fields;" and, at the same time, mingles horrid images with the remorse of the aged debauchee. However strangely the grotesque and the terrible are there united, it is but the copy of nature. A person, who was himself a freethinker, assured a clerical friend of mine, that in the southern part of the United States, he had repeatedly been present with men of loose habits in their last moments; that they again and again said that they saw the Evil one; and, what was very remarkable, that they all described him alike, as a strange, black figure. The same observation has been made by Doctor Nelson. It is but a single instance of that general uniformity of psychological phenomena which is witnessed in the time of departure.

Confining our view to these phenomena, we may thus describe the process which is passing within. Except when the brain is directly oppressed, the mind evinces no decay, but rather acts with greater clearness and intensity, and emits some flashes of a higher intelligence. The recollections of a whole life, the consciousness of spiritual existence, and all which is mightiest and deepest in our nature, become brighter, even in opposition to extreme bodily languor. In the immediate vicinity of death, the mind enters on an unaccustomed order of sensations, a region untrodden before, from which few, very few travellers have returned, and from which those few have brought back but vague remembrances; sometimes accompanied with a kind of homesickness for the higher sphere of which they had then some transient prospect. Here, amidst images, dim images, of solemnity or peace, of glory or of terror, the pilgrim pursues his course alone, and is lost to our eye.

XXXIV.

Higher Agencies in Death.

"On all, the unutterable stillness lies,
Of that dread hour when man must meet his God,
And spirits stand around."

WILLIAMS.

A VERY deep conviction of something in death which extends beyond death, has always disposed the human mind to associate with it an interest on the side of higher and invisible agencies. It has been believed, also, to call out in the soul itself more hidden and mysterious connections with the unseen universe. The mind, in some states, can even weaken and dissolve the links that bind it to the body; and the exhibition of such a power might well prepare us for disclosures still more wonderful.

Death from a broken heart is not a fiction. It has too often occurred to leave us at liberty to sport with so frail a vessel as the life of man. The excitement of strong passion has many a time resulted in the sudden and fatal rupture of some one of the channels of circulation. Men have thus fallen dead under mighty irritation, or from sudden fright, or even, it is said, in excess of joy. A violent passion hurried on the death of Henry the Second of England; and the Emperor Valentinian fell senseless in a fit of anger, and never arose. Some have sunk in the moment of uttering blasphemy, or perjury; and perhaps the providential doom was executed through the prompt reaction of remorse and terror. Still more often, the mind receives a shock, through which the bodily system is not at once broken up, but is made peculiarly accessible to some mortal disease. Margaret, the wife of King Malcolm Canmore, was sick when she heard of his fall, and died of grief almost immediately. The defeat at Solway evidently threw James the Fifth into an extreme depression, which issued in a slow fever and in death. But, without the distinct intervention of disease, life has closed under the operation of extreme sorrow. On an inquest in England, in 1846, it appeared that a woman, whose husband had suddenly died, declared at once, in the violence of her distress, that she would not outlive him; and actually expired within four hours. It may have been by a similar influence of the spirit on the body, when the tie to life was weak, that aged persons have so often expired on their birthdays, or, like three of our chief rulers, on some interesting anniversary.

If the mind have power to produce or hasten death, much more may it be held capable of receiving intimations of its approach, apart entirely from bodily symptoms. The idea of occasional presentiments of this kind has everywhere been found, and implies no improbability. It is true, that the number of unfounded and unfulfilled presentiments would surpass all calculation; but some of those which have been indeed fulfilled, are so striking and peculiar as to be quite decisive. That such a man as Lord Byron should say, weeping, "Something tells me I shall never return from Greece," might perhaps be explained by the power of an excited, saddened, and highly poetic imagination. But Napier, by no means a superstitious writer, mentioning two instances of such a presentiment in officers who fell at the action of the Nivelle, speaks of it as "that strange anticipation of coming death, so often felt by military men." When Bonaparte was before Toulon, the wife of an officer begged that he might be excused from some service. Bonaparte was inexorable. The officer, a brave man, had a presentiment of his fall, and, when the attack began, he trembled, and turned pale. "Take care," said Napoleon, "there is a bomb-shell coming." He stooped, and was severed in two; and his commander told the story with a laugh in Paris. Headley mentions a young midshipman, assassinated at Mahon, who went on shore under the strongest presentiment that he should be attacked, though the origin of the affair was subsequent and purely accidental. Sick persons have predicted, at a considerable distance, the very day of their decease. Such was the prediction of the aged Countess Purgstall, when she entreated her guest, Captain Hall, who relates the fact, to remain a certain number of days longer at her castle: he saw no reason to believe her end to be at hand; and yet she died just within the time which she had designated. It was confidently stated that a divine of Boston, who fell by apoplexy, had on the same day foretold his death.

The second Lord Lyttleton dreamed that he should die at a certain hour, and at that hour he died; and these presentiments assume often the form of dreams. Borrow relates that, in the vessel in which he entered the Tagus, a seaman at his side said, "I have just had a strange dream, that I fell from the cross-trees into the sea;" and, the moment after, being ordered aloft, he actually fell, and was drowned. A Jesuit missionary in South America relates the baptism of an Indian, who just before had dreamed that his deceased mother and sister had visited him and directed him to be baptized, as he was about to come to them; and who, without apparent disease, died the same evening. A young Esquimaux, who was brought to Scotland, and died at Edinburgh, said, just before, that his sister had just appeared to him, and called him away. In 1777, a pious woman died in Connecticut, at the age of ninety-nine, and on her birthday. She had often told that, twenty years before, a venerable and comely person, whom she used to call her guardian angel, appeared to her in a dream, and informed her that she should live to be ninety-nine, and then die. The multitude of such narratives, some of which almost every one has heard from private sources, can hardly be explained without supposing some foundation in fact and in nature. Certainly, too, the Holy Scriptures teach that mode of viewing the time of departure, which regards it as the subject of special determinations. "The very hairs of our head are all numbered;" and of the Saviour it is repeatedly said, that "His time was not yet come;" a language which must be thus justified in its application to all whose life and death He partook.

Whether any have been warned of their approaching end, by direct interposition of spirits from the invisible world, we have, perhaps, no sufficient evidence, except in the instance of King Saul. But it seems established that either the departing spirit itself, or some other unseen agency, or some secret sympathy of nature, has often, at the very time of departure, or immediately after, given intimation of the change to a distant survivor. To a belief of such a warning in dreams, Homer seems to allude:

> "Thy distant wife, Ægiale the fair,
> Starting from sleep with a distracted air,
> Shall rouse thy slaves, and her lost lord deplore,
> The brave, the great, the glorious, now no more!"

Robert of Normandy, son of William the Conqueror, is said to have one morning exclaimed, weeping, to his attendants at Cardiff, where he was imprisoned, "My son is dead;" saying, that in his dream he had seen him slain with a lance; and the fact was, that he had just been mortally wounded in Flanders, by a lance which slightly pierced his finger. Philip de Comines says, that the Archbishop of Vienne said to Louis the Eleventh, immediately after mass, "Sir, your mortal enemy is dead," just at the time when Charles of Burgundy had been slain by the Swiss in battle. Ben Jonson told Drummond of Hawthornden that he saw, in a vision, his child, then in London, with a bloody cross on his forehead, as if cut with a sword; and presently came tidings from his wife of the death of the boy by the plague. Walton tells a similar story of an apparition of the wife of Donne to her husband, with a dead child in her arms, near the very hour when she gave birth to a stillborn infant. Lord Bacon says, that when his father died, he was in France, and, two or three days before, dreamed that he saw the country-house of his father covered with black mortar. The Earl of Roscommon, when a boy in France, suddenly exclaimed, "My father is dead;" and the fact was soon brought by letters. The eloquent Buckminster of Boston died suddenly. On the next morning, his father, in New Hampshire, himself dying, exclaimed, "My son Joseph is dead!" and when those who stood around assured him that it was a dream, he said solemnly, "It is no dream, he is dead;" and presently expired. A sea-captain related to Lord Byron, that he had himself awoke in the night, feeling a wet form stretched across him, which he discovered to be that of his brother in his naval uniform; and that, months after, he learned that his brother was drowned that night in the Indian seas. Six officers in Canada saw, it is said, their friend, Captain Blomberg, enter the room in their midst, in the same hour in which he was slain, at the distance of three hundred miles. A gentleman of New York, who dreamed of the death of a child whom he left in health, hastened home, to find it dead when he entered his door. Another gentleman dreamed of the death of his absent son at the South; and awoke, confident of the fact; which, though unexpected, proved to have occurred at that time. These instances are told from the lips of very near friends of the parties; and it has been stated by the immediate acquaintances of a deceased and very highly revered clergyman, that, though he forbore to speak much of the subject, he yet, when questioned, declared that it was true that he saw his distant daughter in the room with him, at the moment of her decease. The wife of Adams, who was murdered by Colt at New York, dreamed before the murder was discovered, that the body of her husband was found in a box, as it had been crowded in by the murderer. Facts like these, which are probably very numerous, since so small a proportion ever become public, are to be judged, like all other facts, according to their evidence. The universal tendency to such a belief proves that it is not felt to be intrinsically improbable. Numerous as the narratives may be, they cannot substantiate the frequent occurrence of what, if substantiated at all, must still be deemed an extraordinary manifestation of the connection between death and a higher order of laws, beings, and events. But its occasional occurrence we may, with Isaac Taylor, regard as settled.

We see but one side of a great transition: the other side is towards a world which must be spiritual; which must be pervaded by agencies at present inconceivable. That, on the borders of both lands, that at the very line of transition, appearances should occur which seem to belong rather to the other side than this, it is not credulity to imagine; nor is it a superstition of which any wise man need be ashamed, to watch with reverence every indication of that high Providence which conducts a human being from the last hour of this world into the first hour of the world to come.

XXXV.

Intercourse with the Dead.

> "The grave is silent, and the far-off sky,
> And the deep midnight; silent all, and lone!
> Oh, if thy buried love make no reply,
> What voice has earth? hear, pity, speak, mine own,
> Answer me! answer me!"
>
> HEMANS.

IN vain the inquiring heart knocks at the gate of that realm into which the dead have entered. Its most earnest gaze is fixed in vain; its most eager cry is unanswered. But it remains ready to welcome any glimpse, to grasp any evidence which may afford sensible assurance of the nature or reality of a life to come. Such glimpses and such evidences have been offered and asserted in all ages; are any of them worthy of reliance? Can any thing be known, from human testimony or from direct disclosure, of the actual state of the dead? Is any one of a thousand narratives of the apparition of departed spirits authenticated at the bar of impartial judgment?

One, at least, if the spirit of Samuel, and not a delusive phantom, appeared after the incantations of the sorceress at Endor. Had it been satisfactorily known through any other channel than Divine revelation, that Saul saw Samuel on the eve of his own fall, and heard the words, "To-morrow shalt thou and thy sons be with me," it would still have been a fact in the history of mankind, and would have proved, as truly as now, the possibility of such apparitions. That there was a real appearance of Samuel, is the plainest interpretation of the language, was the belief of the ancient Jews, and has been supposed by the best divines. He came, not through any power of the sorceress, it should seem, but to her amazement. Once, therefore, a departed spirit has revisited the earth, and has been seen and heard; and, it is worthy of remark, that he took the form and aspect in which he might best be recognised; that of an old man, covered with a mantle; and seemed to come up out of the earth in which his body was slumbering.

There is another example, yet more unquestionable, though more closely blended with the miraculous facts of the redemption. On the mountain of the Transfiguration, Moses and Elijah, many centuries after their removal to the world of spirits, were seen by Peter, James, and John; spoke in their presence; and were known by them as Moses and Elijah. They were not called back into existence, but only brought within the sphere of visibility. Similar appearances are not in their nature impossible; but they must be interruptions of the common course of events; and the question, whether they have occurred at all, is one of fact and evidence.

Amongst the numerous accounts of such apparitions, apart from the sacred records, not one has been sustained by such evidence as to take its place in history as an acknowledged fact. Many of them fade away before the lamp of investigation, and cannot be traced to any responsible witness. In others, the operation of an excited fancy, or a diseased state of the nerves, is an ample explanation; especially where the apparition has been connected with some spot memorable as a scene of death. The dim and shadowy character of the supposed appearances almost precludes the possibility of proof, beyond the mind of the spectator himself, and of those who are already disposed to receive his statement. It has not been alleged, that clear and full revelations have at any time been made by the visitants. Men have undoubtedly seen, or seemed to themselves to see, the forms of deceased persons, such as they were in life; but they have passed by in silence; and there was too much room for delusions of the fancy or of the senses. Johnson, with every disposition to believe, regarded the question as still, after so many thousand years, undetermined; and another century of inquiry has furnished no addition of testimony.

But, on the other side, as Johnson remarked, was the prevailing notion of all ages. Every history was full of these stories; all the great poets have employed them, from Homer to Shakspeare. The Scriptures suppose such a persuasion. "It is his angel," said the frightened disciples, when Peter, whom they deemed slain, appeared at the gate; and, when they saw the Saviour walking upon the sea, "they supposed it had been a spirit." An universal belief like this is not sufficiently explained by an universal longing for communion with the departed. Its foundation is rather in the actual discourse which our spirits hold with the dead, and which they seem to hold with us, when their images are before us in our solitary contemplations, our reveries and our dreams.

Thoughts of a deceased friend become sometimes, and in some mental constitutions, so vivid for a moment, that the difference between recollection and present reality is all but imperceptible. The departed spirit seems even present to the inward eye; his influence is actually and most powerfully felt; may he not be indeed near, though invisible? This is the question which prepares the mind for a belief in outward though dim and momentary apparitions. Of all this, the most remarkable instance on record may possibly be that of Emanuel Swedenborg, whose grotesque reveries appear to have been so habitually intense that he no longer distinguished between these and the firmest spiritual realities. But Wesley, also, who knew Swedenborg and believed him insane, has spoken of his own clear conviction, that the strong impression on his own mind of the images of deceased friends, at particular moments, was produced by their actual, invisible presence. Oberlin supposed that for many years he enjoyed intimate communications with the dead. It is certain, that, in our dreams, the appearance of a deceased person is sometimes marked by a peculiar vividness, which fixes itself on the recollection, and revives the profoundest feelings. Many have had, like me, a stream of consolation from the beaming, beatified countenance of a friend thus restored in the visions of the night. Johnson hoped for himself some communication with his deceased wife; and Boswell affirmed that he had himself, under a like sorrow, "had certain experience of benignant communication by dreams." The same thing is perhaps still more striking in the waking thoughts of some, under great excitement of the nervous system, but quite without derangement of the understanding. A lady whom grief for the loss of a beloved sister had brought to a highly hysterical state, which continued for several months, was at once and for ever relieved by seeing, as it seemed to her, the clear appearance of her sister, who bade her be comforted, and assured her of her own happiness. Another lady, who was afflicted with a kind of fit that deprived her of sensibility to things around, constantly saw in this state her deceased sister and child, but on her revival recollected nothing.

From such remembrances and impressions, to the thought of visible apparitions, the transition is not difficult. One may often be mistaken for the other; and there is in human nature a strong desire to believe. Perhaps most of the more credible narratives may thus be explained; but the great question itself is not quite solved, when the belief in apparitions visible to the outward sight is rejected.

That the appearance, visible as well as invisible, of the dead, is possible, the instances related in the Bible are decisive. That they have ever appeared to the outward eye, except in those instances, can scarcely be proved from history, to the satisfaction of the skeptical, or even of the indifferent. That, however, the strongest sense of their influence, as if they were present, has often been impressed upon the mind, in those states in which visible objects have least control, is confirmed by ten thousand testimonies. That at such times there is a real communion between the living and the dead, and a real presence of the dead with the living, is a natural conjecture, which cannot be wholly disproved.

XXXVI.

Capacities of the Soul after Death.

"If in that frame no deathless spirit dwell,
If that faint murmur be the last farewell,
If fate unite the faithful but to part,
Why is their memory sacred to the heart?
CAMPBELL.

UNLESS the spirits of the dead can sometimes, visibly or invisibly, make us conscious of their existence and nearness, we have from experience no acquaintance with the realm to which they are gone. A hundred ages have inquired in vain. All which, without the aid of revelation, can be won, are only some inferences from the capacities of the human soul, and some, perhaps, from the traditions or imaginations of different families of nations.

The soul acts, in this life, through its bodily organization, but proves itself essentially capable of acting without such an organization. Its frail, inert, and fleshly body is not only its instrument, but its incumbrance. In those states in which it is least restrained by the connection, it seems to intimate the far greater expansion of its powers and freedom of its movements, which await it when the connection shall be quite dissolved.

Nothing but the weakness of the brain seems to prevent an intensity of attention, a power of surveying several topics at the same moment, a rapidity of mental transition, and a tenacity and comprehensiveness of memory, which would carry us on to a far higher state of intellectual advancement. Even a disordered brain permits the disclosure of some particular faculty with an energy almost superhuman. The flow of expression, the flash of thought, the glimpses of a knowledge beyond the reach of the senses, which are sometimes witnessed when the whole corporeal chain seems almost broken, all speak to us of strength to be developed hereafter.

In sleep, the material world exists only for the mind, which reposes through its own playful activity. Then we scale the steep precipice, and cross the stormy flood, and snatch ourselves from the spot of peril, with but a wish and an effort. Why can we not when we are awake? The body will not obey the spirit; it moves but according to its own heavy nature. Hereafter, this body will be no hinderance; and the power of motion may be unrestrained by the laws of matter. Departed spirits may be near or far, around us or among us, or in the remotest regions of the universe, if they can move with the rapidity of the mind.

The memory is the bond of personal identity and individuality. That portion of our life of which we have no remembrance was that in which the child scarcely existed apart from the care and will of the parent. If we are individually immortal, we must carry with us the recollection of the present state; and there are ample tokens that all which ever fixed the attention is capable of being recalled, and held under one broad survey.

The affections, too, must be immortal, unless the character be changed, or the object lose its attractiveness. Otherwise what has once been loved must be more or less beloved always. It is only the weakness of our present powers that brings one object into competition with another, and for the sake of the later excludes the earlier, and the many for the sake of the few. The mind is like a hospitable house of too small dimensions; it must receive its guests, not together, but in succession. But, could it comprehend all within the same embrace, it would reject none whom it had ever welcomed, unless indeed it had been deceived, for it cannot love a delusion which it has discovered to be a delusion. While, then, on this side of the grave, our love for the departed only gathers strength, devotion, and sanctity from the separation; theirs, in a state where every power, emancipated from the flesh, has gained expansion, cannot have been extinguished.

Of the mode of existence in a purely spiritual world, our conceptions must be vague and inadequate. Disembodied spirits, however, must still possess qualities that have an analogy with form and feature, voice and hearing. We cannot think of them otherwise; till the moment of death they have never existed otherwise; and it is the individual soul which gives to the form and features, to the voice and hearing, their individual peculiarity and identity. Here, it gathers to itself the grosser matter of the body, and moves and acts by slow and heavy contact with the material world. Hereafter, it may employ a more ethereal medium; and its action may be far more rapid, delicate, and powerful.

The whole intellectual man appears, in our present state, to be waiting for a development. There is always a presumption that a development, thus universally and naturally expected, will be accomplished. It may be a development of moral qualities, as well as of mental capacities. Perhaps, the character, here restrained, disguised, or suppressed, may there be all that it tends to be, in good or evil.

The intercourse of incorporeal beings must be free from many of our present impediments. Even now, the word is fleeter than motion, and the glance than the word; and a whole volume of thoughts and feelings is told by a single flash of the eye. When a still lighter and clearer communication shall be possible, the conveyance of knowledge, the participation in occupation, and the joy of love, may be unspeakably multiplied. For this, our souls are longing now; and we feel that, if we could see heart to heart and mind to mind, the good would be severed from the evil, and truth and charity would have their perfect triumph. That, for which the spirit longs, it confidently hopes; and there must doubtless be a fulfilment in the future.

Our acquaintance with the works of our Maker is limited by the imperfection of our present organs. The telescope above, and the microscope below, have opened to us worlds which, without their mechanism, would have been utterly unknown. Our spirits pant to discover more; and, in the words of the Spectator, "It pleases us to think that we who know so small a portion of the works of the Creator, and with slow and painful steps creep up and down on the surface of this globe, shall, ere long, shoot away with the swiftness of imagination, trace out the hidden springs of nature's operations, be able to keep pace with the heavenly bodies in the rapidity of their career, be a spectator of the long train of events in the natural and moral worlds, visit the several apartments of the creation, know how they are furnished, and how inhabited, comprehend the order, and measure the magnitude and distances of those orbs, which to us seem disposed without any regular design, and set all in the same circle; observe the dependence of the parts of each system, and, if our minds are big enough to grasp the theory, of the several systems upon one another, from whence results the harmony of the universe." If the spirit be immortal, these desires must doubtless be gratified; so much even nature would expect with joy and assurance. Henry More says, of the disembodied soul,

> "She is one orb of sense, all eye, all airy ear."

There is, however, something even painful in the thought of varieties of existence so far beyond our present capacity of imagination. But it is softened by the remembrance that this world is as wonderful as any which can open upon us hereafter; and that both are the work of the same power, and under the same supreme control. We know that whatever we are called to meet becomes familiar as we approach; and that our souls are perpetually growing to their natural destiny.

XXXVII.

Natural Consciousness of a Life after Death.

"The soul, uneasy and confined from home,
Rests and expatiates in a life to come."

POPE.

THAT death should be the termination of the existence of a human soul, the very consciousness of that soul in the act of death seemed to deny and disprove. Very often, up to the moment of departure, it resembled much more a bird spreading its wings for a strong flight, than one that folds them for sleep in its nest. Where it was otherwise, the causes were of the same nature with those which, during life, from time to time press on the bodily organs, and produce a temporary or partial unconsciousness.

The continuance of consciousness to the last, itself a strong token of immortality, has been sustained by added proofs, drawn from a multitude of analogies. Plants, fading in autumn, and renewed in spring; insects emerging from the chrysalis, with bright pinions; night, brightening into day, as day has darkened into night; the life that is everywhere blooming up from the very ruins of death: all have furnished comparisons, and some have yielded evidence. Besides, a train of arguments, even such as aided Socrates in his last discourse with his friends, have been borrowed from sources still less reliable; as, from the mere necessity, that as death grows out of life, so life should grow out of death, or from the notion of the pre-existence of souls. To such analogies other analogies may be opposed; to such arguments, arguments scarcely less effective. The breath, or wind, or air, from which the soul or spirit has its name, passes, and is lost as the lightest of all things. In vegetables and in brutes, the species is continued; but the individual, even if renewed from season to season, quite perishes at last. A perpetual succession of beings, rather than the revival of the same being, may be suggested by the course of the seasons. Little is demonstrated by reasons brought from the nature of the soul, as an immaterial, uncompounded essence, incapable of being dissipated or dissolved. The truth is, that these and other arguments, which Plato puts into the mouth of Socrates, are but the efforts of the mind to find a defence for believing what it previously desired, and was even constrained, to believe, by its own consciousness. It wishes, it longs, it expects to live onward; it cannot bring itself to feel that its course is to come at once to an end; it is sensible that the purpose of a being like its own would then be incomplete. To demonstrate this may exceed the wisdom of the profoundest philosopher; to feel it has been the privilege of all mankind, except the subtle and the skeptical. The most stupid amongst the heathen Greenlanders were struck with horror at the idea of annihilation.

It is not difficult, perhaps, to prove, as an abstraction, that the soul does not perish with the body. In vain might atheists, like Fouché, endeavour to crush the instinct of nature, by writing on the churchyard gates, "Death is an eternal sleep." But may not the soul be withdrawn from its personal, individual existence, into that general mass of life from which it was taken at first? May it not be, like the animating principle in vegetables and mere animals, something which may be continued in other individuals or other species, but which ceases to dwell in a single being conscious of his identity? Socrates and Plato contended for the immortality of the soul, because they said that all knowledge was remembrance, and that the soul had existed before its union with the body. But, if so, there was no chain of conscious identity between the present life and the past, and there might be none between the present and the future. Such an immortality was not that for which the human spirit longed, and accordingly the conclusions of Socrates went far beyond his reasonings. He expected a life of personal continuance; his ignorance, he said, would soon be dispelled; but he knew not this from his own argument, and he was as much sustained by representations drawn from the poets as by all his philosophy. He was determined to believe; he followed the dictates of his own nature; and those dictates were expressed in the popular feeling of the ancients, in the aspirations and even in the fictions of poets, and in the solemn meditations of the bereaved.

Frederick Schlegel says, that we can hardly give the name of faith to "the conception of the immortality of the soul among the primitive nations;" for it was "a lively certainty, like the feeling of one's own being, and of what is actually present." In all the ancient world, as in all the modern tribes, except, possibly, the most abject of all, there was always an expectation of a life to come, usually taking a form which connected the future man with his very pursuits in this life. The hunter was buried with his bow, that he might use it in the unseen land; servants were even slain, that they might attend their master; and the Hindoo widow consumed herself on the funeral pile of her husband, in the confidence that their union would be perpetual. In the classic nations of antiquity, the retributions of Elysium and of Tartarus were, to the popular mind, as much realities as the existence of superior beings. Lucretius treated both as equally popular delusions. The belief of the people, in fact, retained the primitive consciousness; a consciousness so universal that, even in the Old Testament, the immortality of the soul was rather presupposed than formally and frequently asserted. It was never a discovery; those who denied it were always the fewer and the later.

The poets described as poets; but their boldest fictions would have been tasteless and powerless, had they not found in the reader this strong consciousness. Some of their images appear to have been borrowed from the patriarchal and Hebrew belief, through uncertain tradition. Other passages spring up directly from the heart. The heroes of Homer pass into a world of deep shadows; and, though the Hades to which he makes Ulysses descend is far less distinct and impressive than that of Virgil, yet the dead have all the traits of the living. "O dearest Harmodius," exclaims an Athenian poet, "thou art not dead; but in the islands, they say, of the blessed, where, they say, are the swift-footed Achilles, and Diomed Tydides." In a lofty and solemn strain, Pindar reveals the deep belief which lay behind all their mythology.

But it is in the personal expectations of the bereaved, and of those who were approaching the grave, that the reality of the ancient belief is most palpably evident. Even in the skeptical verses of Adrian, to his own soul, the sense of continuous life is expressed under all uncertainty of the place and the manner. "I shall part from hence," said Socrates, "and go to enjoy the felicity of the blessed." Neither ancient nor modern eloquence can easily match that sublime expression of the affection and hope of Cicero. "What," says he, "is more desirable than to go to them whom, though dead, we still in life had loved, and to enjoy a perpetual life with those, who so much laboured by precept and example that we might honourably live and cheerfully die! To me it seems, assuredly, that nothing more delightful can befall me, than, if death open an entrance to other regions, to come to those, and be with those whom I have chiefly loved, and never can cease to love and praise. Oh, how shall I exult, when I attain the society of my kindred and my friends! What intercourse can be more joyous, what meetings and embraces more sweet! O blessed death, which shall open the entrance to a life most blessed!" "Thou, therefore," he thus apostrophizes his departed daughter, "now separated from me, not deserting me, but sometimes looking back, lead me, where I may yet enjoy thy conversation and the sight of thee!" This was not rhetoric, but the aspiration of his mind and heart; he says, that he would not willingly relinquish the persuasion, even though it were untrue; and so high, to such a consciousness of immortal life, could the classic Pagans reach, and not philosophers only, but all who could think and feel, here on "this isthmus of a middle state."

XXXVIII.

Heathen Traditions of Life after Death.

> "Guide
> My pathless voyage o'er the unknown tide,
> To scenes of endless joy, to that fair isle,
> Where bowers of bliss and soft savannahs smile;
> Where my forefathers oft the fight renew."
>
> Bowles.

The traditions and opinions of mankind concerning the state after death, have, apart from written revelation, a sufficient uniformity to attest a foundation in the voice of nature, or in truth revealed at the beginning. If they have such a foundation, they cannot but speak a language which, however perverted, has a deep significance; for nature and primeval revelation are equally from God.

On the Egyptian monuments, the soul is represented as brought, after death, into the presence of its judge, attended by accusing and approving spirits. The Greek mythology carried it across the Styx, in the boat of Charon, to the bar of three righteous judges, under whose award it passed to an appropriate abode, according to its works on earth. We have no uninspired writings, apparently, that are older than the poems of Homer. In these, a shadowy gloom overspreads the world of the departed. Achilles, after seeing Patroclus, his dead friend, in a dream, exclaims:

> "'Tis true, 'tis certain; man, though dead, retains
> Part of himself; th' immortal mind remains;
> The form subsists without the body's aid,
> Aerial semblance, and an empty shade!"

The spirits of slain warriors speed through their wounds into air, and hasten to that dim land, where even the joy of virtuous heroes seems almost gloomy. So thick, to heathen eyes, is the mist of futurity.

The Scandinavians said, that the brave were to revel for ever in the halls of Valhalla, and drink mead offered them by maidens, from the skulls of their enemies. Some of the Pagan Arabs said, that of the blood near the brain a bird was formed, which once in a century visited the sepulchre; and some believed a resurrection. The first natives of America, whom the Spaniards discovered, said, that the souls of good men went to a pleasant valley, where the guava and other fruits grew in abundance; that the dead walked abroad in the night, and feasted with the living. Charlevoix says, that the Indians paid great regard to dreams, as embracing intercourse with spirits. They supposed a Paradise in the West, a sunset land. The Mexicans distinguished three places; the House of the Sun, for men who died in battle or captivity, and women who died in childbed; the place of the God of Water, for the drowned, for children, and for those who died of dropsy, tumours, and such diseases, or of accidental wounds; and the place of darkness, in the centre of the earth, or in the North. An Indian told David Brainerd, that he had been dead four days, and would have been buried but for the absence of some relations; that he went to the place where the sun rises, and above that place, high in the air, was admitted into a vast house, miles, he supposed, in length, and saw many wonderful things. The Patagonians call the dead those who are with God, and out of the world. The Tongo people suppose the souls of their dead chiefs to be in a delightful island of shadows, to the northwest,

> "Some safer world in depths of woods embraced,
> Some happier island in the watery waste."

The Yucatanese represented the abode of the good as a delightful land of plenty, under the shade of a mighty tree. The Chickasaws, on the other hand, told Wesley that they believed the souls of red men walked up and down near the place where they died, or were laid; and that they had often heard cries and noises where prisoners had before been burned. The Indians of Cumana supposed echo to be the voice of the departed. It was a common opinion of the Indians of America, that the spirits of the slain haunted their tribe till they were avenged.

But the idea of transmigration has also been found, in Africa, amongst the Egyptians; in Asia, with the Brahmins; and in America, amongst the Tlascalans. Sometimes, even, a higher fate has been assigned to the chiefs and sages, while the lowlier orders of men were supposed to pass into the forms of the lower orders of animals. The idea, however, of transmigration, is itself but an anomaly; and can only be regarded as one of the vagaries of the human mind, in its attempt to penetrate some of the mysteries of existence.

The general current of the traditions of all nations points to a future, spiritual life; to a separation there, according to the character and actions here; to joys awaiting the good, joys, of which the images were borrowed from the knowledge or pursuits of each people; and to a very close connection between this life and that life to come, in the identity of individuals, in the recollection there, in the revival of acquaintance, and in occasional appearances of the departed here, or glimpses of their forms, or echoes of their voices; though all is represented as distant and shadowy. This general belief assures us, either that it is the remnant of a common faith, derived at first from a single revelation; or, that the instincts of our nature prompt everywhere the same conceptions. In either event, the Almighty has imparted, implanted, or permitted this universal persuasion; and, when we have separated the original, common foundation from the accidental and special additions, it is hardly in our power to doubt what all men have believed.

XXXIX.

Natural Prospect of Death.

> "This is the chord of mournful tenderness
> In heathen song, at every parting close
> Returning, while with flowers their heads they dress,
> That like those fading flowers the spirit goes
> But to some unimagined, dread repose:
> Still in the soul sounds the deep under-chime
> Of some immeasurable, boundless time."
>
> WILLIAMS.

So much can the mind reach, without the Christian revelation. The picture will be completed, when we have seen how, without that knowledge, men actually have died. History has preserved the last sayings of many illustrious Pagans. Travellers and missionaries have told us the feelings and expressions of the more barbarous heathen. In various narratives, and in the frequent experience of the day, we can observe the dying thoughts of those who have rejected the faith and hope of the Gospel.

Every sentiment that proceeds from the objects of this life alone would of course be found apart from the expectation of that life which is revealed hereafter. The high preference of heroic death to ignominious life; the affecting farewell of friendship; the firm endurance of extreme pain; the care to fall with dignity; the mighty rally of all the resources that human nature could gather, to meet an unknown future; the suggestions of philosophy; the willing submission to a common lot; the acquiescence in the will of the

Creator, that is enforced by reason and necessity; the weariness of this world, that follows experience of its toils, changes, and sufferings; the occasional flashes of imagination, brightening the scene beyond; all these belong to man in every state, however much they may be developed under the instruction of the word from heaven. More certain prospects, and clearer confidence, and positive joy could hardly proceed from the midst of so much dimness.

It is the remark of Doctor Judson, the missionary, that the heathen of Burmah notice with astonishment the welcome which the Christian converts are enabled to give to death. The Indian savage, however, has often exulted at the very stake, in a kind of frantic defiance of his enemies. The Hindoo woman has sat down to her fate, tranquil and triumphant upon the pile. Regner Lodbrog, king of the pirate Danes in the eighth century, was taken captive by the Saxons, and thrown into a dungeon amongst serpents, to be bitten till he died. A song remains which in that terrible condition he composed; and every line breathes fiery scorn, delight in his bloody deeds, and proud anticipation of the heaven of the Northern barbarians:

> "Me to their feast the gods must call:
> The brave man wails not o'er his fall."

All which has power to kindle the imagination, can nerve men against the mere dread of dying; and the dreams and falsehoods which have been built on the foundation of the natural sense of immortality have power to kindle the imagination. There has never been amongst the heathen any such fear of death as would have forbidden them to brave its terrors in martial contests. The mind, stung by the desire of revenge, or sustained by pride, or exalted into heroism, has dared or endured all which is most terrific, and has even rushed into the arms of destruction.

It was generally true, indeed, of the heathen, that they shrank as they approached the grave, and felt an undefined apprehension. Some mighty impulse was required, to lift them above this apprehension; and then the spirit was, as it were, intoxicated with its wild dream, or overpowering passion. When men sat calmly down to contemplate the prospect before them, they could attain no more than a resigned uncertainty. Socrates spent his last hour in cheerful discourse with his friends on immortality, and then drank the hemlock, as one who was presently to know the truth or falsehood of all which he hoped; and his last words bade Crito sacrifice a cock to Esculapius; for he complied with the observances of his nation, knowing no purer ritual. Cyrus the Great is represented as saying to his sons when he died, "I never could believe that the soul dies, and has no life separate from the body; but if I should be mistaken, still fear ye the gods, who never die;" and if these sentiments are to be viewed as those of the narrator rather than the king, that narrator was Xenophon, the disciple of Socrates. In the verses of the dying emperor, Adrian, he addresses his soul as a fluttering stranger, about to wing its way from its accustomed pleasures to an unknown region. Julian died with expressions of joy, that the purer and better part of his nature was soon to be released from the grosser body, and that he was reconciled to the gods and the stars.

There is, in deaths like these, the vagueness of anticipation, which indeed, without revelation, could never be removed. It is still more striking in modern unbelievers, from the contrast with the prevailing hopes and fears of their fellow-men in Christendom. They have not spoken of any beam of light, across the unfathomable future. But, both in Pagans and in infidels, the human spirit has been found able to look, not with joy, but without agitation, into such a region of shadows, clouds, and darkness. This was not the result of any knowledge of the world after death, which had been drawn from reasoning or from tradition. It is but the natural consciousness of immortality. Man does not expect perpetual extinction; and, gathering all his courage, he goes on; borne up, it is true, by the connection which he still feels between himself and the world which he is leaving. One of the most memorable of such scenes, was that of the last hour of those Girondist members of the National Convention who perished together by the guillotine. They were permitted to hold a kind of banquet in their prison; and till the break of day they prolonged their discourse. Most of them, though educated in the Roman communion, were Deists, and rejected the services of the confessor who was waiting at the door, and who heard their conversation; but a few had not become unbelievers, and one had been a bishop, and one a Protestant minister. They talked of their country, of Europe, of their party, of their enemies; when, towards morning, one of the youngest and lightest said, "Where shall we all be, at this time to-morrow?" Their countenances were overspread with solemnity; they spoke in lower tones; they spoke of the immortality of the spirit; they reasoned, some like heathen philosophers, two or three like Christian believers. At length, one said, "Let us go to sleep; life is not worth the hour which we are wasting in thinking of its loss." "Let us watch," said others; "eternity is too serious and too awful for even a whole life of preparation." The hour drew on; and these ardent, eloquent, intelligent men went to the scaffold, chanting their national hymn of republican patriotism. One by one, they lay down under the blade of death, and the song grew weaker and weaker, till the last, the brilliant Vergniaud, was heard alone. It was the utmost height to which, without a light from heaven, genius and ardour could mount above the common apprehension of death; and, yet, it was also the excitement of men dying together, dying in the face of the world, and dying, as they thought, for their country, and in the issue of a great enterprise.

Not, therefore, the actual terrors of death, but the gloomy uncertainty of the prospect, must most strike us in the concluding hours of ancient error or modern unbelief. The terrors of death belong chiefly to the state of the conscience, and may even be heightened by clearer knowledge and diminished by ignorance. Against death, as a natural event, the soul has proved itself capable of being fortified, by the incitements of the world on which it is looking back, by dreams of fancy or fanaticism, and by the courage of philosophy. "Not only the brave and the wretched," says Seneca, "but even the fastidious can wish to die." Lord Bacon makes the remark, that "there is no passion in the mind of man, so weak, but it mates and masters the fear of death." "Revenge triumphs over death: love slights it: honour aspires to it: grief flies to it: fear preoccupates it." But all these have still only enabled it with difficulty to bear up above the waves; and the common mind has only yielded to insensibility, or acquiesced in an irresistible destiny, wafting it on, it sees not whither.

XL.

Bondage under the Fear of Death.

> "Oh, beat away the busy, meddling fiend
> That lays strong siege unto this wretch's soul!"
>
> SHAKSPEARE.

"It is as natural," says the profound Bacon, "to die as to be born; and, to a little infant, perhaps the one is as painful as the other." The dread of death is chiefly from the conscience, which anticipates the great penalties of guilt beyond. Unquestionably, this dread has been silenced for the time, even in the guiltiest of men; borne down by the excitement of many passionate impulses; and even kept down by the force of a strong will, by soothing doctrines, and especially by such occupation of all the thoughts as might prevent earnest contemplation of the future. But, it is equally certain, that such a dread has been found in all ages; that it is not wholly unknown to the experience of any; that it has increased in power as men have been compelled to pause and think, before they dared to die; and that it has even become most intense where revelation had aroused the conscience, and had partially unveiled eternity.

A punishment, an everlasting punishment, beyond the grave, was feared, even by the heathen, when the thought was banished by no exciting or elevating influence. They painted the unhappy murderer, as possessed by the avenging Furies, and driven towards a terrible abode. Their Tartarus, though its minuter horrors were the texture woven by poetry, was yet itself a state that cast an actual and an alarming shadow over many a conscience. Lucretius, striving against all religion, acknowledges the prevalence of this terror:

> "Now naught of firmness, naught of rest remains,
> Since death to fear unfolds eternal pains."

If less of such dread appears amongst the more barbarous Pagans than in the classic days and lands of Europe, it is because remnants of primeval truth then lingered, which have been almost obliterated where mankind have descended towards barbarism. The terror of the savage is more indistinct, more ignorant, and more easily suppressed. But, always and everywhere, there have been examples of an awful remorse, and "a fearful looking-for of judgment," sufficient to seem, even to the heathen, like the beginnings as well as the warnings of unspeakable wo to come. The revelation of "the wrath of God against all ungodliness and unrighteousness of men" has but given to these apprehensions certainty and intensity.

It is no fiction, that very bad men are often haunted in their dreams by the spectral images of their crimes and their victims. It is no fiction, that their deathbeds are often the scene of horrors which none can see without impressions of unearthly dismay. The solemn awe with which even the good have beheld the grave from afar, and the trembling alarm with which it is approached by the thoughtless, are sometimes exchanged, in the hardened ruffian, for wild agony or infernal despair. Demons sometimes seem gathering around. Sometimes, the spirit of a demon is seen in the ghastly countenance. Dreadful cries of wretchedness, or horrid blasphemies, or broken supplications mingled with curses, or the steady, cold utterance of a hopeless prospect, as if the heavens were brass and the earth iron, or the fierce rejection of every call to prayer, fearfully

> "Tell what lesson may be read
> Beside a sinner's restless bed."

This is not the mere anguish of delirium. It is not to be placed with the fears of the young and light, who are overwhelmed by the sudden prospect of death and judgment. Even such, however, have sometimes seen the divine law written against them in such burning characters, that, like Belshazzar, they have shrunk and shaken, till perhaps they were persuaded to seek their only peace, late but not too late.

Always, where the offered mercy is rejected, men remain in bondage under the fear of death, even though unconscious at present of their chains; for, death remains, an unsubdued enemy; and the consciousness of this may awake with tremendous reality when that enemy is near. But if a vast weight of abominable and atrocious deeds be superadded, each of them may throw a blacker and still blacker feature into the horrid gloom. The soul may slumber through all, till it is aroused by the fiery waves of that ocean on which it is launched for ever. Then, all is hidden from our view; there is no joy in the departure, but there is little wo; the vessel falls with a dull, heavy dash into the bosom of its own dark element. But at other times, the moral sleepers start up with a terrific cry; and it is amidst agonizing shrieks, borne on the everlasting winds, that they are hurried onward to their destiny.

PART THE THIRD.

XLI.

Death under the Redemption.

"But the wide arms of mercy were spread to enfold thee,
And sinners may die, for the sinless hath died!"
HEBER.

DEATH was the consequence of the fall; but the fall was balanced and over-balanced by the redemption. None of its effects are unmitigated or quite triumphant. The earth, though it brings forth thorns and thistles, is yet beautiful even in its wildness, and yields to industry a copious harvest. That very labour which was a part of the curse, becomes largely a blessing. Though a woman has sorrow because her hour is come, yet there is joy that a man-child is born into the world. The very passage from this life, awful as it is to nature, yet is not, probably, what it must have been, had no redeeming mercy intervened. But, more than all, the life to come has been granted; and they who hope for such an inheritance can feel that the death which must first be passed is death no longer.

As soon as the sentence was pronounced that man should return to the dust from which he was created, so soon it was promised, by the same supreme word, that the seed of the woman should bruise the head of the serpent, while his own heel should be bruised by the serpent before the struggle should be finished. It was the image of a contest, in which a slight wound should be inflicted on one side, but on the other an utter destruction. The seed of the woman was the human nature; and emphatically, that nature in the promised Redeemer, the Son of man, "made of a woman," born of a virgin. He was to have enmity against the tempter, the cause of this curse of death, and to overcome in the contest, but not without suffering; and in Him the human nature was to suffer and to conquer. It was, in the language of Holy Writ, "that, through death, He might destroy him that had the power of death, that is, the devil, and deliver them who, through fear of death, were all their lifetime subject to bondage."

Whatever were the effects of the incarnation, they were not dependent on the date of its accomplishment. Time, in the counsels of heaven, is not the element which it must be in the thoughts of the human intellect. Forgiveness and sanctification are the results of the intercession of the One High Priest; yet both were given to multitudes who had died in their several generations before He entered within the veil. His death casts its benign and soothing shadow behind as well as before; and its influence has been felt by those who never heard the story, but lived, in time or place, beyond the sphere of its propagation. The incarnation of the Son of God was the great event to which the whole history of the earth looked forward; and He was incarnate, and "took part of flesh and blood," that He might die and rise again. This was the significance of that original promise, which, diminished of its lustre in the Pagan channels, and brightening with accumulated accessions in the line of the Hebrew patriarchs and prophets, was in both preserved till the fulness of time was come.

A contemplation of death, not merely as the universal fulfilment of the original doom, not merely as it is seen by nature, science, and experience alone, but as it is in the revealed light of God and in the hope of the believer, may best begin at the death of Jesus. But that which made His death so distinct from every other was the union of Deity with the mortal nature, the absence of all taint of sin, and the spontaneous submission of Himself, therefore, to a lot to which He was not liable, neither in His divine nature, which was not mortal, nor in His human, which was not sinful. In assuming our flesh and blood, indeed, which were already under the doom of death, He might necessarily assume mortality, but not that death which He endured, in which His soul was made an offering for sin, and He cried, "My God, my God, why hast thou forsaken me?"

Such a death was the chief of mysteries; and so it stands, amongst all the scenes of death which have been so many millions of times renewed upon this earth. It was worthy to be the close of a life which was itself the close of all preceding history; and to be the beginning of one with which the better life, the life of regeneration, and of resurrection to come, was to be given to man. From the earliest days of our race, the smoke of sacrifices ascended in all lands; the death of a living creature, solemnly celebrated, was the highest rite of religion. It was the worship of the patriarchs, from Abel downward; it was the custom of the classic nations; it was appropriated and hallowed anew by the Mosaic revelation. All religion thus pointed to death; to a death, through which heaven and earth were to be reconciled. When that death had been accomplished, it was remembered and signified in the most sacred ordinance amongst all Christian nations. To the death of Christ, consciously or unconsciously, all who solemnly thought of the destinies of the immortal spirit, have been accustomed, in all ages and lands, to direct their eyes and their hopes, in longing, in inquiry, in wonder, or in trust. The heathen knew not to whom they looked, when they saw in the blood of their sacrifices a propitiation for their guilt. The Hebrews and the patriarchs probably knew only that, like the brazen serpent, it was the appointed type of "things in the heavens," and was to have their reliance, not for its own mere sake, but for some great mystery which it signified. But to all, death, the death of the sacrifice, seemed the only gate of hope, opening from sin, fear, and sorrow, to life, purity, and peace.

Such is it, far more than even to the most enlightened of the prophets, such is it to the faith of the Christian. He sees no death as what death must have been had Christ not died. At this point, this central point, of the history of men he must place himself, when he would survey the flight of ages, and the ceaseless and universal decay of generations, and would look over into the future abodes, and know death by the light of two worlds.

XLII.

Anticipation of the Death of Christ.

"Amidst the visions of ascending years,
What mighty Chief, what Conqueror appears!
His garments rolled in blood, his eyes of flame,
And on his thigh the unutterable name?"
"'Tis I, that bring deliverance: strong to save,
I plucked the prey from death, and spoiled the grave."
"Wherefore, O Warrior, are thy garments red,
Like those whose feet amidst the vintage tread?"

MONTGOMERY.

IT is hard to imagine how the thought of deliverance through the death of a victim, the thought of substitution in sacrifice, should ever have arisen in the human soul, except from divine suggestion. But it was there, when the righteous Abel brought of the firstlings of his flock; and there it remained in all its strength, while the covenant with heaven was renewed successively by Noah, by Abraham, by Jacob, by Moses, by David, and by Solomon. Once, the command, which was not to be consummated, that a promised son should be offered up by a righteous father, intimated still more of an awful, tender mystery. Sacrifice was the chief, the hourly exercise of the great Mosaic ritual, "a figure for the time then present." The victim, too, was always to be spotless, perfect in its kind; and that which was most significant and solemn, for the deliverance which it commemorated, for the universality of the requisition, and for the time of the offering, was a lamb without blemish, the very type of innocence.

To the prophecy of symbols was added the prophecy of words. The primeval prediction betokened a transient injury of the conquering seed of the woman, in the very act of redemption. From the patriarchal times of Job, the eye went forward to the coming of God in the latter day, as a Redeemer, as the next of kin, paying the ransom. David sang of One who was bowed down to the dust of death, whose hands and feet were pierced, whose enemies offered him vinegar and gall, and shook their heads in scorn of his dying anguish; of One who cried, "My God, my God, why hast thou forsaken me?" and who yet, from such humiliation, should be brought out into a triumph that should be shared by all nations, and that should continue for ever. Isaiah beheld One who was wounded for the transgressions of men, and made His grave with the wicked, yet divided the spoil with the strong, even because He had poured out His soul unto death. To Daniel the time was revealed when Messiah should be cut off, but not for Himself. Zechariah foretold that the Shepherd should be smitten; that Israel should look upon Him whom they had pierced; and that, by the blood of His covenant, the Lord should send forth His prisoners out of the pit wherein was no water.

So wonderfully were deliverance and death linked together in prophecy. So they remained through the life of Jesus, tinging the most glorious prospects with a hue of unutterable sadness. Even when the aged Simeon foretold that He should be "a light to lighten the Gentiles, and the glory of Israel," he said to the virgin mother, as if anticipating the day when she should stand at the foot of the cross, "a sword shall pierce through thine own soul also." The cradle of the Saviour was sprinkled, as it were, with the blood of the infants murdered in the coasts of Bethlehem. When He began His ministry, it was with a distinct glance across to the awful end; for He said to the Jews, on His first visit to Jerusalem after His baptism, "Destroy this temple, and in three days I will raise it up;" and said it of the temple of His body. To Nicodemus He said, that the Son of man must be lifted up, as was the brazen serpent in the wilderness. The attempts of His countrymen against His life began when He began to preach, at Nazareth, His own city, and followed Him through all His public way, to the last. He was ever anticipating the day of their success, with solemn, unhesitating calmness. Three days, He said, must the Son of man be in the heart of the earth. It was then no time for the children of the bridechamber to fast; but the days would come when the Bridegroom should be taken from them, and then should they fast. With a sorrowful allusion to the manner of His death, He said, "He that taketh not his cross and followeth after me is not worthy of me." "The bread that I will give," He also said, "is my flesh, which I will give for the life of the world." At the period of His transfiguration, He began to speak directly to His disciples, of His rejection, death, and resurrection, with mysterious awe and sadness, yet as one who went forward willingly and triumphantly to the appointed sacrifice. "My time," said He to His brethren, "is not yet come." "A little while," said He to the Jews, "and then I go my way unto Him that sent me." "I go my way, and ye shall seek me, and shall die in your sins: whither I go, ye cannot come." Once, He admitted His disciples to a sight of His deepest feelings: "I have a baptism to be baptized with; and how am I straitened till it be accomplished!" At other times, with solemn tenderness, He said, "I am the good shepherd: the good shepherd giveth his life for the sheep." "No man taketh it from me, but I lay it down of myself." "I must walk to-day, and to-morrow, and the day following: for it cannot be that a prophet perish out of Jerusalem."

The solemnity deepened as He advanced: one great anticipation was seen through all His discourses; before He could enter into His kingdom, He must "suffer many things," and "give His life a ransom for many." "Can ye drink of the cup that I drink of, and be baptized with the baptism that I am baptized with?" said He at that time to the sons of Zebedee. It was then that He groaned in spirit, and was troubled, and wept, as He went towards the grave of Lazarus. When Mary poured the ointment on His feet, "She did it," said He, "for my burial." After He had entered Jerusalem, amidst Hosannas, yet with tears, He stood in the temple, and when certain Greeks desired to see Him, and when His eye doubtless passed over the whole great harvest of the Gentiles, said, "The hour is come that the Son of man should be glorified: except a corn of wheat fall into the ground and die, it abideth alone; but if it die, it bringeth forth much fruit." In the depths of a struggle which no mortal intellect could ever fathom, He cried, "Now is my soul troubled; and what shall I say? Father, save me from this hour? But for this cause came I unto this hour." "Now," He said, again, "is the judgment of this world: now shall the Prince of this world be cast out; and I, if I be lifted up from the earth, will draw all men unto me." How dread and confidence, how anguish and triumph are blended here; not in the words of a mortal, feeble and sinful, though sustained by faith, but of the Lord of glory, who did no sin, and who was the Conqueror of death and the grave! The intensity of all these feelings breathes throughout His last discourses in the temple and in the circle of the disciples. As He sat down to His Last Supper, He said, "With desire I have desired to eat this passover with you before I suffer." He made the bread and wine, which were before Him, the perpetual symbols of His death, and pledges of a life which belongs to those who eat His flesh and drink His blood. Even there, He was "troubled in spirit;" even while He said, "Now is the Son of man glorified." He felt the vastness of His sacrifice, when, likening it to the utmost proof of human friendship, He said, "Greater love hath no man than this, that a man lay down his life for his friends." Knowing that "it was expedient for them that He should go away;" knowing that "a little while, and they should not see Him, and again a little while, and they should see Him;" knowing that He went to the Father; He yet withdrew to an agony which not even the most favoured three were permitted to witness, except from afar.

There, in the shadow of Gethsemane, His soul was exceeding sorrowful, even unto death. He prayed that, if it were possible, the hour and the cup might pass from Him; He prayed, kneeling and falling upon His face; three times He prayed in the same words, wrestling and struggling, though strengthened by a ministering angel, till "His sweat was as it were great drops of blood falling down to the ground." But His prayer still closed with submission and sacrifice: "If this cup may not pass from me, except I drink it, Thy will be done!" Then, He came forth: He refused to summon one angel from the legions who would have hastened to His deliverance: "This is your hour," He said to His adversaries, "This is your hour, and the power of darkness;" and so passed on to the iniquitous tribunal, to scourging, buffets, and the cross.

XLIII.

Circumstances of the Death of Christ.

"Oh for a pencil dipt in living light,
To paint the agonies that Jesus bore!
Oh for the long-lost harp of Jesse's might,
To hymn the Saviour's praise from shore to shore!"
KIRKE WHITE.

AT the cross, the scene of love triumphant over unimaginable woe, fixes the wonder of men and of angels. Like a mighty Intercessor, the Son of man prays for the forgiveness of his murderers. Like the Lord of eternity, He bestows with a word a place in Paradise. Yet, while the sun was wrapped in darkness, His soul too was dark; and He cried out, at least for a moment, as one forsaken of his God. A few moments after, the final act of submission was finished: He committed His Spirit into the hands of His Father, and all was peace. But, what he endured was still death; death in an intensity which baffles the imagination, and strikes down the heart in adoring amazement.

Mocked, buffeted, scourged, Jesus was led away, bearing His cross towards the common place of execution. The cross was composed of an erect beam fixed in the earth, and a transverse beam towards the top; together with a small projection below. It was probably not the whole immense weight, but only the transverse beam which was borne by the sufferer along the road to His death. This beam was fastened to the other, at the fatal spot; and while the body rested upon the projection, the hands were bound to the transverse beam, and large nails were driven through the hands and feet, deep into the wood. In this constrained position of the body, the least motion under the anguish of such horrible wounds, tore the already lacerated members. Nerves and tendons were pierced; and the most sensitive portions of the human structure exposed to the chilling air. A mighty distress was felt where the blood, unable to circulate freely, accumulated at the vital organs. In all this torture, the victim often survived till the third day, and had been known to linger till the seventh. If the speedier removal of the body were required, the legs might be broken, or some mortal blow or thrust inflicted. But Jesus was already dead, when, towards sunset, the soldiers came to do this office; and though a spear pierced His side at the very seat of life, it was needless. He lived but six hours after His crucifixion; and His bodily anguish was told only by the words, "I thirst," uttered just before He expired. The sufferings of His corporeal frame were doubtless the most intense, but they were less lasting than those of the two malefactors, who were crucified with Him, and of multitudes beside. He would not diminish them by recourse to the somewhat stupifying draught of wine and myrrh, which was placed in compassion at His lips. The prophetic language of the twenty-second Psalm, so closely fulfilled, would indicate the extremity of pain when the body and soul were violently sundered.

In that separation, the soul too suffers, and suffers chiefly. He, the only One amongst all millions who was without sin, was put to death as "a reproach of men," as the most daring of blasphemers. His apostles had forsaken Him: He was betrayed by one, and another had just denied Him, with imprecations.* But His mother, and the disciple whom He loved, and several devoted women, still stood by His cross: He was not alone. In such an hour, when the tenderer feelings predominate, our Lord, who "was made in all things like as we are," uttered no denunciation of sinners, but prayed for His murderers, even in words that softened their guilt to the utmost, "They know not what they do;" granted, and more than granted, the petition of the dying malefactor; and commended His mother to His friend, as a mother henceforth, and His friend to His mother, as henceforth a son. Pain of the body and the soul, the pain of dying, produces, except in hardened minds, some gentleness and meekness, and accords with a forgiving spirit. In Him, it was human tenderness, with divine forgiveness.

As His spirit departed, the veil of the temple was rent from the top to the pavement; the rocks were riven; the earth quaked, and graves flew open. All nature cried with the centurion, "This was the Son of God!" Such stupendous tokens spoke the immensity of the act; and spoke the sympathy of other than visible powers with the Redeemer and the redeemed. Perhaps they were more than tokens. Perhaps the mighty event of that hour actually echoed through the universe.

Whatever we feel in death, except the consciousness of personal guilt, and of danger after death, He felt, who was made "like unto us in all things, sin only excepted." But more, much more was there, than ever darkened the dying hours, or entered into the heart, of mortal man; and all worlds must have bowed down in distant adoration, could they have known the tremendous mystery of that conflict which was decided, when He cried, "It is finished." The Son of God had died, not like a conqueror trampling upon the terrors of the grave; not like a hero, meeting the shock with a dauntless bosom; not like a philosopher, enduring with calm and resolute firmness; not like a saint, smiling in sweet patience, as he walks through the dark valley; but like a willing victim and sacrifice, who feels all, suffers all, to the utmost depth of anguish, and overcomes only because the cup is exhausted.

Great was this mystery of godliness, far too great to be interpreted by any but those who, with humble hearts and sincere faith, learn the interpretation from the word of God; from the Son and from the Spirit. To all beside, Christ crucified must be foolishness; an awful enigma without significance.

XLIV.

Design of the Death of Christ.

> "On thee and thine, thy warfare and thine end,
> Even in His hour of agony He thought,
> When, ere the final pang His soul should rend,
> The ransomed spirits, one by one, were brought
> To His mind's eye."
>
> KEBLE.

THE Saviour of men said of His own death, that He would give His flesh for the life of the world, would lay down His life for the sheep, would give it a ransom for many; and, "signifying what death He should die," said, "Now is the judgment of this world; now shall the prince of this world be cast out; and I, if I be lifted up from the earth, will draw all men unto me." He said, too, that He laid down His life only that He might take it again; and, when He admonished His disciples of His approaching sufferings, He commonly added the assurance of His resurrection or His future glory.

At the institution of the sacrament of His holy Supper, He spoke as one who partly lifted the veil of an unutterable sacrifice. "This is my body, which is given for you:" "this is my blood of the New Testament, which is shed for you, and for many, for the remission of sins." In the discourse which accompanied that last passover and first communion, He uttered many words of similar disclosure. "Greater love hath no man than this, that a man lay down his life for his friends." "For their sakes I sanctify myself, that they also might be sanctified through the truth." "How then," said He, as He was betrayed, and the disciples thought of defence, "how then shall the Scriptures be fulfilled, that thus it must be?" "The cup which my Father hath given me, shall I not drink it?" "The prince of this world," He had also said, "cometh, and hath nothing in me;" and His dying cry, "It is finished," told the close of an awful conflict. But beyond, He saw and promised its transcendent issues. "In my Father's house are many mansions; I go, to prepare a place for you." "Ye now have sorrow; but I will see you again, and your heart shall rejoice, and your joy no man taketh from you." "If I go not away, the Comforter will not come unto you; but if I depart, I will send Him unto you." In His sacrificial prayer, death even bore the aspect of glory: "Father, the hour is come: glorify thy Son, that thy Son also may glorify Thee."

After His resurrection, He instructed Cleopas and his companions in the meaning of the prophets, and said, "Ought not Christ to have suffered these things, and to enter into His glory?" Still later, He said to His assembled disciples, "Thus it is written, and thus it behoved Christ to suffer, and to rise from the dead the third day, and that repentance and remission of sins should be preached in His name among all nations."

The words of the Saviour, therefore, declare that His death was the fulfilment of a divine purpose and of divine predictions. It was at an appointed time that He was to be glorified. It was His own voluntary submission and offering. It was expressly for men, for their life, their ransom, their forgiveness. It was a triumph over "the prince of this world," the devil. It was to be followed by great glory and joy, glory to Himself and joy to His servants; by His entrance into the mansions of heaven; by the mission of the Comforter; and by the attraction of the world to the cross of their Redeemer.

The wider development of His doctrine concerning His own death, as of all others, must be sought, where He has taught us to search, with those to whom He promised all truth, and whom He enjoined to teach whatever He had commanded. "His," said the apostles, "is the blood of the everlasting covenant;" "the precious blood of Christ as of a lamb without blemish and without spot, who verily was foreordained before the foundation of the world." "Herein is love, not that we loved God, but that He loved us, and sent His Son to be the propitiation for our sins." All the types of the law told the divine purpose; and several of the prophets predicted its fulfilment in the sufferings and death of the Anointed. "Him," said St. Peter, "Him, being delivered by the determinate counsel and foreknowledge of God, ye have taken, and by wicked hands have crucified and slain." "These things, which God before had showed by the mouth of all His prophets, that Christ should suffer, He hath so fulfilled." "They that dwell at Jerusalem," said St. Paul, "and their rulers, because they knew Him not, nor yet the voices of the prophets, have fulfilled them in condemning Him; and when they had fulfilled all that was written of Him, they took Him down from a tree, and laid Him in a sepulchre." With allusion to the types, he says, "Christ our passover is sacrificed for us." "Christ died for our sins," are elsewhere his words, "according to the Scriptures." "Saying none other things than those which the prophets and Moses did say shall come; that Christ should suffer."

It was, they all declare whom He sent, His own act of love. He hath "loved us, and given Himself for us," and "washed us from our sins in His own blood." He "gave Himself a ransom for all," and loved the church, and gave Himself for it;" "gave Himself for our sins, that He might deliver us from this present evil world, according to the will of God and our Father." "He humbled Himself, and became obedient unto death, even the death of the cross."

The sacrificial, redeeming, propitiatory character of His death is the very burden of the apostolic epistles and of the Apocalypse. "Christ hath redeemed us from the curse of the law, being made a curse for us." "Christ our passover is sacrificed for us." "Christ died for our sins." "The man Christ Jesus gave Himself a ransom for us." "One died for all, when all were dead, and died for all, that they which live should not live unto themselves, but unto Him which died for them and rose again." God "hath made Him to be sin for us, who knew no sin;" "hath set Him forth to be a propitiation through faith in His blood." He "was delivered for our offences." "Justified by His blood, we shall be saved from wrath through Him." "When we were enemies, we were reconciled to God by the death of His Son." "In that He died, He died unto sin once." "God sending His own Son in the likeness of sinful flesh, and for sin, condemned sin in the flesh." The church of God is that which He hath "purchased with His own blood." They "who sometimes were far off are made nigh by the blood of Christ." He "hath loved us, and given Himself for us; an offering and a sacrifice to God, for a sweet smelling savour." "We have redemption through His blood, even the forgiveness of sins." He "took out of the way the handwriting of ordinances that was against us, nailing it to His cross." "He, by the grace of God, should taste death for every man." As "a merciful and faithful High Priest, He made reconciliation for the sins of the people." As such, He "learned obedience by the things which He suffered;" He "offered up prayers and supplications, with strong crying and tears, unto Him that was able to save Him from death, and was heard in that He feared;" and, "being made perfect, He became the author of eternal salvation unto all them that obey Him; called of God, a High Priest, after the order of Melchisedec." He once "offered up Himself." Of old, the high priest entered within the veil of the tabernacle, bearing the blood of the animal offered in sacrifice: Christ "entered in once by his own blood." His death was "for the redemption of the transgressions that were under the first testament." "Almost all things were by the law purged with blood, and without shedding of blood was no remission: it was therefore necessary that the patterns of things in the heavens should be purged with these, but the heavenly things themselves with better sacrifices than these." "Now once in the end of the world hath Christ appeared, to put away sin by the sacrifice of Himself." He "was once offered, to bear the sins of many." He "offered one sacrifice for sins for ever." We "were redeemed with the precious blood of Christ, as of a lamb without blemish and without spot." He, "His own self bare our sins in His own body on the tree;" "by whose stripes we are healed." He "suffered for sins, the just for the unjust, that he might bring us to God." He "hath suffered for us in the flesh." He "hath loved us, and washed us from our sins in His own blood." He hath redeemed His people "unto God by His blood, out of every kindred, and tongue, and people, and nation." He "is the propitiation for their sins, and not for theirs only, but for the sins of the whole world." "God sent His Son to be the propitiation for our sins." The chosen title of the Son of God in that book which discloses most of heaven, in the Apocalypse of St. John, is "the Lamb that was slain;" and thus is His sacrifice for ever celebrated in the songs of saints on high, as here it is shown forth at His table till He come.

It was a triumph over the Author of all evil; a triumph, complete and everlasting. "Through death, He destroyed him that had the power of death, that is, the devil;" and "delivered us from the power of darkness." "The Son of God was manifested, that He might destroy the works of the devil." "By the blood of the Lamb," the saints "overcome the Accuser of their brethren."

The glorious fruits of the death of Christ are told with a grandeur of apostolic thought and language, which declares how much they exceed all human imagination, even so far as they embrace but the destinies of man; and which even seems to intimate an interest on the side of other worlds. "Being by the right hand of God exalted, He shed forth that which was seen and heard" on the day of Pentecost. "God, having raised Him up, sent Him first unto Israel to bless them, in turning away every one of them from their iniquities." "God hath exalted Him to be a Prince and a Saviour, to give repentance to Israel and forgiveness of sins." "If, when we were enemies, we were reconciled to God by the death of His Son, much more, being reconciled, we shall be saved by His life." He "broke down the middle wall of partition" between Jews and Gentiles, "having abolished in His flesh the enmity." "Having spoiled principalities and powers, He made a show of them openly, triumphing over them in His cross." "Through death He delivered them who, through fear of death, were all their lifetime subject to bondage." "By His own blood, He entered into the Holy Place, having obtained eternal redemption for us;" and, "by means of His death, they which are called receive the promise of eternal inheritance." "We are sanctified through the offering of the body of Jesus Christ once for all." "For, by one offering, He hath perfected for ever them that are sanctified." We have "boldness to enter into the Holiest by His blood, by a new and living way which He hath consecrated for us through the veil, that is to say, His flesh." "The blood of sprinkling speaketh better things than that of Abel." "Our Saviour Jesus Christ hath abolished death, and brought life and immortality to light through the Gospel." Having "washed us from our sins in His own blood, He hath made us kings and priests unto God and His Father." "The Spirit of Christ, in the prophets, testified beforehand the sufferings of Christ, and the glory that should follow." That glory seems to tower above all words, even the words of inspiration. "God hath set Him at His own right hand in heavenly places, far above all principality, and power, and might, and dominion, and every name that is named, not only in this world, but in that which is to come, and hath put all things under His feet, and gave Him to be the head over all things to the church." "Because He became obedient unto death, God also hath highly exalted Him, and given Him a name which is above every name, that at the name of Jesus every knee should bow, of things in heaven and things in earth, and things under the earth; and that every tongue should confess that Jesus Christ is Lord." "For the suffering of death, He was crowned with glory and honour." "When He had by Himself purged our sins, He sat down on the right hand of the majesty on high." "This Man, after He had offered one sacrifice for sins, for ever sat down on the right hand of God; from henceforth expecting till His enemies be made His footstool." As if the utmost issues of His death reached even beyond this world of mortals and their eternal destinies, the voice of inspiration declares that "it pleased the Father, having made peace through the blood of His cross, by Him to reconcile all things unto Himself, whether they be things in earth, or things in heaven."

So died the incarnate Son of God, made for our sake the Son of man; and so, He abolished death.

XLV.

Change in Death through the Death of Christ.

> "There is no death: what seems so is transition;
>   This life of mortal breath
> Is but a suburb of the life elysian,
>   Whose portal we call death."
>
> LONGFELLOW.

THE language of the Scriptures, when they speak of the effect of the death of Christ on the death of men, is the intensest and the broadest. He has "abolished" and "destroyed" death; and "whosoever believeth in Him shall never die;" "shall not taste of death." Still, bodily death reigns over all men, and Christ endured it, and from it no one of His servants is exempted. It must be that death has two senses; that in which it is, through Christ, at an end; and that in which it remains. The sense in which it remains is before our eyes, and will soon be our experience. The sense in which it is, through Christ, at an end, can best be comprehended by reverting to the view of death as it would have been if Christ had not died.

It would have been the extinction of all which makes life life. The body would have been dissolved, "dust to dust." The spirit would have passed, either into nothingness, or into wretchedness without remedy. The separation itself could not be without mighty woe, when, hopeless and comfortless, body and soul were torn for ever asunder. Through Christ, it was decreed that the body should be reanimated; "all should be made alive." Through Christ, the soul, whatever else might be its allotment, should share the same immortal existence. For those who should die before the age of actual sin, and for those who should embrace and hold fast the holy hope in Christ, the world to which death is the passage should be light and glory. The passage itself could no longer be what it had else been; for, the valley on each side stretches up, as it were, into the rough mountain pass between; and when both valleys smile, the one an earthly garden, the other a heavenly Paradise, the pass between them must be less gloomy and less toilsome.

But the blessing, the one stupendous blessing, of redemption, has made even of this life, and for the evil and the good alike, another scene than must have been, had the curse been without remedy. The sun shines and the rains descend on all alike; all see the beauty, and hear the music of nature; to all, the senses are the avenues of delight, and the exercise of the powers is a happiness; and all have exquisite joy in the fellowship of man with man, under a multitude of relations. Life is gladdened, and death, as the mere close of life, is alleviated, for all, through that benefit of the redemption which may be separated from all its spiritual and eternal issues. Men do not die as they must have died, had the sentence been simply, and without qualification, fulfilled. Apart entirely from all inward anguish, death is not dreadful. When the infant and the idiot, or those whose senses at the hour of death are immersed in sleep, or those whose cerebral organs have been oppressed and stupified, sink into its arms, it has no terrors. When the senses and the mind are all awake, it is felt that nothing but alarm of conscience should make the soul recoil from a change which otherwise can bring no peril. Those are deceived, unless they are the victims of a morbid, nervous timidity, who imagine that they are afraid to die, but not afraid to be dead. A mind in health could not so shrink from what must be a mere transition, if the state into which it shall be borne by that transition were utterly without power to excite anxious foreboding. It is the conscience that is awake and agitated; and its apprehensions can only be removed through a persuasion which, whether true or false, shall be adapted to itself, and shall seem to disclose safety beyond the grave. But, while this terror is truly taken away only through the Redeemer, and through Him only for such as have not rejected His love, other terrors of the mere bodily dissolution have been, like the perpetuity of corporeal death, taken away, at least in their most awful forms, for all human creatures.

Only He who was sinless tasted all the bitterness of death; and sinners taste it no more, except it proceed from the consciousness of guilt unforgiven, and therefore of danger beyond. That consciousness could not be His; all else which is in death He exhausted, and the world was relieved. Hence, when the terrors of conscience are allayed, men go down into death and meet the natural change with a tranquillity so common that it cannot be deemed difficult. The terrors of conscience are unfelt by the infant, the idiot, the insensible; they are often braved by the hardened; they are sometimes soothed in the heedless; they are generally suppressed in the unbelieving; and they are banished from the breast of steadfast, humble, hopeful piety. But, in whatever manner these are escaped, the death of Jesus has removed, or wonderfully softened, for all mankind, those other terrors which surrounded the sentence of death; just as His mediation, through which all blessings flow to men, removed or softened the sorrows which were mingled by the same sentence with the cup of the living. When, watched by affection and relieved by science, every pain soothed, and every tie gently loosed, the dying mortal sinks as if into a sleep, whose beginning, perhaps, is hardly discerned, this is the utmost of the simply earthly relaxation of the common sentence; a relaxation which, through the death of Jesus, has been granted to our universal nature.

XLVI.

Christian Prospect of Death.

"I have a sin of fear, that, when I've spun
My last thread, I shall perish on that shore;
But swear by thyself that at my death thy Son
Shall shine as He shines now, and heretofore:
And having done that thou hast done,
I fear no more."

DONNE.

THE incorporation of the Son of God with our nature, and His endurance of death for our sake, removed, incidentally we might almost say, an innumerable host of evils; and this train of effects reached even to the gate of eternity. But there, the soul passes on, from trial to retribution, bearing with it whatever has been acquired through its own inward and voluntary union with its Saviour. Death, as a physical or mental change, is greatly lightened to all by the death of Christ; death, as an event in the life of the immortal spirit, is what it is rendered by the character which in this life that spirit has put on. The physical nature reaps, from the universal union with Him who assumed it, a physical immortality; the sensitive soul shared, for the same cause, a corresponding relief; but the spiritual nature must be spiritually united to Him with its own glad consent, that the spiritual victory which He has won may be its everlasting possession.

This victory is signified at the deathbed of the believer. To faith, the triumph of the love of God in

Christ over all which makes death terrible, is a sublime reality, a fact which in its operation becomes a part of our own history. There exists amongst men a general persuasion that the dying hours of a Christian must manifest, more or less, his participation in the victory. The persuasion is just; for, although there must be exceptions, and there may be many, the results of special counteracting influences on the mind, yet it is the nature of faith to shed around the soul the true light that is come into the world, and that light does disclose the abolition of death for all who are in Christ Jesus.

But if, for the believer, the terrors of death are finally overcome, they are first seen with the clearest glance, in their own vastness. It is perfectly true, therefore, that many a profligate man has been braver than many a Christian. They who think of death as only a momentary shock, or only the end of this life, and think no farther; or they who deride or deny all which has been revealed of a retribution after this life, may advance through years of health, and perhaps to the end, without evidence, perhaps without consciousness, of serious alarm. But hardly can a Christian be found, who has not at some time looked on death with solemn anxiety. Many have borne this load along with them almost to the end; and a heavy and fearful mist has ever hung around their utmost horizon. If their perception of the manner in which a sinner must be justified before God has been indistinct, these fears have been so much the more natural and unconquerable. An illustrious example of this habitual gloom was the devout and most thoughtful and strong-minded Doctor Johnson. It had been very much the frame of the excellent Jones of Nayland. Even the pious Halyburton, whose deathbed was a scene of unsurpassed and utter triumph, spoke then of himself as one "that had been many years under the terror of death." Not without reference to such solemn dread, is a petition placed in the Litany for deliverance "in the hour of death;" and many a pastor has heard from many a conscientious Christian, when that hour arrived, the joyful acknowledgment that a mighty weight of apprehension was now, for the first time, entirely lifted from the soul.

To the eye of the believer, death is the transition from the world of duty to the world of recompense. His mind has been overwhelmed with the unutterable magnitude of that decision which, although not first made at that point, can thenceforth be no more reversed. He is very conscious of a deceitfulness within himself, and still more of the vast distance between his own attainments and the purity of that fellowship to which he aspires. What, then, if this distance should prove impassable at last, and all his hope only a flattery from within? The prevailing sentiment of most believers, throughout their course, is doubtless that of hope and cheerful content; but in our present state every feeling is mingled and shaded; and it is impossible that sin and weakness should not sometimes and to some degree change hope into anxiety. A common experience has been uttered by John Newton: "We may anticipate the moment of dissolution with pleasure and desire in the morning, and be ready to shrink from the thought of it before night."

Still, hope is commonly in proportion to faith; and through his life the Christian, justified by faith, rejoices in hope, looks on to the end, and glories even in tribulation. For him, the cloud which closes the prospect is never a mere uncertain vapour; if it is not dark and awful, it is gilded and enwrapped and pierced with rays of glory. The habitual conviction of his mind is that which was expressed by St. Paul; just so far as he can say, "To me to live is Christ," just so far he knows that to him "to die is gain." He is sure that the victory over death and the grave has been won, and that, if he is but in Christ at last, nothing in life or death, nothing present or to come, can separate him from the love by which that victory was so dearly purchased.

Thus he passes on, with dazzling hopes, sometimes shaded by fears, and always softened by humility. Thousands on thousands of Christian deathbeds admonish him to fear transgression only; since then no other fear will haunt his departure. And there can hardly be a more signal illustration of the vicarious redemption than this, that the event which the sinless Saviour anticipated with a spirit so straitened, a soul so troubled, and prayers so agonizing, should be expected by sinful men with such calm and confiding and exulting peacefulness.

XLVII.

Providences in Christian Death.

> "Thou know'st the secret wishes of my heart:
> Do with me as Thou wilt—Thy will is best."
>
> SOUTHEY.

IT is no part of the common, Providential system that believers, rather than unbelievers, should receive any other than the general, natural warnings of the approach of dissolution. Such knowledge as that of the Lord Jesus, who, though deliverance was in His control, "knew that His hour was come that He should depart out of the world," is not given to His followers. But, in the ages of miracles and of inspiration, St. Paul could affirm as a certainty, while yet in prison, that "the time of his departure was at hand;" and St. Peter could say that he "must shortly put off this tabernacle," in the manner which his Master had shown him by an express prophecy.

Intimations, not wholly dissimilar, are said to have been sometimes given in later ages. Polycarp dreamed that his pillow took fire and was consumed; and, as the persecutors were already seeking him, he inferred, what seemed rather improbable, that his martyrdom would be, as it was, by fire. In prison, Perpetua of Carthage saw in dreams what was interpreted by herself and her companions as indicating their fate and the order of their departure, as it soon befell. Gregory the Great relates that his aunt, St. Tarsilia, the day before she was seized with her last sickness, had a vision in which her ancestor, Felix, one of the bishops of Rome, invited her to a glorious habitation. It was said that Bishop Hall punctually foretold the very night of his death.

More often, sayings have dropped from good men, as they unconsciously drew near to sickness or sudden death, which seemed as if a higher mind had gently led their thoughts to themes that beseemed a pilgrim almost in sight of Jerusalem. In private recollection, such examples will occur to many, and they are frequently noted in the sketches of the lives and deaths of Christians. It may be through the operation of some of the more subtle elements in our corporeal system, suggesting rather to feeling than to thought the approach of change, and the nearness of that incorporeal world which sometimes seems to touch us through our nervous constitution. Or it may be through some actual intimation from invisible ministers of good, as a guardian conducting a child to the home which he had left in infancy, might prepare his mind, without informing him, as he drew towards the end of the journey. However it be, the fact is sufficiently frequent to have been often noted, and is too readily explained to permit the charge of superstition. Doctor Arnold died very suddenly; but the last words of his last lecture, on the preceding day, were a blessed anticipation of waking in the likeness of Christ; and the last entry in his diary, before he lay down to the sleep from which he only awoke to die, was of a solemn review of his whole life, and a sober, pious contemplation of the future. "And then," he wrote, "what is to follow this life?" The last recorded conversations of Bishop Heber, before his sudden transition, were on the highest and most enrapturing themes, the riches of the Gospel, the duty of bearing it to the heathen. Doctor Milnor, a few hours before his not less sudden removal, was congratulated upon his healthful appearance, but said that he had that within which admonished him to be always ready. President Burr, on New-Year's Day, preached on the text, "Thus saith the Lord, This year thou shalt die," and died in the same year; and, when this fact was mentioned to his successor, President Davies, he said that it ought not to be viewed as premonitory, but as very remarkable; and, on the New-Year's Day a few weeks before his own death, preached on the same text, and thus, as he said in his sickness, undesignedly preached his own funeral sermon.

Good men have been permitted, consciously or unconsciously, to choose the place and occasion of their end. In other instances, remarkable correspondences have appeared, which seemed to have a signification and to speak a special appointment. Meletius died during the Council of Constantinople, which had been called for the express purpose of healing the schism in the Church of Antioch, where he presided as one of the rival prelates. So Buonaventura, too, died during the Council of Lyons, at which few were equally eminent. Proterius, Bishop of Alexandria, was massacred on Good Friday in the church where he was at prayers. St. Francis of Paula died also on Good Friday; Conrad Pellicanus on Easter-Day; and Bede on Ascension-Day, just as he had finished the last verse of his version of St. John. St. Benedict was carried into the church, and there died, after receiving the eucharist. St. Columba died there during the office of matins. St. Oswald passed his last night there, then washed the feet of several poor men, and expired. So died there, before the altar, Fructuosus of Braga, after a night on that spot. Pope Celestine the Fifth, a simple hermit, whom others, for their own ends, had placed in the papal chair, and presently displaced, expired while he was engaged in saying his office; and one of the best of the Popes, Leo the Ninth, on the day before he died, delivered a discourse on the resurrection, at the very spot which he had chosen for his burial. Thurstan, Archbishop of York, an iron man in an iron age, celebrated the vigils in commemoration of the dead in Christ, chanted, himself, the *dies iræ*, sank upon the pavement, and in the presence of his monks breathed his last. In the earlier times of the Anglo-Saxon church, Cedwalla, a devout prince, set out for Rome, whence Christianity had come to his people. It was his wish to receive baptism there, and the wish was granted; but he lived but a week after his baptism. Aldhelm, on a journey of duty, sickened, was removed into a church, and there commended his soul to God, and died. Nicholas Ferrar died in an ecstasy of devotion, at the very hour of the night at which he had been accustomed for many years to rise for midnight worship. The pious Countess of Warwick, who had often wished to die praying, died praying. Bishop Jewel, who had wished to die preaching, was on a preaching journey through his diocese, when he was smitten with a rapid disease, and returned no more. The heavenly Archbishop Leighton had expressed a wish that he might die on a journey and at an inn, and it was granted.

It is not rash to believe that He, without whom not a sparrow falls to the ground, should order the fall of His servants with a tender care even for the fulfilment of their wishes, where no higher end would thus be counteracted. No such special adaptation can commonly be expected to be visible. The same experience which discloses a few examples that arrest our notice, includes multitudes that show no peculiarity of circumstance and no striking significance of arrangement. But those few may be designed to remind men, from time to time, of the perpetual guidance of a Providence in whose sight the death of His saints is precious. That we may know the direction of footsteps, it is enough to see them at intervals, even though far between.

XLVIII.

Removal of the Fear of Death.

"For this poor form
That vests me round, I give it to destruction,
As gladly as the storm-beat traveller,
Who, having reached his destined place of shelter
Drops at the door his mantle's cumbrous weight."

BAILLIE.

IT may be stated as an almost universal experience of the pious, that death, as it draws nearer, loses much of that awful solemnity which it wore at a greater distance. In part, this is the effect of a natural law, which governs our passage through all, or almost all, the events of our earthly being. Everywhere, nearness and familiarity prepare the mind to encounter the evils which it dreaded. Some are found far less than their appearance; for others, corresponding resources develop themselves at the shock. Man, as he approaches the change of worlds, meets only what his Creator has given him an inward capacity to bear, unless he dies in his sins, and so encounters that which is more than mere death. But when the sting is actually taken away, when death is really but

———"a path that must be trod
If man would ever pass to God,"

it is not wonderful that the fear also should go by like a mist which the morning sun must dissipate, because it is only the growth of night. Through life, it is often permitted to remain; and the younger we are, and the more remote the grave may seem, the deeper appears its mysterious solemnity. The further we plunge, too, into worldliness, the more depressing is the chill produced by sudden anticipations or imaginations of our latter end. It is necessary that it should be so, lest all thoughts of eternity should be lost. Even when the steps are turned towards heaven, the same cloud must be suffered to retain more or less of its darkness, lest the heart, still too frail, should forget its own manifold dangers. During our exposure to temptation, we need the humility, the caution, the vast seriousness of spirit which such a dread must maintain; to number our days must persuade us to apply our hearts to wisdom. But, when this necessity is past; when the prize is no longer at hazard; a strong and victorious faith sees nothing in death which should inspire anxiety. A certain human weakness remains, like that with which a painful operation is anticipated; and very often, too, distrust of itself struggles in the heart against confidence in God. Still it is generally observed, that good men feel and declare, sometimes even with surprise, that the apprehensions which they have shared with others, and which have, more or less, haunted them through life, are much alleviated, or quite dissipated, as the hour of departure draws on.

Almost all Christian pastors may have heard from some aged believer, yet in health, the declaration of a readiness to bid the hour of death a perfect welcome. Such Christians have spoken of lying down, night after night, with the thought that they might never wake, and with entire willingness that any slumber should be the slumber of the grave. The prayer of Bishop Ken, which they have often repeated, has been fulfilled:—

"Teach me to live that I may dread
The grave as little as my bed."

There are many examples of piety in appearance not less elevated, at a far earlier period of life; but it may be doubted whether this absence of all anxiety is so completely seen in any to whom their age and health permit the thought that their end may be distant. It seems one appointed effect of the approach itself. For, in the aged and the young alike, the mortal sickness, in its later stages, often clears away every alarm.

The excellent Sir William Forbes, the biographer of Beattie, uttered this: "Tell those," said he, "that are drawing down to the bed of death, from my experience, that it has no terrors; that, in the hour when it is most wanted, there is mercy with the Most High; and that some change takes place which fits the soul to meet its God." When the loyal Earl of Derby came to his execution, although he had said in previous times, that he could die in fight, but knew not how it might be on the scaffold, he now said that he could lay his head on the block as cheerfully as on his pillow. "Let my people know," said the pious Archdeacon Aylmer, "that their pastor died undaunted, and not afraid of death: I bless my God that I have no fear, no doubt, no reluctation, but an assured confidence in the sin-overcoming merits of Jesus Christ." So said President Finley, "Give my love to the people of Princeton; tell them that I am going to die, and that I am not afraid of death." "Oh, do not fear to die," said Mrs. East, in dying; "you will find the word of God sure; all will be fulfilled, and you will find it so." Doubtless the aspect of death is softened by exquisite suffering before its arrival: "I were miserable," said Donne, "if I might not die." In the venerable Mr. Adam, of Wintringham, under severe infirmities, it became great weariness of life. While his attendants were moving him, he said, "If I could be sensible what these persons are doing when they place me in my coffin, it would be one of the most agreeable impressions I have ever known." But it is infinitely more than this when one can say, like Halyburton, "I, a poor, weak, timorous man, once as much afraid of death as any; I, that have been many years under the terror of death, come now, in the mercy of God, and by the power of His grace, composedly and with joy to look death in the face." This change is what has been named "dying grace, kept for a dying hour." St. Ambrose said, in words which other saints, like Jewel, have made their own, that he "neither had so lived as to be ashamed to remain, nor, when he remembered the goodness of his divine Master, was he afraid to die." A pious clergyman, half an hour before he died, whispered, "The fear of death is quite taken away." Another expressed a slight anxiety at the very fact that his awe had so departed. A venerable divine of New England, just before his end, declared that he was conscious only of an awfully solemn and intense curiosity to know the great secret of death and eternity. So spake the philanthropist Howard, "Death has no terrors for me." William Jones, of Nayland, who had always looked forward with trembling, said joyfully in the hour of dissolution, that, if this were death, he had never conceived of death before. So said the pious Lady Glenorchy, almost as her last words, "If this be dying, it is the easiest thing imaginable."

It often appears, that exactly those from whom constitutional courage or philosophic firmness could least be expected, go down into the valley of death with most complete triumph over their past apprehensions. In the recollections of many, some such example of a dying friend will occur with convincing power and tenderness. They tell us that this absence of fear is no fruit of nature, of habit, or of strenuous effort; but the gift of Him who gave to death its terrors, when He made it the doom of sin; and who takes those terrors away, when sin is blotted out through the blood of the Lamb.

XLIX.

Conversion on the Bed of Death.

> "Thou didst bear away from earth
> But one of human birth;
> The dying felon at thy side, to be
> In Paradise with thee."
>
> MILMAN.

THAT the approach of death should sometimes be attended by very mighty effects on the human character, is not only not surprising, but quite unavoidable. That these effects should sometimes issue in that inward transformation through which a sinner, till then impenitent and unsanctified, might be made meet for an inheritance with saints in light, would seem, to one who has observed the power of events over the soul, rather probable than wonderful. If the contemplation of death at a distance so often leads men to earnest thought, to prayer and to God, as mighty, at least, might be the contemplation of death at hand. No Christian could well deem a deathbed repentance impossible, even if he should doubt its acceptance.

But its acceptance, or the possibility of its acceptance, can now be doubted by no Christian. One instance is given by Holy Scripture; and it was under circumstances which were plainly designed to teach that, on this side of the grave itself, no mortal shall assign limits to the mercies of his Saviour. The malefactor on the cross blasphemed even after he hung in agony by the side of Jesus; but in those few dying hours repented, sought forgiveness, was forgiven, and obtained the assurance of immediate admission into Paradise. It has been said, and often repeated, that one such instance is recorded in the word of God, that none might despair, and but one, that none might presume. Yet, in that one, such as it was permitted to be, lies the force of a million. Had any dying penitent tasked himself to imagine a sufficient pledge of the possibility and the acceptance of a true repentance at that hour, he could have imagined nothing beyond such an example as that of the thief upon the cross.

Perhaps we fear too much the injury from the perversion of the example. The same injury may proceed from the hope of any future repentance; and among the multitudes who hope some day to repent, very few can distinctly intend to delay it to a deathbed. The Christian church, however, has never hesitated to renew, at the eleventh hour, and even after the eleventh hour, the call of the great Master of the vineyard. Always, the minister of Christ has gone, with the words of pardon for the penitent, even to the scaffold of the most hardened, remembering what manner of death Christ died, and who died with Him and was saved. As little have any refrained from preaching the Gospel at the bedside of the expiring sinner.

Doctor Johnson once quoted, with approbation, an epitaph on a person who died by a fall from a horse:—

> "Between the stirrup and the ground
> I mercy sought—I mercy found."

The supposition may have been a perilous one for thoughtless minds; but it proceeded from a thoughtful mind, measuring, or rather forbearing to measure, a solemn possibility. But, in the more common conversions of the sick-bed, although of those who recover so many turn back to perdition, yet not a few persevere, and prove the depth of their change by its fruits in their subsequent lives. Though those who die can give and receive no such assurance, yet analogy may persuade us that the inward resolution may have been so much the more thorough as the peril was more imminent. "I trust," says John Newton, "the power of His grace and compassion will hereafter triumphantly appear, in many instances of persons who, on their dying beds and in their last moments, have been, by His mercy, constrained to feel the importance and reality of truths which they did not properly understand and attend to in the hour of health and prosperity. Such a salutary change I have frequently, or, at least, more than once, twice, or thrice, been an eyewitness to, accompanied with such evidence as I think has been quite satisfactory. And who can say such a change may not often take place when the person who is the subject of it is too much enfeebled to give an account to bystanders of what is transacting in his mind?" Many a Christian reader recollects the narratives of the last days of Struensee and of John Cowper.

The uncertainty which must almost always hover over such repentance, the frequency of delusive hopes and transient changes, and the mighty weight of improbability, that any one individual will have time, and opportunity, and warning, and strength, and grace for a change like these, are as striking to the reflecting reason as is the guilt of relying on such an expectation to the honest heart. They who can pervert such a truth as the occurrence of these conversions may pervert any other; and the truth must not be disguised for the sake of any perversions, especially when it so magnifies the unsearchable riches of that mercy which is all the hope of all.

L.

Diversity in Christian Death, from Difference of Belief.

> "One army of the living God,
> To his command we bow:
> Part of the host have crossed the flood,
> And part are crossing now."
>
> WESLEY.

EVEN amongst those who abide in the same hope, it is impossible that the feelings, at the approach of death, should not be varied in degree by the diversities of doctrine, opinion, association, and custom. That general removal of its terrors, which is the natural and designed fruit of belief in the redemption, may thus be aided or counteracted. The light shines alike, but it is variously admitted; sometimes only in part, sometimes through a medium by which it is broken and confused, or discoloured and bedimmed.

Amongst pious Calvinists, the tone of peace at the last is very often a particularly firm, though deeply humble, sense of safety; but sometimes, too, it has been a painful struggle against doubt, despondency, and oppressive apprehensions. The mind of Cowper was clouded till his dying day, and, when his features settled into the quietness of the grave, his affectionate friends could do no more than to imagine that they saw in them the index of "a calm composure, mingled with a holy surprise." Under any system of religious belief, his intellect would have suffered from its malady; but the exact form which the delusion took and even in death maintained, was borrowed from doctrines which seemed to distinguish between the secret and the revealed will of the Most High. Amongst pious Methodists, with their prevailing view of assurance, of the witness of the Spirit, and of perfected sanctification, and with the loose rein which they give to all natural expressions of exalted feeling, the common tone is more often than elsewhere one of jubilant triumph. Amongst pious members of the Anglican and the Lutheran communions, the general sentiment of ecclesiastical fellowship, the administration of the sacrament, and the use of fervent forms for committing the sinking frame and the departing spirit to a faithful Creator and most merciful Saviour, have impressed on this peace a kind of joyful, almost liturgical solemnity, so beautifully expressed in that hymn of Theodore Zwinger, composed on his death-bed and translated by Merrick:

> "The festal morn, my God, is come,
> That calls me to thy hallowed dome."

Amongst pious Romanists, while the confession, the absolution, the viaticum, and the extreme unction, may all tend to repress alarm, the peace of Christian hope must yet be deprived of its glow by the dim expectation of they know not what of purgatorial endurance.

In the devout humility of an ascetic spirit, St. Martin of Tours and the royal St. Louis caused themselves to be laid on beds of ashes when the last moment was nigh. In the same or a more superstitious spirit, some, in the Roman communion, have put on the coarse robes of some monastic order, as if to die in that profession. Others have insisted on being laid upon the hard pavement, or even in the attitude and in the depository of the dead, there and thus to die. With a more subdued and tranquil observance of accustomed forms, the celebrated Father Paul Sarpi folded his hands upon his bosom in the shape of a cross, and so expired; and in the same attitude the aged Bishop Jolly, of the Scottish Episcopal Church, was found alone and dead. Like Monica, the mother of Augustine, many have asked the prayers of survivors for their souls when they should be gone; and, in later times, it has been with indistinct and disturbed apprehensions of their need of such intercessions. A certain gloom, more or less intense, may shade the path even of the honest and safe believer, when he has become subjected to the influence of an unscriptural system.

The rigidness of one form of Christian thought and custom, and the warmth of another; the habit of meek submissiveness, and that of eager, affectionate obedience, are seen in their effects to the last. These effects may be united with peculiar traits of temperament; and such traits may incline the mind to one or another view of questions which have been variously regarded by Christians, or to one or another mode of habitual devotion. Charles the First went with calm dignity to the scaffold, after listening to the morning lessons of the Church of England, which, on that day of the calendar, related the crucifixion of our Saviour. Oliver Cromwell, if he can be named amongst those who have died in faith, is said to have strengthened himself in the time of death by recourse to his conviction that he had once been an heir of grace, and to the opinion that an heir of grace could never fall quite away. Some, like Bishop Bull, like Brentius, and like the pious Dr. Bedell, have solemnly affirmed what they had held, or taught, or written, even though their several doctrines may have somewhat differed. Others have even laid upon those whom they left behind, the solemn charge of dying persons, that they should never forsake the doctrine or communion to which they had themselves adhered in death. A lady of my acquaintance, whose piety was fervid, and was joined with a warm imagination, uttered in her last hours the hope that she might be permitted, if it were possible, to hold some guardian influence over an infant child just born into her family circle.

Every portion of the Christian church has furnished to the believer some means of solace and refreshment for his last warfare. From the days of the apostles, the elders have been summoned to pray at his bedside. Prayers and hymns for the chamber of death, and for the use of the dying themselves, are found in liturgical books and manuals of devotion, especially in those of Germany. The Holy Communion has been, by a custom very general in Christendom, the crowning preparation for the passage. So dearly has it been prized, that one of the martyrs under Queen Mary, a layman, made in his prison such arrangements as he could, and, praying that, as far as might be possible, his participation in the elements before him might be to him the enjoyment of the Lord's Supper, went thus to his crown with an invigorated spirit. The great Schleiermacher, in his last moments, sat up in his bed and administered to his friends and himself this sacrament of faith. It has been sometimes a relief to pour into the breast of a spiritual guide some special confession, and to receive the authoritative declaration of absolution on the supposition of true penitence; a declaration which cannot increase the real certainty of forgiveness, but only confirm the inward conviction of those whose heart condemns them not; and thus it is permitted by Protestant churches. The abuse of such aids may be serious and frequent; but nowhere does the Christian minister more feel his need to lean directly on the words of Scripture and the ordinances of Christ, and on the collective piety and experience of the universal church, than in the presence of death, and under the knowledge that scarcely a few days or hours are left for all which his labours can impart. If he sees, as he must, the influence of peculiar modes of thought and belief, or of various ecclesiastical usages and systems, in giving a tone and hue to the hope which triumphs at such a season, so much the more must he bless the lot which enables him to speak simply there the words of Holy Writ, to offer the prayers which have been uttered by innumerable saints, and to administer the cup of redeeming grace at the command of the Redeemer.

LI.

Diversity in Christian Death, from Temperament and Disease.

> "One after one shall follow thee,
> As pilgrims through the gate of fear,
> Which opens on eternity."
>
> WHITTIER.

WE can conceive that the transforming grace of God might, in life and in death, remove or suppress every influence of natural peculiarities or accidental associations; but such is not its custom. Sometimes, indeed, the most marked traits of the original outline seem quite to disappear, and the timid become undaunted, and the harsh have the meekness of little children. But, except where these natural traits have been very closely allied to such as were decidedly moral, the man has generally retained to the last much of that mental individuality which has such a colouring effect on the pure light of piety. This individuality gives to many a Christian death-bed a character quite distinct from that of others as evidently Christian.

John Newton and Thomas Scott were friends, and held the same doctrines; but the Christian life and death of Newton were like the balmy air of June; those of Scott like the bracing and often chilly breezes of November. Payson, nervous, imaginative, eloquent, variable, passed, at the approach of death, from many a long valley of humiliation, if not from the precincts of the fortress of despair, far up into what he termed the "land of Beulah," and the "delectable mountains." The pensive poet, Wilcox, struggled with fears at the very close. "I have some hope," he said; "pray for me that I may not be deceived; all my hope is in the promises of God in Christ Jesus." Bishop Dehon, dying still young, yet, after a life of patriarchal pureness from his youth, breathed forth, as almost his last words, "God of Abraham, Isaac, and Jacob!" and then, as his temper had always been lovely, "lay silent, with great loveliness in his eyes." Simeon, whose peculiar cast of mind had always prompted quaintness of expression and even an unusual enjoyment of the ludicrous, throughout a life of almost unsurpassed zeal and usefulness, carried this with him into his chamber of death; and said in his own way, just before he expired, "Do you see any sting here?" A most learned and conscientious man, Bishop Burgess of Salisbury, but of an unimaginative mind, said, in his last illness, "Oh, what a comfort there is in looking to Christ! I scarcely like to speak of looking to the cross; that is figurative; I want something substantial." On the other hand, Tasso, in the monastery where his closing days were spent in prayer, died clasping a crucifix; and multitudes of saints have delighted to have the image of the cross before the eye of the spirit in the act of departing.

An influence, like that of the natural temperament or of accidental associations, may be also ascribed to the character of particular diseases. Some, like paralysis, weakening the nerves, weaken also the power of self-control, and sometimes cause an appearance of great depression. Others, with the remedies which are applied, exalt the fancy by exciting the brain, and thus prepare the sufferer to utter glowing thoughts in glowing language. Some are attended with such prolonged and severe pain, that the wish to die becomes eager and habitual; others bring such exceeding languor, that the face of death is, even without an effort of faith, easy and placid, but no feeling appears ardent or vigorous. The disease which was fatal to Robert Hall had subjected him for many years to the torments of martyrdom; and, when the last moment rather suddenly came, it seemed almost an agreeable surprise. Whitefield, struggling with asthma, awoke in the night, saw himself unable to preach, as he had intended on the next day, soon felt himself dying, and passed his few remaining hours in a kind of wrestling conflict with his malady, and of wrestling prayer for his family, college, friends, and congregations. In the midst of delirium, many have rejoiced in the brightest glimpses of unearthly glories. Even then the mind of Bishop Wilson was filled with visions of angels. The thoughts even of those who seemed quite insensible, have disclosed, when for a moment of revival they could be seen, a sacred communion and peace to which, except for such a moment, the inactive senses denied all avenues of observation or expression.

But what a diversity in Christian death is thus effected by the diversity of disease! From him whose sentence of triumph is interrupted by the very stroke, and finished perhaps in another world, to him who sinks into a dream of years from which he only wakes for an instant while his soul is passing, peace has a thousand forms; but each is peace. There is frequently a tumultuous rushing of wild and troubled thoughts, the offspring of corporeal maladies; they pour along like clouds in a windy night, breaking the light of the moon, which yet pursues beyond them its calm, clear way. It has even been known, yet perhaps scarcely known, that disease should produce in men whose lives had left no room for doubt in a single witness of their faith, a gloom and even an apparent despair that enfolded their minds till reason disappeared. Scarcely can the triumph of the inner man of the heart, even over the worst darkness of the intellect, be more signally exemplified than in the consoling reflections which one of the brightest minds of a recent age communicated to another, Mackintosh to Hall, when the great divine feared the recurrence of a mental malady, from which he had suffered previous derangement. His friend brought to him Christian strength, which he, as a Christian, knew how to receive. They thought and spoke of passing into the temporary loss of intellect itself, as into a sleep, through which the protection of Him who slumbers not would not be wanting, and from which the spirit would emerge with elevated and expanded pinions. Even so perfect a victory is given to faith, over all the peculiar fears with which some forms of disease may encompass the season of departure. They can but be for a little while: their beginning is preceded by a filial submission, and their end is beyond all sorrows.

LII.

Conflicts in Christian Death.

"Oh, fear not Him who walks the stormy wave;
'Tis not a spectre, but the Lord!
Trust thou in Him who overcame the grave;
Who holds in captive ward
The powers of death. Heed not the monster grim,
Nor fear to go through death to Him."

CONDER.

OUR Redeemer said of His own night of agony, "this is your hour, and the power of darkness." It has been the persuasion, and doubtless the experience, of many of His followers, that some special contest with the temptations of their adversary, especially in the forms of distrust and despair, often awaits the dying. Perhaps it was for this cause, that the Reformers of the English Church, in that most solemn service which is performed at the grave, placed such words as these: "Suffer us not at our last hour for any pains of death to fall from thee." It might well have been believed that they who should be kept till the last hour in faith and obedience, would not then be forsaken. But, even if salvation itself could not then be endangered, the comfort and peace of the Christian might be much impaired; his testimony to the power of grace shaken by the onset; and at least a parting sting might be given by the serpent beneath his heel.

Of no such contest do many Christian deathbeds afford any intimation. Not seldom, all which is seen or told is peace; peace from first to last. The appearance, however, of a peculiar struggle within is sufficiently frequent and sufficiently marked, to be justly viewed as one of the spiritual phenomena of death. When Bucer, on his deathbed, was warned that he should be armed against the assaults of the devil, he answered, "I have nothing in common with the devil; I am only in Christ; God forbid that I should not taste the sweetest consolation." The Viscountess Falkland, a lady of exalted piety, had much feared these assaults, but was quite exempt. But the mild and placid Melancthon said at one time, "I have been in the power of death; but the Lord has graciously delivered me." George Herbert "fell into a sudden agony," and presently said "that he had passed a conflict with his last enemy, and had overcome him by the merits of his Master, Jesus." Hervey spoke of a great conflict which he felt within; but at last said, "The great conflict is over; now, all is done;" and said scarce any thing more, except that, now and then, he exclaimed, "Precious salvation!"

The occasions of this conflict may probably be very different. It may be a struggle with the innate love of life; for youthful piety, especially, can still enjoy the glory and beauty of this world beneath the sun. Even such a struggle will not be condemned by those who have seen the fading bloom of that most beautiful period, when all joys are most joyful, and have meditated much on the Saviour and His agony. Still more intense may be the strife of soul in fathers and mothers, before a young and dependent family is calmly left behind. In mothers, the victory, once won, is often so complete as hardly to leave a trace of the conflict, and scarcely is there any higher victory of faith; but the conflict itself may often have been proportionably severe, unless, indeed, the tender and compassionate Comforter had made it easy. Many pious hearts, too, shrink, at times, with an appalled timidity, from "the wide, the unbounded prospect" of an eternal existence; and an hour of heavy conflict may succeed the conviction that all is at hand. With others, "a horror of great darkness," altogether indistinct, may be the inward oppression. John Wessel was even tempted with doubts of the truth of that religion which he had loved and served; but, an hour after, said, "I thank God all my vain disputations are vanished; I now know nothing but Jesus and Him crucified." But commonly, perhaps, it is the conflict with that which makes the sting of death; with conscious sin, with recollections of guilt, and of the law, which is the strength of sin; a conflict in which, if the soul lose its hold upon the hand of the Redeemer, it must sink beneath the waters.

At such a time, such a conflict may well bear some resemblance to the agony in Gethsemane. The cup is felt to be one which, were it possible, the fainting, overwhelmed, quivering soul would wish to pass by its lip untasted. It is one of the most awful struggles of faith, probably the most awful, but the last.

LIII.

Reliance on Christ in Death.

> "And oh, when I have safely passed
> Through every conflict but the last,
> Still, still unchanging, watch beside
> My bed of death; for thou hast died!"
>
> GRANT.

THE reliance of the heart upon the love and grace of Christ becomes even simpler, firmer, and more intense in its last trial. If we need the mediation of the Son of God, then surely, if ever, must the need be felt; and if He is indeed the Saviour of sinners, how can a penitent sinner fail to cling then with all His soul to the assurance of His love, when all other supports fall all around? The Lord who loved us and gave Himself for us; who ransomed us with his blood; who went before us, for our sake, in the path of mortal suffering; who died, and dying overcame and abolished death; is seen by the eye of faith as the Good Shepherd, and guides with His rod and staff along the dark valley.

"I know whom I have believed," was the thought of the imprisoned apostle, when he expected his summons to martyrdom. "Yes, He is very precious to me," are the accents that are but whispered by one dying believer. "I am going to my Lord," exclaims another as he departs. "This day," said Bishop Jewel, just before he expired, "this day let me see the Lord Jesus." "Blessed Jesus," were the last words of the good Bishop Horne, whose sweet book on the Psalms has been the companion of so many prayers. "Come, Lord Jesus, come quickly," has been the cry of thousands, while each has sunk, as it were, into His everlasting arms. Other thousands have taken upon their pale lips the dying words of Stephen, "Lord Jesus, receive my spirit." The last words of the learned and pious Doctor Good were the completion of a sentence begun by another: they spoke of Him "who taketh away the sins of the world."

Even here, however, it is not commonly that spectacle of ardent, eager looking, as to the brazen serpent, which may have been earlier witnessed. Faith has become the habit of the soul, and thus is calmer and more like a natural, spontaneous sentiment. It is not so much the almost desperate grasp of the drowning man, who must perish if he lose but this one hold; it is rather as when a friend leans on a tried friend, and commits to him every interest, and life itself, without a question. But, as a testimony to that Gospel which has brought him thus far, and now more than ever lights the way, and for the satisfaction and instruction of all around, as well as to invigorate his own faith and hope by recurrence to their first principles, many a dying Christian disclaims all trust in his own righteousness, and declares his sole confidence in the atoning Mediator. To Him, indeed, all the holy ordinances which at any time surround the deathbed point alike. No prayer is offered there, but in His name; no other would accord with the inward pulsations of him who dies, or of those who see him die. The sacrament, which is taken as if in preparation for the last journey, is that of His body and blood. From him who clasps a crucifix to his bosom, with sincere though misguided devotion, to him who, also misguided, refuses the aid of all visible ordinances, but still believes Christ is "the only name given under heaven;" and the suggestion of any other hope would result in faintness of spirit and in shrinking dismay. The heart, in death, receives and bears an irrefragable testimony to those two sayings of the Lord, "No man cometh to the Father but by me;" and "Him that cometh to me I will in no wise cast out." Faith alone overcomes; the faith which unites to Him that giveth the victory.

LIV.

Love in Christian Death.

> "Oh, dearest friend, death cometh! he is here,
> Here at my heart! Air! air! that I may speak
> My hoarded love, my gratitude sincere!"
>
> SIGOURNEY.

THE softening influence of suffering and of the parting hour makes the chamber of death a scene of tender love. If at such a season the roughest hearts are melted, much more must Christian charity be then more than ever affectionate and complete. The difference in death-beds is not generally that between love and hate, but that between love which is merely earthly and love which is also heavenly. With the dying Christian, it is the very spirit of the skies. It tells how near he is to the land whose air he already breathes, drawing in health for the soul while the body sinks away.

What a tenderness spreads itself over the love of a believer for his friends, when he is to leave them behind! Every word of counsel is so precious, every request so sacred, at that hour, not only because it is the last, but because it is full of a love stronger than death. Oswald, a pious Saxon king, breathed out his soul on the field of battle with the words, "Spare, Lord, the souls of my people!" "Peace be with you," said the Reformer Musculus, and crossed his hands on his breast and died. "In this love and communion we are and remain one," said Schleiermacher to his family, just as he expired, after partaking with them the Lord's Supper. The great Lord Burleigh, in a letter written just before his death, expressed his desire to be in heaven, a servitor for his Queen and for the church. Whitgift, palsied and dying, could only say, "*Pro ecclesia Dei!*"—for the church of God! Who has read without a feeling of strong and admiring sympathy, how one of the English martyrs under Queen Mary, a married priest, clasped his wife and children, and said that he were no man who would not be content to die for such, for their legitimacy and fair fame? The inexpressibly affectionate looks of the dying, fix sometimes a recollection more precious than any treasures. Tender messages to the absent, grateful glances in return for little attentions, the fervent kiss, the sweet, indescribable smile, the grasp of the hand in the act of departure, who has not witnessed all these, if he has been often at Christian deathbeds?

This dying love for friends reveals itself peculiarly in the desire, the hope, and the assurance of future reunion. It reaches to the dead as well as the surviving, and exults with a peculiar rapture in the approaching meeting with such as stand already on the everlasting shore. A few hours before the death of Luther, he rejoiced in this prospect. "We shall, I think," said he, "be renewed in the other life, through Christ, and shall much more perfectly recognise our parents, wives, and children." Melancthon, a few days before his death, told Camerarius that he trusted their friendship should be cultivated and perpetuated in another world. Cruciger, another of the school of the Reformers, spoke in his last hours, of meeting and recognition. Caspar Olevianus, a divine of Heidelberg, when his son had been summoned to see him before he should die, sent to him also the message, that "he need not hurry: they should see one another in eternal life." So Joseph Scaliger spoke of "soon meeting and embracing, no longer the subjects of age and infirmity." "What pleasure there is," said the pious Mrs. East, "in the thought that we shall together adore the Saviour; and that, if permitted, I shall gladly welcome you on your admittance into heaven." Recollections of dear, departed friends come often with such a vividness that, looking on, we are almost persuaded to deem them near. The aged Hannah More, in her last distress, stretched out her arms, as if catching at some object, uttered the name of her deceased sister, cried "joy!" and sank into a state from which she never revived.

But the same heavenly love reaches to enemies, and forgives and prays, as Jesus prayed and forgave. The first martyr, Stephen, followed in this the very footsteps of his Lord, beseeching Him that the sin might not be laid to the charge of the murderers. It has been the prayer of many and many a Christian on the scaffold and at the stake and in the dungeon. The martyr, St. Lawrence, on his bed of coals, is said to have prayed for the conversion of Pagan Rome. "O Lord, open the King of England's eyes," said Tyndal, as the flames rose around him at Antwerp; flames lighted through the machinations of that king to consume, even on a foreign shore, the translator of the New Testament. It has even become a custom with those who have suffered innocently, or for political acts for which they were not condemned by their own conscience, to declare their forgiveness of such as had brought them to their end. All Christians deeply knew, in the hour of leaving all, that for the unforgiving there could be no forgiveness, and no home in the world of peace. But no Christian, on the verge of glory, can feel a less heavenly wish than that his worst enemy may be, by his repentance, the occasion of joy in heaven.

That same celestial spirit goes out, at such an hour, in longing prayers for the triumph of the kingdom of God on earth and the salvation of all. An aged Christian, when his pastor inquired for what he should specially pray at his bedside, answered,

"With love which scarce collective man can fill,"

and as if all was granted already for himself, "pray for the whole family of mankind." Edward the Sixth, with his dying breath, supplicated that his kingdom might be delivered from "Papistry." "Let the whole earth be filled with his glory," were the words with which the gallant Earl of Derby gave the signal that the axe should fall. Almost the same words broke from the lips of a sweet, pious child just as her spirit passed. It is the utmost ascent of the human heart, before it has lifted its anchor for the voyage of eternity.

LV.

Contrite Peace in Christian Death.

"The last end
Of the good man is peace. How calm his exit!
Night-dews fall not more gently to the ground,
Nor weary worn-out winds expire so soft."

BLAIR.

WHETHER emerging from conflict, or spared it entirely, the soul of the dying believer is generally irradiated with a peculiar grace and peace. If this be in its nature no more than what he has often enjoyed, its degree is higher and more perfect. Already, he seems in spirit to rest from his labours. The world of temptations has passed by. All gentle and pure feelings have undisturbed control; and the most exalted of his thoughts and the sweetest of his affections alone remain. Shut by the necessity of his weakness, as well as by his own wishes, from all except a few friends, he communes with another world and prepares to go forth.

It is of the nature of Christian peace to be profoundly humble; for it flows from the hope or sense of forgiveness, and forgiveness supposes a most abasing conviction of unworthiness. If this be strong in life, it can but gather fresh strength when the soul is waiting its speedy call into the more immediate presence of the Lord of glory. The fifty-first Psalm, known as the *Miserere*, has often been the prayer of dying saints. Rogers said it on the way to the stake. It was repeated by Bullinger on his departing day. It was read at the bedside of Arnold a few moments before he expired. When a minister spoke to the illustrious Grotius, in his sickness far from home, of the prayer of the publican, he cried out, "I am that publican; I place all my hopes in Jesus Christ." The innocent and saintly Archbishop Usher, after a very long life of godliness, uttered these as his last words, "O Lord, forgive me, especially my sins of omission."

But it is not to be supposed that the lowliest depths of confession would be trodden at the very last. Those whose repentance has been delayed till then, if, touched indeed, they obtain the pardon which they passionately implore, yet can hardly be cited as examples which may illustrate "how a Christian can die." Through the regrets and pains of penitence, the faithful Christian has passed, before he lay down for his final rest. Humility, rather than humiliation, is the character of his experience, after he has withdrawn within himself and contemplated the close. When his sickness began, or when it first wore the aspect of approaching death, he may have bowed his spirit in one solemn act of confession. If he received the Holy Communion, he earnestly sought to bring that cordial penitence for all his guilt, which has the promise, as well as the seal, of perfect pardon through the blood that cleanseth from all sin; but on that promise he relied, and, though he feels himself a sinner, he feels himself a sinner forgiven. Not to the deathbeds of the pious must we look for anguish and deep shame, for the return of the prodigal or the lamentations of Peter when the cock crew: these are already past. The prodigal is in the arms of his father; the penitent has heard from his Saviour the blessing, "Peace be with you:" and the contrite lowliness which remains, though the deepest and tenderest, is no longer pain.

LVI.

Light in Christian Death.

"Stronger by weakness, wiser men become
As they draw near to their eternal home:
Leaving the old, both worlds at once they view,
Who stand upon the threshold of the new."

WALLER.

THE idea that the departing spirits of good men are at times favoured with intimations, visions, or assurances which would on other occasions be held supernatural, is one which has often occurred to the thoughtful, and which is attended by no appearance of improbability. They who are on the border of two worlds might well look over from one, and catch some glimpses of what lies just within the other. Little proof would be asked by minds not firmly fond of incredulity. Is that little afforded by the last earthly hours of the saints?

The Saviour, in that parable which was designed to afford a glance beyond death, the parable of the rich man and Lazarus, intimated an approach and nearness of higher spirits at the season of departure. The patriarchal ancestors of Israel were possessed at that season with a divine power of prophecy, and spoke the destinies of their posterity. There is, therefore, a foundation for the belief that immortal faculties may receive some development before the boundary of death is crossed. To St. Stephen, certainly, a vision was displayed and heaven was really opened. To St. Peter it shown, that he must shortly put off his mortal tabernacle. We are easily prepared to suppose that something not dissimilar may have been granted to the faithful but uninspired followers of such leaders. Many are the narrations which sustain a belief so natural and so authorized. Even if some remain unconvinced, and although extraordinary instances are not to be cited as proofs of an ordinary rule, it will still be difficult for most Christians not to recognise a design in a class of facts so numerous and of such surpassing interest.

Basil of Ancyra, who was put to death in the time of Julian the Apostate, foretold the approaching death of the emperor; and George Wishart, at the stake, foretold that of his persecutor, Cardinal Beatoun. The words of Latimer may be regarded as uttered in the same spirit, when he said, "We shall this day light such a candle in England, as, by God's grace, shall never be put out." To John Knox, his friends confidently attributed a power of prophecy.

It is related of the death of St. Ambrose, that Honoratus, Bishop of Vercelli, was at the time in the house, in a distant room, and three times heard a voice, "Arise immediately, he is at the point of departure;" on which he hastened, gave him the sacrament, and saw him expire. Whether the voice was outward or inward, an actual interposition or a powerful impulse, the event has been in many an instance substantially repeated. Clergymen have hastened, under such an incitement, to the bedside of the dying; and friends have felt themselves irresistibly prompted to an interview which they have always remembered with thankfulness. It is impossible, when we speak of death and its circumstances, to discriminate accurately between the natural and the supernatural. What belongs to this world is natural; what belongs to the future world is supernatural; and in death they meet.

More interesting by far is the question whether the dying Christian has, before he crosses the boundary of worlds, experience of such "powers of the world to come" as are perceived by none but the dying. Often, like St. Augustin, such have requested, after their farewell words, to be no more disturbed, as if they were intent on something of indescribable earnestness. They have folded their hands, and fixed their gaze, and a calm smile, or an ecstatic joy, or a deep, deep intensity of contemplative adoration, has settled upon their features. So, Gellert died in silent prayer. Such scenes will be in the remembrance of many by whom they have been watched, and who felt as if they saw while one was passing in at the porch of the celestial temple.

Others, as they drew nearer to the end, have uttered their astonishment and joy at the new consciousness which was dawning. "Light breaks in!" exclaimed the pious Blumhardt of Basle, a little before he expired, "Light breaks in! Hallelujah!" Mrs. East, with "a look of dazzling and indescribable lustre," said at midnight, "He made the stars also," sank into sleep, and never awoke again. Melancthon requested not to be interrupted; when asked if he wanted any thing, said, "Nothing else but heaven;" and begged them "not to disturb his delightful repose." Rivet said, "I am come to the eve of a great and eternal day; I have learned more divinity in ten days than in fifty years before." Doctor Maclaine said, "I can now contemplate clearly the grand scene to which I am going: it appears to my mind very magnificent and very awful; there is no cloud in the prospect." Doddridge said, "Such delightful and transporting views of the heavenly world as my Father is now indulging me with, no words can express." Hooker fell into a kind of rapturous reverie, meditating on angels, their number, order and harmony. The countenance of Sargent, the biographer of Martyn, kindled into holy fervor; he spoke of "glory, glory," and of "that bright light," and, when asked, "what light?" answered, "the light of the Sun of righteousness."

With many, however, there has been a distinct denial of sensations beyond the sphere of common joy in the Holy Ghost. When Doctor Bedell was asked if he saw Jesus, he was already speechless, but answered significantly by pointing to his heart and to heaven, as if he had said, "there only." "I have no rapturous joys," said Rowland Hill, "but peace, a good hope through grace—all through grace." Œcolampadius, laying his hand upon his heart, as the rising sun broke in at the casement, said, "There is light enough here."

But others have seemed to themselves to feel and perceive much more. Nicholas Ferrar assured his friends that he had seen a heavenly entertainment. The Countess of Carbery had fears, but "passed into a kind of trance," and then "cried out aloud, Glory be to God on high! now I am sure I shall be saved." That excellent person, Lady Elizabeth Hastings, a little before she died, cried out, with sparkling eyes and an elevated voice, "Lord, what is it that I see? Oh, the greatness of the glory that is revealed in me! that is before me!" The accomplished Olympia Morata, an exile for her faith, said, as she sank in death, smiling with inexpressible sweetness, "I distinctly behold a place filled with ineffable light;" and her last words were, "I am perfectly happy." Doctor Bateman, a little before he died, said, with the sensations of a Christian physician, "I can hardly distinguish whether this is languor or drowsiness which has come over me; but it is a very agreeable feeling;" and died, crying, "What glory! the angels are waiting for me! Lord Jesus, receive my soul! Farewell!"

Gregory the Great tells that his aunt, in her agony, called out to make room for the Lord Jesus, whom she saw coming towards her; and so died. In just the same manner, Doctor Nelson relates, how a pious lady of St. Louis, after a strong spasm, that was strong enough to have been the last, said to her pastor in a faint whisper, "I was in sight of home, and I saw my Saviour!" Such instances, more or less striking, are innumerable, and something of this nature has perhaps fallen within the knowledge of almost every observer. We must not be bold in speaking of what none but the dying can have seen and felt; but certainly there is enough to persuade us, that many of those who, with clear minds and organs unoppressed, approach the shadowy barrier between two worlds, do breathe some airs from that which is beyond; have a solemn, joyous experience till then, in that degree, quite unknown; and perceive, as if within a curtain, the motions of forms, whose outlines and features they cannot discern.

LVII.

Last Words of Dying Christians.

> "With lifted eyes,
> And aspect luminous, as with the light
> Of heaven's opening gate, he strove to join
> His voice with theirs, and breathe out all he felt;
> But in the effort feeble nature sank
> Exhausted; and, while every voice was hushed,
> His fluttering spirit, struggling to get free,
> Rose like the sky-lark singing up to heaven."
>
> WILCOX.

THE boundary is now reached; the soul is ready to cross. We stand, and gaze eagerly, to watch the very last of those signs which the faithful leave behind; the utmost link between their pilgrimage here and the world of angels. Their last, last words, though perhaps less significant than many earlier sayings, are yet treasured with a peculiar sense of sacredness. But when they have been uttered with the consciousness that they were the last, they must indeed have a mighty attraction for those who know that they are to pass by the same spot, and who long to pass in the same hope or triumph.

No other words, probably, have been so often heard from that spot, as those, or nearly those, with which our Lord commended His spirit to His Father, and with which the first martyr called on the Lord Jesus to receive his spirit. These were the last words, substantially, of Basil, of Luther, of Tasso, of Edward the Sixth and Lady Jane Grey, of Latimer and Ridley, of

Cranmer and Hooper, of Herbert, of Martin Boos; and it might almost be said that they had become an established form, where the approach of the moment of departure could be perfectly recognised. An established form, indeed, of commending the spirit into the hands of "a faithful Creator and most merciful Saviour," is said at many bedsides; and, like Beza, many have died during such a prayer, or, like Bishop Bull, have only survived to breathe a single or a repeated Amen. Another closing cry of devout hearts has been, as with Bishop Abbot, in the words of St. John, "Come, Lord Jesus; come quickly." "Depart, my soul, depart," said the ascetic Hilarion, "why this delay? Dost thou fear death, after almost seventy years spent in the service of Jesus Christ?" Two Protestant martyrs, Esch and Voes, sang Te Deum in the midst of the flames; it is told of Huss and of Jerome of Prague, that they died singing hymns in the fire; and more than one pious minister of Germany has expired on a deathbed in the act of singing. The last words of many are simple expressions of readiness, or testimonies of peace, or affectionate farewells, or ejaculations of prayer. "Peace! peace! victory! victory! faith and patience hold out!" were amongst those of Payson. With the single exclamation, "My God! my God!" the spirit of Gustavus Adolphus passed from the storm of battle into the world of rest. The last words of Doctor Sharp, Archbishop of York, were from one of the divine poems of Herbert. Those of Sir Edward Coke were, "Thy kingdom come, thy will be done!" Doctor Hammond exclaimed, "O joyful day!" and never spoke again. So said Cardinal Baronius, "Now is the hour of triumph and of joy," and drew his feet together, and placed his hands upon his bosom, and expired. The poet, Earl of Roscommon, in the moment of expiring, cried out fervently, in the words of his own version of the *Dies Iræ*,

> "My God, my Father, and my Friend,
> Do not forsake me in my end."

James Andreæ breathed his last in answering to the question whether he believed a crown of life to be reserved for him, "Yes;" and Brentius, in the same word, in answer to the question whether he held the faith of the Gospel. Myconius died invoking the Son of God; Cruciger, in the act of supplication. The expiring breath of Lady Falkland was spent in two words of exhortation, embracing the whole duty of man, "Fear God, fear God!" Mrs. Shepard, whose prayer for Lord Byron, communicated after her death, so much moved him, whispered, last of all, "God's happiness! God's happiness!"

It is very often seen, however, that consciousness survives the power of utterance, and we watch to observe what feelings may possibly be signified, when the saint is thus actually in the very depth of the valley. Sir Matthew Hale, when he could no longer speak, was constantly lifting his eyes and his hands. When Knox was asked for a sign that he remembered the precious promises of God, he raised his hand, and died immediately after. Bishop Ferrar, before his martyrdom, declared to a friend that, if he saw him move or heard him utter any cry of pain in the flames, he might reject his doctrine; and he was enabled to fulfil the sign.

There are many who can tell with what strange joy and awe they have felt the pressure of a hand, or seen the ecstatic glance or illuminated countenance, when death had already so far prevailed, that no other token of what passed within was possible. Halyburton said to his friends, "When I fall so low that I am not able to speak, I will show you a sign of triumph, if I am able;" and, accordingly, when he could no longer speak, he lifted and clapped his hands. Doctor Nelson relates an example which, though but one amongst many, had in it circumstances singularly striking and convincing. An aged and exemplary Christian man remained, in faith, but without exhilarating readiness for his change, even till his sight and his hearing had ceased, while his anxious daughter sat by, painfully longing for that issue of the sun from behind the cloud, through which all might glorify the Redeemer in whom he had trusted. While he could yet hear, it was agreed between them, that if, at any stage of the passage, a foretaste of heavenly delight should be granted, he should give her with his hand a certain token. After his senses were all closed, and his breath had become obstructed, and he was plainly at the gate of eternity, he gave the token, and a smile of exultation lighted up his countenance.

Often, we seem to see the trace of such joy in the look of him who is already in his coffin, as if the last beam that played on the house of clay was the first from a brighter sphere. The face of Stephen, when his hour approached, was "as it had been the face of an angel," and so, no doubt, it appeared to the devout men who bore him to his burial. For the human eye there is no more; we should linger around the bed or watch the bier in vain.

PART THE FOURTH.

LVIII.

Transition in Death.

> "Gently—so have good men taught—
> Gently, and without grief the old shall glide
> Into the new: the eternal flow of things,
> Like a bright river of the fields of heaven,
> Shall journey onward in perpetual peace."
>
> BRYANT.

THE progress of the departed spirit is imagined with an intense eagerness of conjecture. Does it open its eyes at once, with sudden rapture or alarm, on a scene of unutterable wonders? Does it awake, as we awake, from the sleep of night, so gently that the mind is conscious of no struggle, and scarcely of the change from activity to slumber, and from slumber to activity again? Does it carry on a continuous thread of perception, and know at once the world which it has left, and the world which it has entered? Does it feel itself alone or amongst companions? Does the separation from this earth become wider and wider as it advances on the journey beyond the eternal hills? Can we attain to any conception of its sensations, its condition, or its prospects?

A strong impression of the human mind is, that the spirit which has departed is not at once very far removed. An influence seems still to hover near us: thoughts and dreams of strange distinctness seem like the spiritual presence of the dead. We linger long over the subsiding features which we have loved; and a communion which may be rather felt than proved appears prolonged for a little while.

There seems no reason to deny that those pious persons who have been restored after they had all but passed the gates of death, and those who have spoken when they were standing there, were really admitted to glimpses, though faint, of the nature of that joy into which one moment more must have opened their entrance. Their expressions are uniformly descriptive of a state of deep, ineffable, holy peace, and more than peace. Such is probably the state of the pardoned soul so soon as it is released from the body.

"This day," said One who was dying, to another who within a few hours was to die; "this day shalt thou be with me in Paradise." The transition, therefore, from earth to the place of bliss must be almost immediate; for it was not till just before sunset that the legs of the penitent malefactor were broken, and he expired. There is no indication of an interval.

But that there is an interval between earth and Paradise, however brief to the disembodied spirit, is apparently told us by the passage of Lazarus from one state to the other. "The beggar died, and was carried by the angels into Abraham's bosom." A natural supposition is here confirmed by the language of our Saviour. He speaks of transportation, and thus there must be transition.

He speaks, too, of companions and guardians; the

angels or messengers who carried Lazarus to his abode of bliss. They are present to receive the departing spirit; they accompany and guide it; they are ministering spirits still.

> "Thou art not alone; on either side
> The portal, friends stand guard."

It is no dream of the fancy, no poetic imagery, that shows them hovering near the deathbed of the just; but the very word of Him at whose birth and at whose departure into the skies angels were visibly present, and talked with men. In that spiritual state they are doubtless visible to the spirit. Often before the departure, it has seemed to hear unearthly music; and, in many legends, such strains are related to have been heard by the spectators.

An apostle, too, was once caught up into Paradise, and, without death, passed where death is the common passage. He knew not whether he was in the body or out of the body; but he "heard unspeakable words, which it is not lawful for a man to utter." It is probable that the very remembrances were but such as could not be communicated in language; perhaps such as no human thought could even convey in a distinct form across the boundary of worlds. We need not forget that such have been the dimly glorious recollections of those who have seemed to die, yet returned. Like Tennant, they have forborne to speak often of what they remembered; yet have felt a certain home-sickness for the land which they had but seen from afar. The employments and joys of that land seem too different from our own sphere to be here described or even with clearness conceived; but not too different to be capable of being united for a moment with the experience of mortal man, whether, like Paul, he enter in, or, like the others, stand on the borders.

But there is nothing in their experience to persuade us that the spirit opens its eyes in eternity, as with a shock of surprise, allied to alarm. The apostle was caught up, without even knowing whether he had left behind him his earthly tabernacle. If, as is probable, the soul in death feels the same transition, it is but as the continuance of life in another scene and sphere; as an unbroken thread passing gently up, though passing swiftly.

The rest is hidden.

LIX.

State of the Just after Death.

> "Isle of the evening skies, cloud-visioned land,
> Wherein the good meet in the heavenly fold,
> And drink of endless joy at God's right hand;
> There kings and subjects meet, and young, and old,
> Pure virgins, matrons chaste, and martyrs bold,
> Prophets, apostles, patriarchs, great and good,
> Many yet one, in union manifold."
>
> WILLIAMS.

THE souls of the just are blessed, from the period of their death, as the souls of the wicked are wretched; the former in Paradise, the latter in torments. So much the Holy Scriptures have revealed of the life which immediately follows death, and they have revealed little more.

When the ancients spoke in general terms of the world of spirits, without allusion to any diversity of abodes, they called it the unseen land, or gave it some similar designation, which repeats itself in their different languages. In the Scriptures of the Old Testament, this general designation of the general state of the dead is employed with the same wideness of significance. It was a vast unseen world; and usually, from its alliance to the grave, was described as if it were below.

In that world, the dead princes are poetically represented as welcoming the fallen sovereign of Babylon; in that world, too, the rich man sees Abraham and Lazarus far across the impassable gulf of separation.

In that world are "the spirits in prison." Into that world passed the soul of the Redeemer, though there it was not left. That world embraces alike the Paradise of the penitent malefactor and the chains and dungeons in which the lost await their final portion.

How different, how opposite, how inseparable, must be the regions of that one world, we could imagine from the extremes which are found in this, and we can learn from all that is told of their inhabitants. St. Paul exulted that "to depart and to be with Christ" was far better than to abide here, useful and blessed as he was, in the flesh; that though to him "to live was Christ," yet "to die was gain." But Judas Iscariot, after Satan had entered into him, after his guilt had been consummated, went, driven by despair, through the awful path of suicide, "to his own place." "The souls of the wicked, in their separate state," says Owen, "are perpetually harassed with the disquieting passions which they have impressed on their minds by their corrupt fleshly lusts." It is a thought which has often been urged, and sometimes has been expanded into an immense theory. The foundation is truth; and that truth is peculiarly terrible. Of those "who came out of great tribulation," it is written that "they are before the throne of God, and serve him day and night in his temple;" that "they shall hunger no more, neither thirst any more, neither shall the sun light on them, nor any heat;" that "the Lamb shall feed them, and lead them unto living fountains of waters, and God shall wipe away all tears from their eyes." Of one who "in hell lifted up his eyes, being in torments," it is written that he asked, and asked in vain, for one drop of water to touch the tip of his tongue and cool him in the flame. So different are the inhabitants, so different the habitations. Words and images could not be devised which should more thoroughly express joy and woe than those which are employed to describe the state of the soul after death. Its state, still later, when all is consummated, is expressed by the very same images and words. The prospect beyond the resurrection is only that of the same joy and woe, prolonged and made more intense, like twilight passing into day.

In all Christian ages, the mind, clinging to the substantial reality of these scriptural disclosures, has yet sought to give them a definitiveness more than their own. Irenæus was content to say that, since the soul of our Lord departed in that shadow of death where are the souls of the dead, the souls of his disciples also shall go into the place assigned them by God. But Tertullian, in his gross, literal spirit, supposes it to be beneath the earth; yet reckons Paradise higher than hell. Augustin distinguishes Paradise from heaven, though St. Paul was certainly caught up into Paradise at the same time as into the third heaven; and in this distinction he is followed by Bull, Whitby, and Doddridge, in their interpretations of that very passage. But the language of St. Paul decides that Paradise, the abode of the just, is not more scripturally represented as below than as above. Many of the early fathers, as Eusebius, Cyril, and Ambrose, carried out the Pagan imagery of Hades as a shadowy realm, into which Christ descended as a conqueror or a preacher of deliverance. Thus "his preaching to the spirits in prison" is interpreted by Clement of Alexandria, Athanasius, and Cyril. One of the earliest Christian writers says that there is one passage into Hades; but that, after passing this gate, the righteous journey towards the right, to the place called the bosom of Abraham ; the wicked towards the left, to a place of misery. Jerome describes all the patriarchs and Hebrew saints as below in Hades, and the gate of Paradise as closed against them, till Christ descended and burst it open, and something like this seems the opinion of Owen, who supposes them till then in a qualified bliss. So Chrysostom says that death before conducted into Hades, but now to Christ. Justin Martyr even supposed that all of them, like Samuel, were under the power of such evil spirits as were allied with the woman of Endor. Augustin, however, doubted whether the name "hell" was anywhere in Scripture employed of the abodes of the just. Hilary gives to the gulf, between the just and unjust, the designation of chaos. A certain confusion has ensued, as soon as even the wisest and holiest of men have attempted to divide and bound what the word of God has left indistinct.

But, amongst all this confusion, the general faith of Christians, drawn from that word, has ever been that, after death, the souls of the faithful live in the world unseen, in rest and joy; the souls of the wicked in remorse and despair ; that the former are in Paradise, in the bosom of Abraham, with Christ, in the blessed company of the just made perfect; the latter in the bondage and anguish which are emphatically and only within the gates of hell.

For both alike, this state is intermediate, as between death and the resurrection; and intermediate, as between this life and the consummated happiness or woe of the life which follows the judgment; but not intermediate, as if for either it were between bliss and misery. It was indeed a very ancient custom of the early church to include the blessed dead within the embrace of its general prayers, asking for them no more than their perpetual peace and glorious resurrection; and this in token of unbroken communion, not of needed intercession. "Not having any doubt at all," were the words of Charlemagne concerning Pope Adrian, "that his blessed soul is at rest; but that we may show faithfulness and love unto our most dear friend." Such prayers, and even the later prayers of the Roman communion, that the faithful departed "may not be condemned unto the everlasting pains of hell," are justified by Cardinal Bellarmine, the great defender of that communion, "Not as if it were not certain that they should not be condemned unto those pains, but because it is God's pleasure that we should pray even for those things which we are certain to receive." An idea found in St. Augustin, however, that those who "are saved, yet so as by fire," might endure a kind of purgation in the flames which shall precede the final judgment, grew in the course of ages into the unfounded conception of purgatory. Of that fiction it is only to be wished that it were as harmless as it is baseless.

The language of St. Ambrose fitly expresses the general belief of the earliest as well as the latest time concerning each of the pious dead. "Theodosius," he says, "being freed from doubtful fight, doth now enjoy everlasting light, and continual tranquillity; and, for the things which he did in this body, he rejoiceth in the fruits of God's reward; because he loved the Lord his God, he hath obtained the society of His saints."

LX.

Paradise between Death and the Resurrection.

"The dead are like the stars by day:
Withdrawn from mortal eye,
But not extinct, they hold their way
In glory through the sky."
MONTGOMERY.

THE abode and the condition of the departed just have indeed been disclosed but by glimpses, through the divine oracles. Still, a few most interesting features, which the longing mind would have imagined, have thus an ample confirmation.

Our thoughts would turn to the pure skies for the destined habitations of pure spirits. One of our race went visibly, without the common form of dissolution, to a glorious rest; and he was borne into the skies. Was he at once admitted into a higher world than saints who die and leave their bodies to the sepulchre? Here, the lines between Paradise and "the third heaven" fade away. The Saviour ascended in the body; but those who depart in Him are with Him, though their bodies rest in ten thousand graves. Moses died on Mount Nebo, and was buried in a valley of Moab, by unseen hands of angels; but he came with Elias, to bring together the law, the prophets, the Gospel, and the apostles on the mountain of the transfiguration. It would be difficult to avoid believing that either the body of Elias was left behind when he ascended, or that of Moses had been raised and glorified. They came to the summit of a hill, to a spot nearest to the skies, and from the skies they came; the skies, to which Elias had visibly gone; the skies, to which the Lord Jesus afterward ascended; the skies into which Paul was caught up; the skies, from which the Lord will come again, bringing with Him those who sleep in Jesus. Not in delusion, therefore, nor merely in poetry, do we speak of such as gone upward, as in heaven.

The appearance of Moses and Elias is also a proof of some knowledge of terrestrial events amongst the saints above. At that one point at least, on that one great occasion, the worlds of the departed and of the living were in contact. There is no cause for affirming that single instance to be the one sole exception on that side of the veil, as well as on this. Their state is higher than ours, and must embrace wider and deeper knowledge. They do not come to us, and therefore can tell us nothing which happens there; but we go to them, and therefore they may well receive information of all which happens here. They are exhibited to us in Holy Writ as "a cloud of witnesses," by whom we are compassed about; a mighty mass of spectators, like those who, as if in one thick cloud skirting the horizon, encompassed and overhung the lists where the racers toiled on towards the prize. Witnesses they assuredly are; and they seem to be represented rather as witnesses who evermore look down upon the struggle, than merely as those who are soon to know its issue. St. John "saw under the altar," or at the foot of that towering structure in the celestial temple, "the souls of them that were slain for the word of God, and for the testimony which they held: and they cried with a loud voice, saying, "How long, O Lord, holy and true, dost thou not judge and avenge our blood on them that dwell on the earth? And white robes were given unto every one of them; and it was said unto them that they should rest yet for a little season, until their fellow-servants also, and their brethren, that should be killed as they were, should be fulfilled." Both the cry and the answer suppose a knowledge of the course of events below; a knowledge and an interest. The interest, indeed, could never be doubted; for no pure and hallowed affection dies.

That it should ever have been doubted, whether the inhabitants of the spiritual world recognise each other in that abode, is but an example of the wide influence of unbelief, suggesting the strangest dimness wherever the Scriptures had not spoken in the most explicit words, even though the obvious reason for which the words had not been spoken was, that to speak them was needless. Why should not the departed recognise and be recognised? How can their very nature and being be so utterly changed that they should be able to exist in the same world, to remember, and to be a general assembly, a church, a society, without recognition? If the future life is the sequel and result and retribution of the present, how can recognition fail? Not a step can we proceed, not a conception can we form, not a statement of divine revelation can we clearly embrace, in our contemplations of the future life, without admitting or involving the necessity of mutual recognition as well as mutual remembrance and affection. Were Moses and Elias unknown each to the other? Did the martyrs below the altar utter the same cry, without knowing the history of their companions, each a stranger amongst strangers? Was Abraham a stranger to Lazarus, or was Lazarus seen and known by the rich man only? Could those who watch for souls render account for them, with joy or grief, and yet not know their doom? Could Christian converts be the "glory and joy" of an apostle at the coming of the Lord, if he knew them not? Could the patriarchs be seen in the kingdom of God by none but those who should be shut out? All proceeds on the supposition of just such knowledge there as here. It is probable, indeed, that the human soul must always clothe itself with form, even in the separate state; and such a form would bear the same impress which had been given to the mortal body. There is no extravagance in the wish of Doctor Randolph to know Cowper above from his picture here, or in the same thought as expressed in the verses of Southey on the portrait of Heber.

Only one objection is urged in reply: it proceeds from the feelings. It asks, how we could be happy, and know the objects of our earthly love to be absent. But with equal stress it may be replied, that it would be just as difficult to be happy while we could not know them to be sharers of our happiness. The dreaded sorrow of missing one cannot be escaped by supposing a state of forgetfulness towards others, through which we should miss all. For, if a still intenser forgetfulness were imagined, in which our own history in this life, with all recollection of all men should be lost, there could no longer be that identity of consciousness without which there could be no reward, or punishment, or individual immortality. Such suggestions should be met with a simple, humble faith, in that all-providing wisdom which can enable the human soul to forget all which it might be distressed to remember, can fill it with all holy and joyous meditations, and can, in a thousand ways, preserve the flowers of memory without its thorns.

Of the events of that long sojourn, of the progress of the soul, of its employments, for events, and progress, and employments there must be, only the slightest glimpses are afforded. "The veil," says Arnold, "is purposely drawn, that we might not seek to hold too close communion with the dead." Whatever may be the delusion of those who forget or disregard the great and impassable gulf which is fixed by death itself between the just and unjust, we need not hide from ourselves that centuries and even thousands of years cannot well be fruitless in the world of spirits. In a comparative infancy all enter there; in real infancy, many. A mighty development must be accomplished; perhaps a high and blessed education, the complement of all which was left unfinished here. "As we are here," says Owen, "in and by the word and other ordinances prepared and made meet for the present state of things in glory, so are they by the temple-worship of heaven fitted for that state of things when Christ shall give up the kingdom unto the Father." But it is hidden from us now, under general images of rest and peace; that state is shown, even in revelation, only by glimpses; glimpses, through which many have delighted to perceive, though uncertainly, a guardian instrumentality of the departed just in still serving the kingdom of God and the souls of their brethren here.

Even in glimpses of such a state, all which is deepest within us rejoices and will rejoice. The imagination and the heart long for more; but sanctified by Christian hope, they catch with exquisite delight the few, bright rays which the word of God reflects, as they fall from the scenes of Paradise.

LXI.

Resurrection of Christ.

"When by a good man's grave I muse alone,
Methinks an angel sits upon the stone;
Like those of old, on that thrice-hallowed night,
Who sat and watched in raiment heavenly, bright;
And with a voice inspiring joy, not fear,
Says, pointing upward, that he is not here.
That he is risen!"

ROGERS.

THUS death has reigned over all men, and must reign; and even the triumphant departure of the redeemed spirit, and its separate abode in the joys of Paradise, are still tokens of the fulfilment of the universal sentence. The Redeemer of the world has promised a consummation yet more complete, and in His own person has given the earnest. It was not possible that He who came to destroy death "should be holden of it;" that the body which was prepared for Him, and in which He bore our sins, should remain in the power of the grave; nor was even the common victory permitted, that His flesh should see corruption. Receiving but, it as were, a slight and momentary wound, such as a serpent may inflict on the heel that crushes its head, He conquered death, and him that had the power of death.

The resurrection of Jesus was probably instantaneous; but it had no human witnesses. When His followers approached the tomb, He was no longer there;

the guards had been smitten with a stupor of terror which was like death itself; and probably they neither saw nor heard while the stone was rolled away by an angel. The moment of reanimation was veiled from mortal view; we only know that the earth quaked; that angels were near; and that, when men beheld the spot again, He was risen.

A few hours after, at the utmost, he was seen by Mary Magdalene, near the sepulchre. He met the other Mary, and Salome, and they "held Him by the feet." On the same day He was seen by Peter, by Cleopas and another disciple, on the way to Emmaus; and, in the evening, by ten of the apostles, assembled at Jerusalem. With them He ate, and breathed upon them.

A week after, He met the whole eleven; and Thomas was permitted to touch the print of the wounds in His hands and His side. Again, He was seen on the shore of the lake of Tiberias, by Peter and Thomas, Nathanael, and James, and John, and two other disciples. At that time, He again took bread with them at their humble repast. Afterwards, on an appointed mountain in Galilee, He appeared to no less than five hundred believers, most of whom survived many years, to relate that wonderful meeting, and to convince mankind by their own readiness to suffer for what their eyes had witnessed. Once he was present, too, with one apostle alone, either James the son of Zebedee, or James the son of Alpheus. Through a period of forty days, He thus "showed Himself alive," by many signs, under many circumstances; and carried on with His apostles long and most interesting conversations, expounding to them the prophecies which had foreshown His death and resurrection. At the end of forty days, He was for the last time with the eleven; gave them His parting commands, and going out with them to the Mount of Olives, and to Bethany, thence in their sight ascended into heaven, and a cloud received Him from their gaze.

If the vision of St. Stephen in his dying moments can be explained without allusion to the resurrection of the Lord Jesus, not thus can we explain His appearance to St. Paul on the road to Damascus; for the apostle himself relates it amongst the instances in which the Redeemer had been seen after His resurrection.

Such a body of witnesses attest the great victory over the grave. It is attested, however, not only by pure apostles and faithful martyrs, who spoke that which they had seen, but also by every token of the presence of God in the Gospel and the church of Christ. That fact of facts is rather the keystone than the cornerstone of revelation; all the parts sustain it, and it upholds them all. "The Lord is risen," said the apostles; as the angels had said before, "He is not here, but is risen;" and every Sunday, and every Easter-day, and every baptism, in which men are "planted in the likeness of His death, that they may be in the likeness of His resurrection," and every Christian burial, transmits the same tidings with one more testimony. "If Christ be not risen," says every preacher, with Paul, "then is our preaching vain, and your faith is also vain." "But now is Christ risen from the dead." From that hour when the tomb of Joseph was opened to the first rays of the dawn, death was no more what death had been since the last sunset shone on Eden. Before, two human forms had been borne into the skies, without yielding to the common doom which consigns the body to the grave. Now, the grave had prevailed, and yet had been compelled to relinquish its prize. Body and spirit were reunited after their painful separation; and henceforth it was a part of the knowledge which rests not on faith alone, but on human sight, that both are immortal.

LXII.

Resurrection of Man in Christ.

> "Then, then I rose; then, first humanity
> Triumphant passed the crystal ports of light,
> Stupendous guest, and seized eternal youth,
> Seized in our name."
>
> YOUNG.

THE relation between the resurrection of the Lord and the everlasting destinies of men must be learned, if learned at all, solely from the Scriptures.

There His resurrection is ascribed to a special operation of Omnipotence. Our faith is in "the operation of God, who hath raised Him from the dead." God "loosed the pains of death," and "raised up the Lord Jesus;" and with remarkable frequency is the act named as that of the Father. "This Jesus hath God raised up;" "being by the right hand of God exalted." It was "according to the working of His mighty power, which He wrought in Christ, when He raised Him from the dead, and set Him at His own right hand in the heavenly places." He "brought again from the dead our Lord Jesus, that great Shepherd of the sheep, through the blood of the everlasting covenant." He "raised Him up from the dead, and gave Him glory."

But our Saviour also asserted that the power to effect His own resurrection dwelt in Himself. "Destroy this temple," said He of the temple of His body, "and in three days I will raise it up again." "I have power," He said of His own life, "to lay it down, and I have power to take it again: this commandment have I received of my Father."

He was, too, though "put to death in the flesh, quickened by the Spirit." "Made of the seed of David according to the flesh, He was declared to be the Son of God with power, according to the Spirit of holiness, by the resurrection from the dead." Thus, like the creation of the first man, Adam, the resurrection of the second man, the Lord from heaven, as well as His incarnation, is at different times ascribed to the Father, the Son, and the Holy Ghost.

The end of His exaltation was, "to be a Prince and a Saviour, to give repentance to Israel, and forgiveness of sins." He "was raised again for our justification." He "is ever at the right hand of God, and maketh intercession for us." "God raised Him up, and showed Him openly," and commanded His apostles to "testify that it is He which was ordained of God to be the Judge of quick and dead;" and "to Him give all the prophets witness." God "hath given assurance unto all men that He will judge the world in righteousness by that man whom He hath ordained, in that He hath raised Him from the dead." He "died, and rose, and revived, that He might be Lord both of the dead and living." "God also hath highly exalted Him and given Him a name which is above every name, that at the name of Jesus every knee should bow, of things in heaven, and things in earth, and things under the earth." He "is gone into heaven, and is on the right hand of God; angels, and authorities, and powers, being made subject unto Him."

It is in our nature that He has returned from the grave, and is exalted even to the throne of heaven. He took that nature upon Him that He might suffer with it, and then might lift it to life and immortality. His own promise was, "I go to prepare a place for you:" "where I am, there shall my servant be." He is raised from the dead, now no more to return to corruption:" He "dieth no more; death hath no more dominion over Him." He "died unto sin once, but in that He liveth, He liveth unto God." In this resurrection and life, He only precedes His people; and what they believe of Him, they must now believe of themselves. "I would not have you to be ignorant," says the apostle Paul, "concerning them which are asleep, that ye sorrow not, even as others which have no hope; for, if we believe that Jesus died and rose again, even so them also which sleep in Jesus will God bring with Him." "If the dead rise not, then is not Christ raised;" "but now is Christ risen from the dead, and become the first-fruits of them that slept. For since by man came death, by man came also the resurrection of the dead. For as in Adam all die, even so in Christ shall all be made alive." "The last Adam was made a quickening spirit;" "as we have borne the image of the earthy, we shall also bear the image of the heavenly." Thus, "if by one man's offence death reigned by one, much more they which receive abundance of grace and of the gift of righteousness shall reign in life by one, Jesus Christ." "If we be dead with Him, we shall also live with Him." "If so be that we suffer with Him, we shall be also glorified together." "He shall change our vile body that it may be fashioned like unto His glorious body." "To him that overcometh," is henceforth His promise, "will I grant to sit with me in my throne, even as I also overcame, and am set down with my Father in His throne."

Raised, therefore, from the dead, and exalted to the

right hand of the Father, for the justification and salvation of His people, He bears with Him the nature which He had assumed; and is the second head of the human family. In Him and with Him all men have the resurrection of the body. They die as the first Adam died: they shall rise again as the second Adam rose. If, here on earth, they have been morally renewed after His image, they shall rise to everlasting life: if they have rejected His mercies, to shame and everlasting contempt.

LXIII.

Body of Christ after his Resurrection.

"Heavy and dull this frame of limbs and heart,
 Whether slow creeping on cold earth, or borne
On lofty steed, or loftier prow, we dart
 O'er wave or field: yet breezes laugh to scorn
Our puny speed, and birds, and clouds in heaven,
 And fish, like living shafts that pierce the main,
And stars that shoot through freezing air at even—
 Who but would follow, might he break his chain?
And thou shalt break it soon; the grovelling worm
 Shall find his wings, and soar as fast and free
As his transfigured Lord, with lightning form
 And snowy vest—such grace He won for thee,
When from the grave He sprung at dawn of morn,
 And led through boundless air thy conquering road,
Leaving a glorious track, where saints new-born
 Might fearless follow to their blest abode."

KEBLE.

MANY questions of vast interest gather around the theme of the resurrection of Jesus. His body was the type of that which shall be received in the general resurrection; for He "shall change our vile body, that it may be fashioned like unto His glorious body."

In that body He was seen, was heard, was touched. He walked, He ate, He breathed upon the apostles. These offices and functions, natural in the present body, cannot be, in the future body, miraculous. They were performed with the express design of convincing the disciples that they really beheld their Lord in the body, and not an impalpable apparition. "Handle me," said He, "and see; for a spirit hath not flesh and bones, as ye see me have." The argument was not deceptive;

and such must be the body of the resurrection as was that body which they beheld and handled.

It was recognised, too, as the same which had bled upon the cross. The same wounds were seen in the hands, the same in the side; they were demanded by Thomas as the signs of identity; and as such they were displayed. Had this identity been merely apparent; had the marks of these wounds been assumed, through an exercise of divine power, the proof would have been an illusion. The body which shall rise must thus be distinguishable as the same which here lived and died.

But in this body many acts were done by the risen Saviour, which exceeded the common functions of our present nature. He was not known, at the first glance, even by the familiar eyes of Mary Magdalene; so that, it should seem, His person must at His will have sustained some change of aspect. He was not known by the two disciples with whom He walked to Emmaus, till He broke bread with His accustomed gestures, and "their eyes were opened." At His pleasure, He appeared, and He vanished. During forty days, He was only manifested from time to time, but commonly remained beyond the reach or sight of enemies or friends. When He at last departed, the manner of His departure transcended the laws which bind all earthly bodies. This moment, He stood amongst the apostles on the hill which they had so often visited together, near the groves of olives; the next, He passed upward, with His hands stretched in blessing; and, while they looked earnestly after, His form was lost in the brightness of the skies.

All these powers, however, though far exceeding all with which our present natural bodies are endued, might have been exercised by our Lord while He was yet in the present body, through His miraculous dominion over nature. He did walk upon the sea; He passed, as some interpreters have supposed, unseen through the crowd of His adversaries; He was transfigured, so that His face shone as the sun, His raiment became white as the snow and glistering, and the fashion of His countenance was altered. Can it be inferred, from the exercise of such powers after His resurrection that, in any measure, they belong to the body of the resurrection?

The exercise of powers which are miraculous is the exception, even where they most abundantly reside. Our Saviour, before His death, wrought miracles only as exceptions, but commonly acted under the general laws to which corporeal nature is subject. But these wonderful circumstances after His resurrection were not exceptions, but the ordinary operations of each day and hour. If, before His death, He once walked on the sea, He ordinarily lived and moved upon the earth. But if, after His resurrection, He came and went invisibly, appeared or disappeared at His pleasure, was known or unknown as He might desire, stood in the midst of His disciples without warning of His approach, and was borne into the heavens spontaneously, this seemed but the common action of the new life which was now begun. That He should at all appear after death, was something entirely beyond the ordinary course of present nature, but was the commencement of another order of things, which is to be realized hereafter, and is henceforth natural. His life after the resurrection was, in its circumstances, like His life before: only so far miraculous as its ordinary course was interrupted for special ends. We know not that any one of those circumstances, which to our present bodies would be preternatural, was such to His risen body; we cannot conceive it possible that such was the character of all.

Something, then, is proved by the resurrection of Jesus, beyond the mere fact of the future resurrection. It proves that the future body is identical, and can be visibly perceived to be identical, with the present. It proves that the future body can perform the functions of the present. It proves that the future body, however, has other functions, embracing far more commanding relations towards surrounding nature, than those of the present. The character of some of these functions may be inferred from the wonderful appearances and the wonderful departure of the risen Redeemer. When our body shall be fashioned like unto that in which He went up into heaven, these powers, no doubt, amongst many others, must be a part of its glory.

LXIV.

Interval before the Final Resurrection.

> "The groans of nature in this nether world,
> Which heaven has heard for ages, have an end."
>
> COWPER.

THE succession of that great harvest of which the death of our Saviour was the seed, is thus described: "Every man in his own order; Christ the first-fruits; afterward, they that are Christ's at His coming." As a great pledge, many bodies of saints that slept arose, and came out of the graves at His resurrection; but thenceforth there is an interval. It is that space during which the Christian destinies of the world are to be accomplished; then cometh the resurrection; and then the end.

At first, it was easy for the believers to imagine that the rapid result of the triumphs or struggles of the Gospel was to be the preparation of the way of the Lord for His early return. He was at hand; every eye should see Him; it might be to-morrow; it might be to-day. His words had been such as to create perpetual expectation, and to enjoin incessant watchfulness. The first believers watched, and waited for the sound of His coming, as of a thief in the night.

But soon it was revealed to the apostles that much remained to be seen on earth before the sign of the Son of man should be seen in heaven. For this, time, many years, perhaps many centuries, must be demanded in the common course of Providence. When the canon of sacred books was closed with the Apocalypse, numbers were even assigned, expressive of periods still to come; numbers and periods which, when they were compared with those of the older prophecies, seemed to point to a long, long development of events in the future.

That development, too, has in great part been realized. Much, and probably most, of all which was predicted is now in the past. But it is, and must continue to be, as true as ever, that "of that day and that hour knoweth no man," when the last enemy, which is death, shall be trodden under the feet of the returning Deliverer.

Thus much, however, we know from the only source of such knowledge. A succession of great and of disastrous events would spread their clouds over the face of society. Nation would rise against nation: earthquakes, famines, pestilences, would follow each other, from age to age; and history would be the narrative of wars, of pestilences, of temporary victories won by the powers of darkness, and of human sufferings succeeded by no general repentance. Still, the word of God should have its course; the Gospel should be preached, sooner or later, to all nations; and the kingdoms of the world should at length become the kingdoms of the Lord. But in the mean while, gigantic powers were to rise against the truth; an Antichrist, a Man of Sin, exalting himself above all that is worshipped; a city on seven hills, corrupting the nations; an army like locusts, laying waste the earth; adversaries, who should trample down the outer courts of the sanctuary; Gog and Magog, and the nations gathered against the holy city. All these enemies should be overcome, before the subjugation of the last enemy.

Periods of a thousand years, and of a thousand two hundred and threescore days or years, appear in the sacred vision. It should seem that the latter is nearly past: it must be that the former is yet to come. When these are over, with all which precedes or follows or lies between, that "day for which all other days were made" shall come suddenly. The lightning, the approach of the thief, the twinkling of an eye, are the comparisons that illustrate the suddenness of its coming.

Thus much we know, while generation after generation are gathered to their fathers. The work of death must be complete; the number of the elect finished. Each generation must watch, like those before; and, whatever probable calculations may be made, to prove a greater or less distance, it was not intended that any mortals should be permitted to close their ears against the sound of the chariot-wheels. Scoffers, it was foretold, would cry, "Where is the promise of His coming?" but they would all lie down in their turn in the grave. Good men, observing "the signs of the times," would again and again be disappointed, and cry, "How long?" and they too would go to their rest. Death must prevail over every generation but one, before death too shall die.

The last sun will rise or set, rising on one region of the earth and setting on another, without creating, we may presume, any new hope or alarm. All nature will pursue its appointed course, and all human society will be engaged as always before, eating and drinking, marrying and giving in marriage, or watching and praying, under the same calm skies, till in a moment, fixed from eternity, the last of all that shall sleep will expire, the sentence, "Unto dust shalt thou return," will have been accomplished, and "the trumpet shall sound."

LXV.

Promise of the Resurrection.

Of the appointed hour our Lord has said, "The hour is coming, in the which all that are in the graves shall hear His voice, and shall come forth." It was the first occasion on which He is recorded to have spoken of the belief in the resurrection of the dead, which generally prevailed amongst the Jews; and He both confirmed it by His word, and connected it with His person, mission and authority. "As the Father raiseth up the dead, and quickeneth them, even so the Son quickeneth whom He will; for, the Father judgeth no man, but hath committed all judgment unto the Son."

The resurrection of the body itself was a part of the hope revealed to the patriarchs, and cherished by the faithful in Israel. At this day, the very words chosen to utter our hope over the graves of our brethren, are those in which Job uttered his own: "Though after my skin worms destroy this body, yet in my flesh shall I see God." That hope had come down from father to son; and the bones of Jacob and his sons were, in that hope, carried from Egypt to the land of promise. To the patriarchs, God was "not the God of the dead, but of the living;" all lived to Him; and they believed, with Abraham, that He was able to raise them from the dead. The thought that the flesh should not be given over to corruption; that the wicked should lie in Hades, and the righteous should have dominion over them in the morning, was familiar to the Psalmist, and to those who sang his melodies. When Ezekiel, in his vision, saw the dry bones starting up into an army of living men, it was no strange figure, but only what his faith foresaw at that "end of the days," when, as was told to his contemporary, Daniel, "many of them that sleep in the dust of the earth shall awake, some to everlasting life, and some to shame and everlasting contempt." In such a faith, that mother, whose story is found in the records of the Maccabees, assured her seven sons while they were dying in torments, that "doubtless the Creator of the world would of His own mercy give them breath and life again." It was the common faith of all the Jews, except the Sadducees, who denied all spiritual existence. Some readily believed that John the Baptist was risen from the dead; others, that one of the prophets had returned. In their assembly, therefore, St. Paul appealed confidently to the hope of the resurrection of the dead, as that which he held with his countrymen, and with their fathers.

To a people thus taught, our Saviour said that He would raise up every one that should believe on Him; every one that should eat His flesh and drink His blood. "I am the resurrection and the life," He said to Martha, when she had professed her belief that her brother should "rise again in the resurrection at the last day." In reply to the Sadducees, He declared that the resurrection of the dead was implied even in the promises to the patriarchs. He intimated it in the assertion that God is "able to destroy both soul and body in hell." To His disciples He gave the assurance, in every form, that the life which He was to enter at His resurrection should be theirs; that He would prepare a place for them, and would come again, and receive them to Himself; that where He would be they should be also; that they should share His glory, His throne, His marriage-supper. Every such promise was a promise of the resurrection unto life.

The apostles preached at once that Christ should be the Judge of the quick and dead; a distinction which could not but import a return of the dead to stand with the living at His judgment-seat. They preached "Jesus and the resurrection," "the resurrection of the dead." "Of the hope and resurrection of the dead," cried Paul, "I am called in question." "I have hope towards God," he said to Felix, "which they themselves also allow, that there shall be resurrection of the dead, both of the just and unjust." He had taught, from the prophets, not only that Christ should rise, but that He "should be the first that should rise." The first must be followed by others; and they are the whole multitude of mankind.

What the apostles preached, they wrote with greater distinctness of detail. They constantly spoke of their own attitude as one of waiting for the coming of the Lord Jesus Christ with all His saints. "If we believe," they said, "that Jesus died and rose again, even so them also which sleep in Jesus will God bring with Him." "If there be no resurrection of the dead, then is Christ not risen." "Christ is risen from the dead, and become the first-fruits of them that slept." "As in Adam all die, even so in Christ shall all be made alive." "This corruptible must put on incorruption, and this mortal must put on immortality." "He which raised up the Lord Jesus shall raise up us also by Jesus." "When Christ, who is our life, shall appear, then shall ye also appear with Him in glory." Among the foundations of apostolic doctrine, are named those of the "resurrection of the dead, and of eternal judgment." They condemned, as a corrupting canker, the pretence "that the resurrection is past already."

"I saw the dead, small and great," says St. John, "stand before God:" "the sea gave up the dead which were in it, and death and hell delivered up the dead which were in them."

So from Enoch, who prophesied, "the Lord cometh, with ten thousand of His saints," to him who died but yesterday in the faith of Christ, the grave has never seemed the last resting-place of the just. They repose in hope: they are buried in sure and certain hope; a hope which is built simply and solely on the revelation of God. All things around might speak only of decay and perpetual dissolution. These very bodies are reduced to their first elements, to fragments, to dust, to gases, to imperceptible principles; and are mingled with the vast system of corporeal nature; with earth, air, water, with winds and woods and the organization of reptiles, birds, and insects. Faith only, the faith of the Gospel, can assure us of any other life from the grave; and simply and only because we believe in Jesus and His resurrection, we believe that all these dead shall rise.

LXVI.

Body of the Resurrection.

> "Through his veins,
> In lighter current, ran immortal life;
> His form renewed to undecaying health,
> To undecaying health, his soul. * * *
> The good and evil, in a moment, all
> Were changed, corruptible to incorrupt,
> And mortal to immortal, ne'er to change.
>
> POLLOK.

"BUT some man will say, How are the dead raised up? and with what body do they come?" The answer is given by an apostle; but it is preceded by a rebuke of the folly of the questioner, and it is drawn from the observation of the course of nature. "Thou fool, that which thou sowest is not quickened, except it die; and that which thou sowest, thou sowest not that body that shall be, but bare grain, it may chance of wheat, or of some other grain; but God giveth it a body as it hath pleased Him, and to every seed its own body." The divine oracle seems to bid us look out upon the face of the universe and see the mysteries there, and doubt no longer. There is a reference to natural reason and to natural illustrations; and therefore these are to assist us, even while the word affords the only decision.

The comparison of the seed intimates a diversity of frame, an identity of existence, and a permanence of vitality. "Thou sowest not that body that shall be:" the seed and the plant have a widely different aspect.

But the seed is nevertheless the same thing with the plant; and the whole plant is virtually enveloped in the seed from which it is to be developed. The very life itself is something permanent; for, although the seed substantially dies, although its whole body of lobes becomes dead earth, yet the germ which they enclose does not perish, but is quickened, and receives its first vegetative nourishment from this very earth. In the same manner, the human body is deposited in the ground, and all its visible frame is dissolved. But it is impossible to say that there remains not somewhere, amidst the elements to which it is reduced, a germ, however imperceptible, from which the immortal body may yet develop itself in an instant. Too little is known of that wondrous principle, whatever it be, which remains through life, and gives to the body the same peculiar, individual form, aspect, and identity, distinguishing it from all others, though every perceptible particle be repeatedly changed and removed. We can only say that, whether there be such a germ or not in the physical nature of corporeal man, such a germ there is in the more general system which embraces all the divine arrangement for his immortality; and the more exact analogy between this process and that of the revival of the seed is suggested by the very language of the Scriptures.

St. Paul proceeds to say that, as there are such varieties of bodies here in the flesh, bodies of fishes, beasts, and birds; and such varieties in the larger universe, bodies celestial and terrestrial; so the body of this life and that of the resurrection are various. "There is a natural body, and there is a spiritual body." One belongs to this present state, and is adapted to its animal and physical necessities; the other belongs to that state in which the spirit is to wield a far more ethereal organization. Indications of the powers of such a spiritual body are seen not only in the acts of our Saviour after his resurrection, but also in His assurance that the children of the resurrection are made like and equal unto the angels.

That spiritual body, in contrast with the body which was sown, is described as glorious, powerful, and incorruptible and immortal. It is to the body in the grave what the rich, waving tree, with its broad branches, its green foliage and its golden fruit, is to the dull, dead atoms of the little seed under the furrows. The bodies of the just shall be fashioned like unto that glorious body, of which some glimpses were given in the transfiguration. Of that body it is told that it was brighter than the sun, and that the raiment outshone the light. When angels have appeared, it has been, at least often, in white apparel, in shining garments. Perhaps there is an alliance between the ethereal element of light and all which is most glorious in the higher worlds from which it emanates; perhaps it is the nearest approach in this earthly state to the splendours of a state of which no actual resemblance can here be attained.

A spiritual body must exercise far mightier powers than the present body over the material elements, since it is not restrained by its own fetters. What capacities of motion and action belong necessarily to the spirit, were the organs through which it must operate less gross and earthy! Every sensation, every perception, every operation in which the mind employs the body, must then be inconceivably subtler, quicker, more comprehensive and more intense. To the corruptible body alone belong inability, weariness, pain, disease, obstruction, by the necessity of its constitution.

But, vast as is the change, all that are in the graves shall come forth; each body the same, by a law of identity, with that which slept; the same, yet another, as the butterfly, the soaring emblem of immortality, is the same with the worm and the chrysalis. One generation, we know, will not even suffer the change of the grave, but another change, by which, in a moment, in the twinkling of an eye, the present mortal nature shall rather be clothed upon than unclothed, and mortality be swallowed up of life.

The resurrection in the last day is one in which "all that are in the graves shall come forth:" but whatever is more minutely said or intimated of the body of the resurrection is spoken of those who have slept and lived in Jesus. They that come unto the resurrection of damnation are also endued with an immortal body, prepared for the endurance of that just doom which sends them "away into everlasting punishment."

So little can we know of the deepest seeds of even the corporeal organization, that it is impossible to say or judge whether the germ of the immortal body, mysteriously enclosed in the mortal, may or may not be made, through the direct effect of holiness or of sin, the germ of necessary bliss or woe hereafter. The body of the believer is the temple of the Holy Ghost. They that sow to the flesh shall of the flesh reap corruption. How deep that sanctification or that corruption may now reach into the depths of our corporeal being, is known to the Author of that being. The blessing and the taint are corporeal as well as spiritual, both now and in the resurrection; and both perhaps may extend their electric chain through the very darkness of the grave.

LXVII.

Death of Death.

> "The isles
> With heaving ocean, rocked; the mountains shook
> Their ancient coronets; the avalanche
> Thundered; silence succeeded through the nations
> Earth never listened to a sound like this.
> It struck the general pulse of nature still,
> And broke for ever the dull sleep of death."
>
> HILLHOUSE.

THE events of the last resurrection are painted in the Scriptures with a peculiar grandeur. From various portions of the New Testament a mighty picture is formed, on which the eyes of successive generations were to be fastened, in the sure knowledge that every eye should see the stupendous reality.

In a day and an hour of which no man or angel knoweth, the Lord Jesus shall return from heaven as He ascended into heaven. "He shall come in His own glory, and in His Father's." The presence of the angels, of all the angels, and the magnificence of His train, is everywhere signified, in contrast with His former humiliation. Some amazing sign shall herald His coming: "Then shall appear the sign of the Son of man in heaven; and then shall all the tribes of the earth mourn; and they shall see the Son of man coming in the clouds of heaven, with power and great glory." They "shall see Him sitting on the right hand of power," clothed with the might and majesty of the Godhead. "The heavens must receive Him until the times of restitution of all things." We "wait for the Son of God from heaven;" from heaven we look for the Saviour, the Lord Jesus Christ."

It is particularly told us, that He shall come "with all His saints." They who have "slept in Jesus" shall be "brought with Him" as a part of His shining train, so that those "who are alive and remain" shall not "prevent," or precede, "them which are asleep."

He "shall descend from heaven with a shout, with the voice of the archangel, and with the trump of God." "For the trumpet shall sound, and the dead shall be raised incorruptible." It was with the same sound that the presence of God on Mount Sinai, when the law came to man, was proclaimed in the ears of Israel. The trump of the archangel, whatever else it be, must be a summons that shall be heard by innumerable beings; one that shall echo, like a thousand thunders, through this visible universe. An archangel may utter such a summons by means which, could they be named, might be regarded as sudden and tremendous operations of nature; for what are all such but effects proceeding from causes which lie behind, in the hands of angels and of the Lord of angels?

The word of God covers these mighty events with an awful indistinctness; the characteristic, from necessity, of all which connects the finite with the infinite. At one time, it is the voice of the archangel, which seems to ring in our ears; at another, the voice of Christ, at which, like Lazarus of old, the dead come forth from their graves. "The sea gives up the dead which are in it; and death and hell deliver up the dead which are in them;" body and soul are united; wherever the seed of the immortal body may have fallen, wherever the spirit may have had its unseen abode.

Of all the dead, "the dead in Christ shall rise first:" "Christ the first-fruits, afterward they that are Christ's at His coming: then cometh the end." They are named first in all the descriptions of the resurrection and the judgment; and it is declared that the saints shall judge the world, and that the apostles shall sit upon twelve thrones, judging the twelve tribes of Israel. For, He shall sit upon the throne of His glory; and before Him shall be gathered all nations of the quick and dead. To gather them, too, He will send His angels, whose office it especially is, to gather together His elect from the uttermost part of earth to the uttermost part of heaven. They are the reapers, who separate the tares from the wheat in that great harvest.

Then, those who were mingled on earth must be for ever divided; and when the righteous shall have been welcomed by their Judge and Saviour to His kingdom, the wicked also shall hear their sentence. The scene of the universal judgment would seem to be upon the earth; possibly on a vast valley or plain, which, if literal, is fast by the walls of Jerusalem; and, if symbolical, has its name, "the valley of Jehoshaphat," "the valley of divine judgment," from the events of that day.

Divided, as the sheep and the goats, the righteous first, and then the wicked, shall be judged according to the deeds done here in the body. Their Judge is the Son of man: "Him hath God ordained;" and by Him "the dead are judged out of those things which are written in the books, according to their works:" "And another book is opened, which is the book of life," in which are written the names of all the final heirs of salvation. A book may be a figure; but it can be a figure of nothing but a record; and this record is one in which every idle word, and every cup of cold water given in the name of Christ, is accurately preserved. "There is nothing covered, that shall not be revealed."

They whose names are in the book of life, the penitent, the believing, the renewed in soul, the diligent in well-doing, are recognised as washed from their sins through the blood of the atonement, and as sanctified by the Holy Spirit. They are acquitted for Christ's sake; and the good which they have done receives the recompense which their Lord had promised. They become, as it were, assessors with Him while the more fearful portion of the judgment is transacted. The wicked also of all ages are gathered in one mighty multitude, and await and receive their doom.

There, on one side, are patriarchs, prophets, pure priests, and righteous kings, and holy apostles, and a noble army of martyrs; true confessors, patient sufferers, pious champions, venerable recluses, faithful matrons, constant wives, devoted virgins, fervent preachers, diligent teachers, earnest writers, watchful pastors, honest men, upright servants, dutiful children, innocent babes without number, generous bestowers, energetic lovers of their fellow-men, humble men of prayer, conscientious labourers in every private sphere of duty, last who were first, and first who were last; the sower and the reaper, the example and they who followed the example, whole families and companies who had journeyed together; and those who had stood alone, "faithful found among the faithless." There, on the other side, are murderers, and liars, the abominable and the bloody, tyrants and robbers, and adulterers, and extortioners, the drunkard, and the reveller, and the blasphemer, the ravisher, the pirate, the manstealer, the parricide, the bold unbeliever, the false priest, the remorseless persecutor, all that lived to themselves only, all that forgot God, the hypocrite, the proud and hard-hearted, the corrupter and the corrupted, they who sinned always against the Holy Spirit, and they who began well and turned back to perdition. From him who made the pyramid his tomb to him whose bones were torn bare by the wild beasts of the desert, from those who slept with their fathers under the eaves of the village church to those who were floated too and fro,

"Full many a score fathom, down deep in the main;"

all have appeared again, to part no more, or to part for ever.

The separation of the Judge parts them for ever, or for ever unites them; and to Him the righteous come, and from Him the wicked go away. Those who shall be for ever with Him are caught up together, to meet the Lord in the air. The wicked are cast into that lake of fire, which is the second death; that bottomless pit, where is weeping, and wailing, and gnashing of teeth. In what part of the universe lie these awful abodes, it may be in vain to conjecture. But it is certain that then, from the bosom of the earth, the flames so long hidden under its volcanoes must burst forth; and the heavens and the earth that are now must pass away with a great noise, and the elements must melt with fervent heat. Fire is the predicted agency; and fire lies waiting in all the secret chambers of nature. The elements, the atmosphere which enwraps the earth, and forms its firmament, or lower heavens, are subject to this agency; and they shall pass, with a tremendous shock and explosion, while under the same mighty agency, the solid globe is transformed.

Then, the new heavens and the new earth appear, for which we wait according to His promise. In that lake of fire, death and hell are swallowed up for ever. The corruptible has put on incorruption; the mortal immortality; the last enemy is destroyed; there is no more death.

LXVIII.

The Second Death.

"Regions of sorrow, doleful shades, where peace
And rest can never dwell, hope never comes
That comes to all."

MILTON.

BUT beyond, there remains the second death; and they who would wisely contemplate the end of man must not shrink from sending on their eyes as far as any beams of present light from heaven may penetrate the darkness of hell. The most terrible of all that is feared in death, is its power to lead to everlasting punishment. He who would so look on death that he shall see at last the face of a friend, must learn to look first on death as it can be, to those for whom Christ died in vain. The path to eternal peace must pass within sight of the tremendous portals from which all hope is banished for ever.

A soul which is not saved must be lost. A soul which is not by some means purified can but proceed ever onward in iniquity, and therefore in misery. But not only are no means known to us, through which it can be purified after rejecting the Holy Spirit in this life, but it is also distinctly declared that no other means remain, in this life or in the life to come. Were but the Spirit withdrawn from this world, this world would soon be an image of what must be beyond the grave of the wicked, and beyond the resurrection to damnation. Sin, perpetually renewed, and never counteracted, must create perpetual woe; and, in the dominions of a righteous Sovereign, the outward condition will answer to the inward.

The state into which the wicked shall in the last day depart, is "everlasting fire, prepared for the devil and his angels." Those angels "are reserved in everlasting chains, under darkness, unto the judgment of the great day;" for that day decides not the doom of men alone. The place is called "the valley of Hinnom," "where the worm dieth not, and the fire is not quenched." It is called, too, "the lake of fire and brimstone, where the devil, with the beast and the false prophet, shall be tormented day and night for ever and ever." It is called in parables, outer darkness, as if without the joyful palace of the Great King; and from that darkness are heard the sounds of weeping and wailing. In parables, too, it is likened to the sentence on him who is delivered to the tormentors, or him who is sawn asunder, or him who is cast into prison till he shall pay the uttermost farthing.

All which is thus told is little; but all speaks in one deep and solemn tone; a tone which can at times alarm and affright every human spirit. No sorrow is more mournful than that of exclusion from joys which we behold from far; and they who shall be cast out from the kingdom of heaven shall see Abraham and all the faithful entering into the inheritance which themselves have lost. No restraint is more galling than that of the strong prison; and theirs is a prison from which there is not even the most distant hope of release. No pains are more terrible than those with which oriental princes have avenged themselves on crime; and with these are compared the pains of the condemned hereafter. No power in nature inflicts such torture as fire, and fire is the chosen and usual figure of their punishment. No object is more loathsome than the worm that feeds on the corruption of the corpse, and theirs is a worm that dieth not. No society can be so horrid as that of those towards whom there can be no confidence or love, nothing but utter abhorrence, dread, and scorn; and theirs is the place prepared for those evil spirits of whom all that we know is that they hate, and that, with all their present power, they are degraded below every human conception of vileness and of more than brutality.

But what we do not know may fill us with even deeper awe than all that is within our knowledge. Eternity, though but one vast word, embraces innumerable events, stupendous histories, and an infinite progress. Begun without hope or love, what can it, or what can it not, disclose as its cycles pursue their course! It is a mystery of mysteries that, in the dominions of God, that dark and dreadful region should continue to exist, where all is evil and only evil. Enough if from these shores of time we behold it with a glance of boundless dread and horror, and turn away, fixing our eyes with steadfast determination on the safe mountains of the land above.

One alleviating whisper is blended even with those most awful denunciations which reveal these depths of despair. There are those who shall be beaten with few stripes, as well as those who shall be beaten with many. It shall be more tolerable in the judgment for one race of transgressors than for another, for Tyre and Sidon than for the Galilean hearers and rejectors of Jesus. Where degrees of suffering exist, the cup of all is not alike intense in its bitterness. This is the single soothing thought which has been breathed from heaven into our meditations on the final world of woe beyond the second death.

LXIX.

Eternal Life.

"I will tell thee even more,
Ten thousand years from now; if but with thee
I too reach heaven, and with new language there,
When an eternity of bliss has gone,
Bless God for new eternities to be."

COXE.

DEATH leads the just through the intermediate Paradise, through the joyful reunion of the resurrection, and through the blessed award of the last day, to all which we are taught to name most fully heaven and the life eternal. This is the dazzling consummation of all hopes; the manifestation for which the earnest expectation of the whole creation waits and longs, and death, as

"the path which must be trod
If man would ever pass to God,"

is welcome to the feet of those who, "in the confidence of a certain faith, and the comfort of a reasonable, religious, and holy hope," look on to this close of all.

The divine oracles exhaust the imagery of earthly joys and splendours and glories, to afford inspiring glimpses of heaven. There shine the gates, the walls, the domes, the pinnacles of a celestial city: its battlements are jasper, its pavements are gold, its foundations are jewels, its portals are pearls. Within flows the pure river of the water of life; and fast by it grows the tree, whose leaves are for the healing of the nations. The ransomed are there, with songs, with harps, with crowns, with palms, with spotless, resplendent robes; they shine as the stars and as the brightness of the firmament; they go in to the marriage-supper; they are placed over cities and peoples; they sit with the Lord in His throne; they rest in the peace of an everlasting Sabbath.

Figures have no value except as they express realities; and the figures which the Holy Spirit has employed must be the nearest and truest of all possible expressions, even though the realities be both unseen and inconceivable. Therefore, the simple mind which reposes entirely in the figures, and imagines heaven as merely such a scene, is in no error, except that it thinks as a child, and sees through a glass darkly; and it is less in danger of delusion than the stronger intellect which casts the figure, and with it the reality, entirely away.

But all is not spoken in figures. The state of the blessed is always described as one where those shall rejoice together, who together have laboured here. Their reward shall be according to their works; and in that kingdom there shall be least and greatest. The reward is enhanced by all those works of love, which lay up in store a good foundation against the time to come, a treasure in heaven; and by all sufferings patiently endured for the sake of righteousness. Its delight consists much in the immediate presence of the Lord of glory, and in the perfect enjoyment of His love. The mourners are comforted; the meek inherit the earth: the pure in heart see God.

With even more distinctness, it is told us that, though "it doth not yet appear what we shall be," yet, "when

He shall appear, we shall be like Him, for we shall see Him as he is." "So shall we ever be with the Lord;" with whom to be "is far better" than all beside. That nearness to the Lord incarnate, that presence with the Son, even after He also shall Himself be "subject unto Him that put all things under Him, that God may be all in all," can now be no further comprehended than as we know that God is in Christ, that God is love, and that therefore to be with Him is to be in perfect love, which is perfect joy. To be with a dear friend and benefactor, with one who is worthy of much love, must always be a high happiness. But in heaven the redeemed are with Him who is "worthy to receive power and riches and wisdom and strength and honour and glory and blessing." All love Him who loved them, and redeemed them with His blood; and therefore their voices are lifted to a strain of rapture unspeakable and full of glory.

They are "come, too, to the spirits of just men made perfect." Heaven has been assembling to itself, through all the ages, whatever of true wisdom, virtue, and excellence had been seen and admired below. The fellowship of heart with heart, and mind with mind, is, as we feel, something that should be immortal; something, than which there is nothing deeper in our being except its foundation in its Creator. That fellowship is perfect where, out of every kindred and tongue and people and nation, from every age and every dispensation, no longer exposed to the divisions, the misunderstandings, and the weaknesses of this world, every barrier removed and every fault purified, while the whole government of a Providence, from first to last, shines in the light of its own manifest wisdom, and can no longer be mistaken, the righteous behold with one another the wonderful works of God, and learn, and adore, and in all the depths of their desire, and the height of their powers, are satisfied.

That we shall see our Lord "as He is," that we shall "see face to face," is promised in contrast with our present ignorance and its dim and discoloured vision. It is a joy of which we have intimations here, in all that brings us near to God, or that enables to behold His footsteps in His earthly ways; in all true wisdom and knowledge, in study and contemplation and worship. These foretastes can but intimate, like all earthly enjoyments, mingled as they are, the inherent capacities of the soul: the rest is left for the land of fruition.

But though now we see but through a glass, this earth has things that are made after the pattern of heavenly things, such as Moses saw in the mount. The ordinances of the Jewish covenant had such a resemblance: such a resemblance, and more than resemblance, must there be in the ordinances of Christ; and such, we may well believe, is this great temple of nature in which "are clearly seen the eternal power and Godhead." To the heavenly world sanctified hearts must carry their affections, and doubtless some of their employments. When our Lord sat at His last supper, He said, "I will not drink henceforth of this fruit of the vine, until that day when I drink it new with you in my Father's kingdom." He surely pointed forward to some scene of holy joy from which they might point back to that sacramental feast, and recognise the unity of the cup on earth with the cup above. It is hard to avoid believing that the charm of consecrated music, so subtle, so spiritual, so linked from the beginning and in its very nature, with worship and praise, and so mingled with the loftiest descriptions of the occupations of heaven, is really to be there prolonged. Of heaven an excellent writer has said that we only know two things which are there, holy love and holy music; and another has remarked that "it may be boldly assumed that nothing in the whole compass of nature bears so near a resemblance as music to the celestial mode of thanksgiving." But probably we know many more elements of joy, which here are in their infancy, and there shall be mature; which here are dim, and there henceforth in perfect radiancy.

"They neither marry, indeed, nor are given in marriage:" the relations of earth are preserved in memory and in affection, but have ceased to be actual, with the necessities of a state like this. The ties, if such there shall be, which shall correspond with those that now bind us in families, orders, and commonwealths, can no more be now imagined by us than the scenery of the new heavens and earth themselves. Yet the very names of earth and heavens, of a kingdom, cities, mansions, suggest and signify something that is more like what they express on earth than like any thing which bears a different name, unconsecrated by such applications.

The angels are the highest, noblest, holiest beings who have ever been disclosed to human thought, below the everlasting throne. In that angelic name all purity and loveliness, all dignity and might, all fervour and energy, all obedience and favour and joy, are represented to the soaring conception. The wings of the morning, the white robes of peace, the glow of celestial love, the glory of superhuman intellect, the ministry of perfect benevolence, the impossibility of death, the unfailing, unfaltering fulfilment of that will which is the life of all that live, these are with the angels, and with those who die and rise, to be made equal to the angels, and like the Son of God.

So may God grant to such as, through these pages, have traced the triumph of death, and the triumph over death, that, "through the grave and gate of death they may pass to their joyful resurrection, for His merits who died, and was buried, and rose again for us, His Son Jesus Christ our Lord.

THE END.

CATALOGUE.

A List of Books from which a selection can be made suitable for family, parish, and Sunday-school Libraries. A liberal reduction from publishers' prices to libraries. The selection is by no means complete, but the publisher can supply any books in the market, at the lowest prices.
H. HOOKER.

ADAMS, Rev. Wm., Mercy to Babes. 12mo.
Advice to a Young Christian. 18mo., clo.
Andrews, Bp., Devotions. Various edit.
A Kempis, Thomas, Imitation of Christ. Various editions.
Arnold, Thomas, D. D., Rugby School Sermons. 18mo.
—— Life and Correspondence. 8vo., cloth.
Aged Christians' Companion. 8vo.
Anglican Ordination, Essays on.
Barrow on the Pope's Supremacy. 8vo.
Baxter, Saint's Rest. Various editions.
—— Care to the Unconverted.
—— Dying Thoughts.
Berrien, Rev. Wm. D. D., Family Prayers, 12mo.
—— Enter into thy Closet. 12mo.
—— Devotion for the Sick. 12mo.
—— Treatise on the Sacrament. 12mo.
—— History of Trinity Church, N. Y.
Beveridge, Bp., On Public Prayer.
—— Sermons on the Church.
—— Private Thoughts.
Blunt's, Rev. Henry, Lectures on the Life of Christ.
—— St. Paul and St. Peter.
—— Elisha.
—— Abraham and Jacob.
—— Seven Churches in Asia.
—— Sermon and Discourses on the Articles.
—— Commentary on the Pentateuch. 3 vols.
—— Rev. J. J., History of the Reformation.
—— Coincidences of the Old and New Testaments. 8vo.
Bradley, Rev. Chas., Family and Parish Sermons.
Brownwell's, Bishop, Commentary on the Book of Common Prayer. 8vo.
Bowden, Rev. John, D. D., on Episcopacy. 2 vols.
Bridges, Rev. Chas., on the Ministry.
—— On Proverbs.
—— On 119th Psalm.
Burnet on the Thirty-nine Articles.
—— History of the Reformation.
Burton, Rev. Dr., History of the Church.
Butler's Analogy of Religion. Various editions.
Book of Homilies. Complete edition.
Burder's Village Sermons. 8vo.
Buds, Blossoms, and Fruits of the Church.
Bickersteth's Questions on the Thirty-nine Articles.
Booth's, Dr., Reign of Grace.
Burder, Self-Discipline.
Carmichael, Rev. Dr., Early Christian Fathers.
Cary, Rev. H., Testimonies of the Fathers of the First Four Centuries.
Cave's Lives of the Apostles.
Cave's Primitive Christianity. 8vo.
Cecil, Rev. Richard, Whole Works. 3 vols.
—— Remains of.
—— Memoirs of Newton.
Chapin, Rev. A., Primitive Church.
Chapman, Rev. Dr., Sermon on the Church.
Chillingworth's Religion of the Protestants.
Churchman Armed. By Palmer and Hobart.
Churton, Rev. E., The Early English Church.
Clark, Rev. J. A., D. D., Pastor's Testimony.
—— Walk About Zion.
—— Young Disciple.
—— Gathered Fragments.
—— Awake, Thou Sleeper.
—— Gleanings by the Way.
Coit, Rev. Dr., Puritanism; or, The Church's Defence against its Aspersion.
Charnock on Divine Providence.
Cooke, Dr. J. E., Presbyterian Ordination Invalid.
Cotterill's Family Prayers. 18mo.
Coxe, Rev. A. C., Christian Ballads.
Croswell, Rev. Dr., Family Prayers.
Cruden's Concordance. Various editions.
Churchman, The Reasons for his Faith and Practice.
Doctrine of the Cross; A Memorial of an Humble Follower of Christ.
Dorr, Rev. Dr., Churchman's Manual. New edition.
—— Recognition of Friends.
—— History of a Pocket Prayer-Book.
Devout Churchman's Companion.
Duy, Rev. Samuel, Sermon and Remains.
Dixon and Smith, on the Catechism.
East, Rev. John, My Saviour; or, Meditation on the Names and Titles of Christ.
—— Peace in Believing; or, A Memorial of his Wife.
Episcopal Tracts of the Diocese of Massachusetts.
Eusebius's Ecclesiastical History. By Cruse.
Evidences of Christianity. By Watson, Leslie, Paley, &c.
Evans's Rectory of Valehead.
Faber, Rev. George Stanley, On Election.
—— on Romanism.
—— on Trinitarianism. 2 vols.
—— on Primitive Sacrifice.
Family at Bethany. 18mo.
Fox's Book of Martyrs.
Fry. Mrs. Elizabeth. By Timpson.
Fry, Mrs. Caroline, The Listener.
—— Christ, our Example.
—— Christ, our Law.

CATALOGUE.

Fry, Great Commandment.
—— Sabbath Musings.
—— Daily Scripture Readings.
—— Table of the Lord.
Foster's Essays on Christian Morals.
—— on Decision of Character.
—— on Morality. By Dimond.
Gaston's Scripture Collection, in the form of a Concordance.
Goode's Better Covenant.
Good Samaritan; or, The Sick Man's Friend.
Godolphin, Mrs., Life of. By Evelyn.
Gaussin, on Plenary Inspiration of the Scriptures.
Graham, Mrs. Isabella, Memoir of.
—— Miss Mary Jane, Memoir of.
Gregory, Dr. Olinthus, Letters on the Evidence.
Gresley, Rev. W., on Preaching.
—— Early English Church.
Griswold, Bp. of Massachusetts. Memoir of his Life. By Rev. Dr. Stone.
Hamilton's Harp on the Willows.
—— Life in Earnest.
—— Mount of Olives.
—— Happy Home.
Harris, Rev. James, Great Commission.
—— Great Teacher.
—— Man Primeval.
—— Mammon.
Henry Venn's Life and Letters. 12mo.
Henshaw's Discourses on the Catechism.
Herbert, George, Temple and Country Parson.
Hill, Rev. Rowland, Village Dialogues. 2 vols.
—— Memoir of.
Hook, Rev. W. F., The Cross of Christ.
Hooker, Richard. Whole Works. 2 vols. With Selections. By Keble.
—— Rev. Herman, Philosophy of Unbelief.
—— Uses of Adversity.
—— Christian Life.
—— Portion of the Soul.
—— Maxims and Thoughts.
Hopkins, Bp. of Vermont, The Primitive Church.
—— The Church of Rome.
—— Primitive Creed.
—— Lectures on the Reformation.
Horne, Bp., Commentary on the Psalms.
—— Whole Works. 2 vols.
Horne, Thos. Hartwell, Introduction to the Study of the Holy Scriptures. 2 vols.
—— Same work, abridged.
—— Protestant Memorials.
Hammond on the Canons. 12mo.
Hawke's Contributions of American History. 2 vols., 8vo.
Hobart's Companion to the Altar.
—— Fasts and Festivals.
—— State of the Departed.
—— Christian Manual.
Hymns for Little Children. Just published.
Jackson, Sanderson, and Cosin, on the Church.
—— Rev. Wm., Life and Reminiscences. 8vo.
Jarvis, L. F., Introduction to Church History.
—— Sermons on Prophecy.
—— Reply to Milnor's End of Controversy.
Jay, Rev. Wm., Morning and Evening Exercises. 2 vols., 12mo.
Jones, (of Naylor,) Catholic Doctrine of the Trinity.
Kip, Wm. J., Christmas Holidays in Rome.
—— Early Conflicts of Christianity.
—— Double Witness.
—— The Lenten Fast.
—— Recantation; or, the Confession of a Roman Convert.
—— Early Jesuit Missions.
Keble's Christian Year.
Keith's Evidence of Prophecy. 12mo.
Law, Rev. W., Serious Call to a Devout and Holy Life.
Melville, Rev. Henry, Sermons. 2 vols.
M'Cullock, Rev. Dr., The Dead in Christ.
M'Ilvaine, Bp., Evidences of Christianity.
Moberly, Rev. Geo., Sayings of the Great Forty Days. 12mo.
Neff, Felix, Memoir of. By Gilley.
Night of Toil. By the author of Peep of Day.
Note Book of a Country Clergyman.
Nelson's Practice of True Devotion.
Newton's Prayers of the Church.
Odenheimer, Rev. W. H., Devout Churchman's Companion.
—— Origin and Compilation of the Common Prayer Book.
—— The True Catholic no Romanist.
Ogilby, Rev. J. D., D. D., Lectures on the Church.
—— On Lay Baptism.
Paget, Rev. F. E., Sermons on the Duties of Daily Life.
—— Tales of the Village. 3 vols.
Palmer, Rev. Wm. Treatise on the Church of Christ. 2 vols, 8vo.
—— Compendous Ecclesiastical History.
—— Letter to Wiseman.
Pastoral Letters of the House of Bishops.
Pearson, Bp., Exposition of the Creed.
Perfect Peace, Memorials of Howell.
Penanzabuloe; or, The Lost Church Found.
Pilgrim's Progress. Various editions.
Plain Sermons. 2 vols.
Philosophy of the Plan of Salvation.
Portrait of an English Churchman.
Records of a London Clergyman.
Richmond, Rev. Leigh, Memoir of, by Grimshaw.
—— Annals of the Poor.
Romaine, Rev. Wm., Life, Walk, and Triumph of Faith. 12mo.
Scougal's Life of God in the soul of Man, and other works.
Secker's Lectures on the Church Catechism.
Sewell, Rev. Wm. Christian Morals.
Sherlock, Rev. Richard, The Practical Christian.
Sherwood, Mrs., Stories on the Church Catechism.
Shorts, Bp., History of the Church.

CATALOGUE.

Slater's Original Draught of the Primitive Church.
Southgate's, Bp., Tour through Arminia, Persia, &c. 2 vols.
—— Visit to the Syrian Churches.
Spinckes, Rev. M., Churchman's Companion.
Sutton's, Christopher, Learn to Live.
—— Learn to Die.
Sewell, Miss, Amy Herbert.
—— Margaret Percival. 2 vols.
—— Gertrude.
—— Walter Lorimer.
Southey's Book of the Church. 8vo.
—— Abridged.
Spear, Rev. M. W., Illustration of the Catechism.
Stevenson's Christ on the Cross.
—— The Lord our Shepherd.
Staunton's Dictionary of the Church.
Spencer's English Reformation.
Thornton Henry, Family Prayers and Commentary.
Trench, Rev. R., Notes on the Miracles.
—— Notes on the Parables.
Taylor, Jane, Contribution of Q. Q. 2 vols.
—— Jeremy, Episcopacy Asserted and Maintained.
—— Holy Living and Dying.
—— Rev. C. B., Margaret; or, The Pearl.
—— Mark Welton.
—— Lady May.
—— Thankfulness.
Venn, Richard, Complete Duty of Man.
Walton, Isaac, Lives of Donne, Walton, &c.
Weeks' Preparation for the Communion.
What is the Church? Edited by Bp. of Maryland.
White, Bp., Comparative Views of the Calvinistic and Arminian Controversy. 2 vols.
—— Memoir of, by Bird Wilson.
—— Commentaries on the Ordination Ordinances.
—— Rev. Hugh, on Prayer.
—— Second Advent.
—— On Confirmation.
—— The Believer.
—— Profession and Principle.
—— On True Happiness.
Wilberforce, Wm., Practical View.
—— Prayer for Families.
—— Life, by his son. 2 vols.
—— Correspondence. 2 vols.
—— Bp. History of the American Church. 12mo.
—— On the Lord's Supper.
—— Robert Isaac, on Holy Baptism.
—— On Incarnation.
Wilson, Bp., Sacra Privata.
Watson's, Bp., Apology for the Bible.
Wake's Apostolic Fathers.
Wilson, Bp. Lecture on the Collossians. 12mo.
—— Evidences of Christianity. 2 vols.
Butler's History of the Prayer Book.

☞ Depository of all the books of the Protestant Episcopal Sunday-school Union, sold wholesale and retail, by

H. Hooker.

www.ingramcontent.com/pod-product-compliance
Lightning Source LLC
LaVergne TN
LVHW020213110826
845151LV00003B/698

* 9 7 8 1 4 2 5 5 3 4 3 5 6 *